AN   LAS
OF   RE

THE
UNIVERSITY
OF HULL
PRESS

Cover Illustration: Map of the East Riding of Yorkshire by Herman Moll, 1724.
                      Reproduction by courtesy of Artlynk Gallery, Wednesday Market, Beverley.

Rear Pocket: This contains a key map showing East Riding parishes and townships in the mid-nineteenth century,
                  which can be used to identify unnamed places on the maps with parish outlines appearing in the atlas.

AN HISTORICAL ATLAS OF EAST YORKSHIRE

edited by
Susan Neave and Stephen Ellis

Maps drawn by Keith Scurr

The University of Hull Press
1996

© The University of Hull Press

British Library Cataloguing in Publication Data.

A catalogue record for this book is available from the British Library.

ISBN 0 85958 652 9
Published 1996

Phototypeset in 10 on 12.3pt Times and printed by the Central Print Unit, The University of Hull.

This atlas is dedicated to the memory of

Alan Harris (1928-1995)

geographer, historian, colleague and scholar of the East Riding

CONTENTS

LIST OF CONTRIBUTORS

Rodney W. Ambler   Senior Lecturer in History, University of Hull

Arthur G. Credland   Keeper of Maritime History, Hull Museums

Janice E. Crowther   Part-time Lecturer in Regional and Local History, University of Hull; Associate Lecturer, Open University

George de Boer   Formerly Reader in Geography, University of Hull

Stephen Ellis   Lecturer in Geography, University of Hull

D.H. Evans   Archaeology Manager, Humber Archaeology Partnership

Roy Gregory   Mill historian and conservationist

Alan Harris   Formerly Reader in Geography, University of Hull

Roger Kain   Montefiore Professor of Geography, University of Exeter

B.R. Kirk   Honorary Secretary, Hull Natural History Society

Peter G. Los   Member of the British Brick Society

W. Ann Los   Member of the British Brick Society

Richard Middleton   Experimental Officer, School of Geography and Earth Resources, University of Hull

David Neave   Senior Lecturer in Regional and Local History, University of Hull

Susan Neave   Research Fellow, Department of History, University of Hull

Margaret Noble   Head of Educational Development, University of Lincolnshire and Humberside

D.M. Palliser   Professor of Medieval History, University of Leeds

J.J.N. Palmer   Reader in History, University of Hull

J. Allan Patmore   Formerly Professor of Geography, University of Hull

Mike Rogers   Archivist, East Riding of Yorkshire Council Archives and Records Service

Robert Van de Noort   Research Officer, School of Geography and Earth Resources, University of Hull

M. Trevor Wild   Senior Lecturer in Geography, University of Hull

Alison Williams   Sites and Monuments Record Assistant, Humber Archaeology Partnership

LIST OF ILLUSTRATIONS

The illustrations on the title pages of the thematic sections of this atlas are as follows:

ENVIRONMENT

Danes Dyke, Flamborough (from T. Allen, *A New and Complete History of the County of York*, 1829)

ARCHAEOLOGY

Plan of the excavation at West Furze (from R.A. Smith, 'Lake-Dwellings in Holderness, Yorkshire', *Archaeologia* 62 (1911), 593-610)

POPULATION AND SETTLEMENT

Kingston-upon-Hull (from T. Gent, *History of Kingston-upon-Hull*, 1735)

LANDOWNERSHIP AND LAND USE

High Hall, Bishop Burton (from G. Oliver, *History and Antiquities of Beverley*, 1829)

TRADE AND INDUSTRY

Saturday Market, Beverley (from G. Oliver, *History and Antiquities of Beverley*, 1829)

COMMUNICATIONS

The first timetable of the Hull and Selby Railway, June 1840

RELIGION AND SOCIAL PROVISION

St James' chapel-of-ease, Lissett (from G. Poulson, *History and Antiquities of Holderness*, 1840)

RIOT AND REBELLION

Title page of a Civil War newsletter, 1642

ADMINISTRATIVE UNITS

Sessions House, Beverley (from G. Oliver, *History and Antiquities of Beverley*, 1829)

PREFACE

This atlas, commissioned as a companion volume to the recently published *An Historical Atlas of Lincolnshire*, deals with the area of the historic East Riding of Yorkshire (as it was before the local government re-organisation of 1974), and the city of Kingston-upon-Hull, the two areas together being referred to as East Yorkshire. It is intended as a general work of reference for anyone interested in the region's rich and varied past, but we hope that it will also be of great value to those teaching or researching aspects of social, economic and landscape history.

The East Riding, the smallest of the three historic Yorkshire ridings, covers some 750,000 acres (303,750 hectares). It is bounded by the North Sea to the east, the Humber estuary to the south, and the rivers Ouse and Derwent to the west and north. With the exception of the chalk escarpment of the Yorkshire Wolds, which runs in a great arc from the Humber to the coast at Flamborough Head and rises to a height of around 800 feet (240 metres), the region is one of generally subdued relief, with much of the land lying only a short distance above sea level. Hull, created a city in 1897, stands on the north bank of the Humber estuary. Its historic core lies adjacent to the tributary river Hull, close to its confluence with the Humber, but the city now extends westwards to the edge of the Wolds, northwards up the Hull valley and eastwards on to the Holderness plain.

In planning this atlas, a great many potential topics were considered, but unfortunately space considerations, and in some cases the unavailability of contributors, have not allowed them all to be covered. Nevertheless, the final selection of topics is still broad in range, and reflects the expertise of historians, geographers and archaeologists currently working in the region, thus bringing together a wealth of recent research into a period spanning more than 10,000 years.

The maps, each accompanied by an explanatory text, are grouped under nine major headings. The first group provides an environmental background to the region and this is followed by a series of maps showing the archaeology of the area from the time of its first inhabitants through to the early historic period. The next six groups of maps, which form the greater part of the atlas, focus on aspects of the history of Hull and the East Riding from the middle ages to the twentieth century under the headings of population and settlement, landownership and land use, trade and industry, communications, religion and social provision, and riot and rebellion. The final set of maps shows the various administrative units into which the region has been subdivided for different purposes and at different periods. Notes and guidance on further reading can be found in a consolidated form towards the back of the atlas. These are followed by an index which, because each map and accompanying text deals with a specific topic, is confined to place-names.

The atlas focuses primarily on pre-twentieth century topics, and the maps, where appropriate, therefore show the boundaries of the historic ecclesiastical parishes (the basic unit of local government before 1894), rather than those of the modern civil parish. The key map, bound in the book but also provided as a loose copy in the rear pocket for ease of reference, also shows the smaller township boundaries. The modern civil parish in which each township lies is given on the accompanying key.

ACKNOWLEDGEMENTS

We are grateful to all the contributors for their willingness to be involved at the outset of this project and for their co-operation at all stages of production. Particular thanks in this respect must go to David Neave, who, in addition to being a major contributor, has been of great editorial assistance. We are also grateful for the advice and assistance provided by Phil Holmes and Jean Smith on behalf of The University of Hull Press. For the production of the maps and for typesetting of the text we are indebted to Keith Scurr and Paul McSherry respectively, and for photographic work we thank John Garner. We also gratefully acknowledge the assistance of Steve Wilson and Carl Schofield of the University's Print and Design unit. The map which appears on the cover was generously loaned by Artlynk Gallery, Beverley, and photographed by the University photographic service. The maps appearing on pages 5 and 11 have been based on maps published by the Ordnance Survey (© Crown copyright). The cost of publishing the atlas has been partially met by generous contributions from the Marc Fitch Fund, Northern Foods plc and Smith & Nephew, for which we and the publishers are most grateful.

Susan Neave and Stephen Ellis
October 1996

ENVIRONMENT

PHYSIOGRAPHY
Stephen Ellis

The East Riding of Yorkshire can be divided into four main physiographic regions. To the east lie the lowlands of Holderness and the valley of the river Hull, to the west and north of which are the Yorkshire Wolds which form an escarpment of chalk running in an arc from the Humber estuary to the North Sea coast. To the north of the Wolds lies the Vale of Pickering, whose southern portion falls within the East Riding, and to the west lies the Vale of York.

The escarpment of the Wolds is the major relief feature of the region, rising to around 160 m above sea level in the south, 240 m in the north and 140 m in the east. Its scarp slope, facing west and north, overlooks the Vales of York and Pickering respectively, and its dip slope runs east and south to meet the Hull valley and the Holderness plain. Where the Wolds reach the coast they terminate in the steep cliffs of Flamborough Head. The origin of the escarpment dates to the Tertiary period, when the chalk was uplifted, folded and tilted towards the south and east. It has been suggested that a number of planation surfaces developed on this feature, as a result of either river or marine erosion, although these have subsequently become obscured by the lowering of the chalk surface by solution, and their age is unclear. The Wolds are incised by networks of often steep-sided valleys, most of which no longer carry surface-flowing water, due to a lowering of the water table as a result of climatic change. The main exception is the Great Wold Valley, which carries the stream of the Gypsey Race, although even this has sections which are dry except at times when the water table is very high. The natural vegetation of the Wolds has been progressively cleared since prehistoric times and the landscape is now dominated by arable farming, with grassland being largely confined to the narrow floors and steep sides of the dry valleys, and woodland mainly occurring as small plantations established within the last few centuries.

The gently undulating plain of Holderness rises only to around 30 m above sea level, and to the west, in the Hull valley, there is little relief and most of this area lies at less than 10 m above sea level. In addition to the natural river, the valley of the river Hull contains a number of artificial drainage networks, the earliest of which were constructed in the medieval period. Many of the drainage systems of eastern Holderness reach the North Sea by flowing westwards to the Hull valley and thence via the Humber, rather than by flowing directly to the coast; this is because the highest parts of Holderness, which form the main watershed, generally lie only a short distance inland. Topographic and place-name evidence indicates that around 70 small lakes, or meres, once occurred throughout Holderness, although all but one of these - Hornsea Mere - have now become silted up or artificially drained. In the southernmost part of Holderness much of the land has been reclaimed from the estuary during the last few centuries. The smooth curve of the Holderness coastline comprises low cliffs, notorious for their rapid rate of erosion, and possesses no

natural anchorages. At its southeastern tip lies Spurn Point, a sand and shingle spit extending some 5 km into the mouth of the Humber estuary. As in the case of the Wolds, progressive vegetation clearance has resulted in much of Holderness now being under arable farming; grassland is largely confined to the wetter, more poorly drained areas, and woodland occurs mainly as small plantations.

The floor of the Vale of Pickering lies at around 20 m above sea level and has, like the Hull valley, been artificially drained in more recent times. The northern boundary of the East Riding is marked by the river Derwent, which flows from the North York Moors across the Vale of Pickering and through the Kirkham Gap, where the Wolds meet the Howardian Hills of the North Riding. From here it traverses the Vale of York before reaching the sea via the rivers Ouse and Humber. This circuitous course occurred as a result of blocking of the more direct route to the sea by glacial deposits in the eastern Vale of Pickering. The Kirkham Gap has been interpreted as an overflow channel from an ice-dammed lake which once occurred in the Vale, but it is also possible that it was cut by subglacial meltwater. At the eastern end of the Vale, between the promontories of Filey Brigg and Flamborough Head, lies Filey Bay, whose cliffs are higher and much less rapidly eroding than those of Holderness. Following drainage improvements, the Vale is now, like Holderness, largely under arable farming, with only limited areas of grassland and woodland.

The Vale of York has generally little relief and much of this part of the East Riding lies at less than 10 m above sea level, although a notable exception is Church Hill, Holme-upon-Spalding Moor, which rises to around 40 m in the east of the Vale. The Derwent and Foulness are the main rivers, along with the Ouse, which forms the southwestern boundary of the riding. As in the other low-lying areas, there are also many artificial channels for drainage improvement, and consequently much of the Vale is now under arable land use, with relatively few areas of grassland and woodland.

The river Humber, which forms the southern boundary of the East Riding, is one of England's major estuaries. Its freshwater drainage area exceeds 24,000 square kilometres, around one-fifth of the area of England. It has a tidal length of approximately 140 km on the river Ouse and a maximum tidal range of 7.2 m. After the first 3 km of its length it is between 2 and 10 km wide, and in the lower part of the estuary the channel depth exceeds 18 m at high water.

Bibliography on page 140

2

PHYSIOGRAPHY

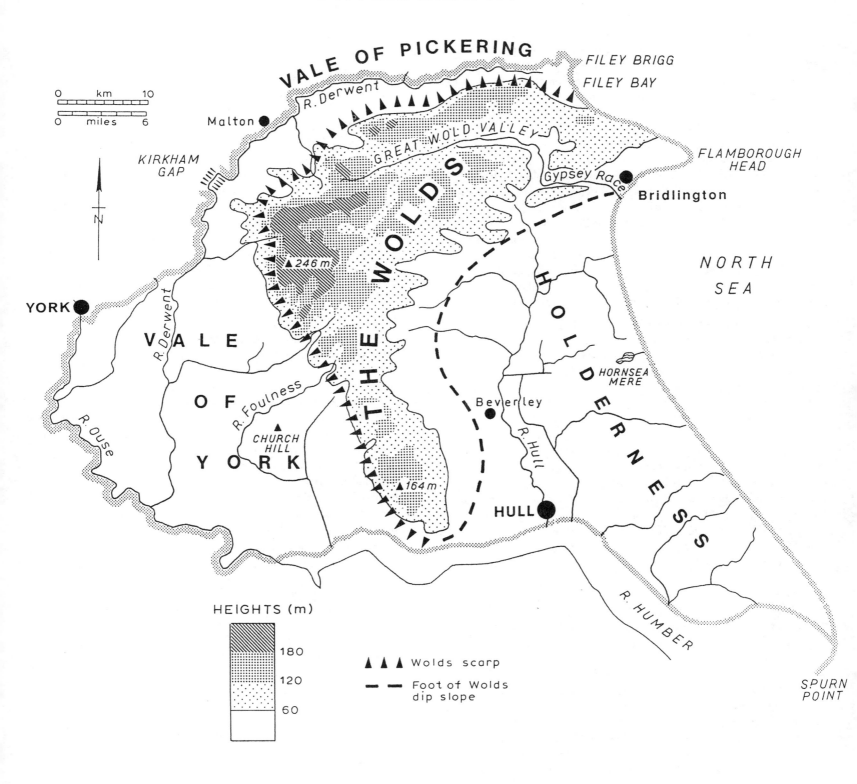

VALE OF PICKERING

FILEY BRIGG
FILEY BAY

R. Derwent

Malton

KIRKHAM GAP

GREAT WOLD VALLEY

FLAMBOROUGH HEAD

Gypsey Race

Bridlington

▲ 246 m

T H E   W O L D S

YORK

V A L E

O F

Y O R K

R. Derwent

R. Ouse

R. Foulness

▲ CHURCH HILL

▲ 164 m

N O R T H

S E A

H O L D E R N E S S

HORNSEA MERE

Beverley

R. Hull

HULL

R. HUMBER

SPURN POINT

HEIGHTS (m)

180
120
60

▲▲▲ Wolds scarp

- - - Foot of Wolds dip slope

GEOLOGY
Stephen Ellis

The geology of the East Riding can best be considered under two headings - *solid geology*, which relates to the bedrock of the area, and *drift geology*, relating to the more recent, superficial deposits which overlie the bedrock. The solid geology of the region comprises sedimentary rocks dating to three main geological time periods - the Triassic (248-213 million years ago), Jurassic (213-144 million years ago) and Cretaceous (144-65 million years ago). The oldest (Triassic) strata occur in the Vale of York and comprise mainly sandstones and marls, dipping gently towards the east. On the eastern margin of the Vale the Jurassic strata are encountered, comprising clays, shales, limestones and sandstones, which also dip gently eastwards. Jurassic rocks, in the form of Kimmeridge Clay, also occupy the Vale of Pickering. The Wolds themselves comprise Cretaceous strata which have been folded into a syncline whose axis runs northwest-southeast and dips gently towards the southeast; this is responsible for the arcuate form of the Wolds escarpment, with west- and north-facing scarp slopes. The strata are mainly chalk, although smaller outcrops of Speeton Clay occur below them at the northern margin of the Wolds.

There are no rocks dating to the Tertiary period (65-2 million years ago). If they did occur, they have been eroded away, or such deposits may never have been laid down because at this time the coast may have been much further to the east of its present position. There are, however, many types of deposit representing the subsequent, and most recent, period of geological time - the Quaternary (the last two million years approximately) - and it is these which comprise the *drift geology*. The majority were laid down during the most ice age of the Quaternary, known as the *Devensian*. Towards the end of this period, around 18,000 years ago, an ice sheet advanced westwards over Holderness and the lower part of the Wolds dip slope, depositing glacial sediments over the chalk bedrock; this episode is known as the *Dimlington Stadial*. Two units of till (boulder clay) have been recognised from this period - the Skipsea Till (formerly known as the Drab Till), which covers most of the area, and the Withernsea Till (formerly known as the Purple Till), which overlies the Skipsea Till and is confined to the southeastern part of Holderness. A third till unit, the Hessle Till, was also formerly thought to occur, but this has now been shown to be the post-glacial weathering zone within whichever of the other two tills occurs at the surface, rather than a separate sedimentary unit. Devensian ice also moved into the Vale of Pickering, and southwards across the Vale of York, forming ice-dammed lakes - Lake Pickering and Lake Humber respectively. This resulted in the deposition of fine-grained lake sediments, whereas elsewhere in these areas the ice deposited till (a mixture of different sized materials, ranging from clay to boulders) and meltwater sediments (mainly sands and gravels). The Wolds were largely unglaciated during the Devensian, but the cold, dry periglacial conditions occurring beyond the advancing ice margin caused mainly silt-sized material to be blown on to this upland area, forming a veneer, typically 30-50 cm thick, over the chalk. Such material is known as loess. More local wind transport also occurred round the margins of the Wolds and in the Vale of York, depositing mainly sand-sized material.

Pre-Devensian Quaternary deposits are much more limited in extent, but a variety of such sediments has been recorded. At Sewerby, for example, deposits from the Ipswichian interglacial period occur beneath the Devensian till, and these include the fossil remains of a number of exotic fauna, such as elephant, rhinoceros and hippopotamus. Interglacial deposits also occur near Speeton on the north side of Flamborough Head, and in the Vale of York near Market Weighton. In Holderness, a glacial deposit known as Basement Till, which underlies the Skipsea Till, was also, until recently, considered to be pre-Devensian in age, relating to the previous Wolstonian glaciation; however, this material has now been suggested to be of Devensian age. On the Yorkshire Wolds, the presence of erratic stones is thought to relate to one or more pre-Devensian glaciations, and small pockets of a material known as Clay-with-flints, which may be of an earlier Quaternary origin, are also found, preserved in solution hollows within the chalk surface.

The most recent deposits in the East Riding date to the Post-glacial period, also known as the Flandrian or Holocene, which started around 10,000 years ago, characterised by rapid warming following the melting of the Devensian ice sheet. This resulted in a rise in sea level, and consequently in river base levels, which caused riverine and estuarine alluvium to be deposited on the floors of the valleys. The many small lakes, or meres, which had developed in kettle-holes in the deglaciated surface of Holderness, gradually became infilled by mineral and organic sediments, and in other poorly-drained, low-lying areas peat also started to accumulate, although such deposits are generally of a limited extent and thickness. At the southeastern tip of Holderness, material accumulated by longshore drift, forming the feature now known as Spurn Point. Most recently, during the past two centuries, artificial drainage and reclamation around the upper part of the Humber estuary has resulted in the accumulation of a material known as warp. This is produced by channelling sediment-laden estuarine water into embanked areas and allowing the sediment to settle out as the water drains away; the repetition of this procedure can accumulate as much as a metre of sediment in a single year, thus raising the level of the land and improving drainage. Within the East Riding, warp occurs in the southern Vale of York, overlying the alluvial and lacustrine deposits, but extensive areas also lie to the south, in the Humberhead Levels. Another form of reclamation occurred in southern Holderness, where, since the seventeenth century, the construction of embankments has allowed the natural accretion of estuarine sediments in the area around Sunk Island.

Bibliography on page 140

GEOLOGY

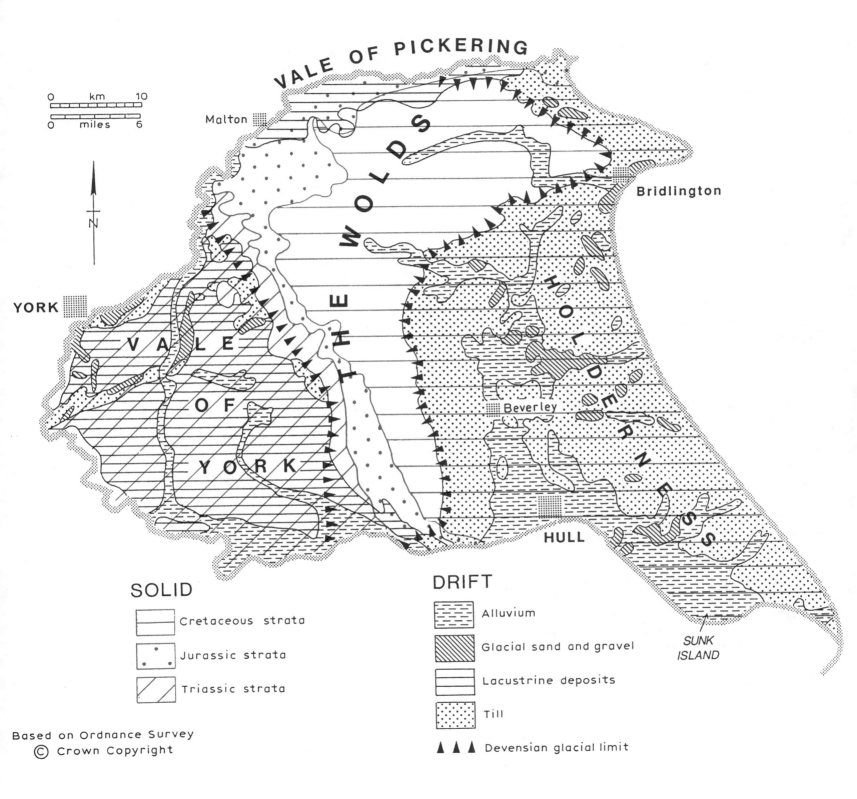

VALE OF PICKERING

Malton

York

THE WOLDS

Bridlington

VALE OF YORK

HOLDERNESS

Beverley

HULL

SUNK ISLAND

0 km 10

0 miles 6

N

SOLID

	Cretaceous strata
	Jurassic strata
	Triassic strata

DRIFT

	Alluvium
	Glacial sand and gravel
	Lacustrine deposits
	Till
▲ ▲ ▲	Devensian glacial limit

Based on Ordnance Survey
© Crown Copyright

COASTAL EROSION OF HOLDERNESS
George de Boer

Erosion of the East Riding's glacial till (boulder clay) coast of Holderness is notoriously severe, as an abundant literature testifies. High, steep waves, generated and propelled by northerly gales are the prime cause, and whatever shelter Flamborough Head affords extends only a limited distance southwards along the coast. More than four-fifths of the cliff material is clay, which is washed away completely. The small remainder - potential beach material - is swept southwards along the shore by these waves, and consequently, away from the artificially protected stretches of coast, the beaches are narrow and offer little protection to the cliffs behind them. In the past, this was aggravated by the regular removal of shingle and cobbles until this practice was prohibited from the mid-nineteenth century onwards.

Coastal erosion is enhanced by the fact that the till loses virtually all its strength when thoroughly wet. Heavy rainfall and water draining out through the cliffs from the land can turn the till into mud which sludges down and is easily washed away. The cliff foot retreats and the whole cliff becomes steeper and less stable. The removal of material operates in an irregular manner, being concentrated at points where cliff instability produces large slips. This irregularity is exemplified by a recession of about 6 m in a single night in 1967 at Barmston where the annual average is 0.8 m, and near Easington where between 1951 and 1966 retreat in individual years varied from 0.15 m to 10.3 m though the annual average is 1.8 m.

Nevertheless, when considering the loss of land in Holderness during the historical period, it is necessary to try to establish long-term average rates of recession and perhaps the overall fairly smooth curve of the Holderness coast gives some justification for this by showing how these local irregular events even out over time. From a comparison of the 1852 and 1889 editions of the Ordnance Survey six-inch map, a British Association Committee in 1895 concluded that over those 37 years erosion amounted to 182 feet (55.5 m) near Hornsea and 273 feet (83.2 m) near Holmpton, these figures equating to annual averages of 1.5 m and 2.25 m respectively, or 1.78 m for the whole length of coast examined. Valentin's survey of erosion from 1852 to 1952 (Map A) also showed an increase southwards: 0.29 m on average from Sewerby to Earl's Dike, rising to 1.75 m from Withernsea to Kilnsea. For over two miles from Easington to Kilnsea, the mean rate exceeded 2.0 m and in two places reached 2.75 m, which Valentin reported as being 'a figure among the highest to be recorded over a comparable period anywhere in the world'. His diagram of these results also shows how erosion decreases north of stretches of protected coast, but rises sharply to high levels south of them, especially near Hornsea and Withernsea which have had some protection since about 1870.

Any attempt to reconstruct former coastlines must be highly speculative. Sheppard favoured a figure of 7 ft 1 in (2.16 m) as the average rate of retreat of the whole coastline and concluded that at this rate a strip of land 2.5 miles (4.0 km) wide would have been lost since Roman times. However, the Roman coastline shown on his map is, according to the scale of the map, just under 1.5 miles (2.4 km) from his modern coastline. This coastline and one 2.5 miles offshore are shown on Map B, together with a third suggestion which uses Valentin's figures to estimate the position of the coastline 2,000 years ago. This also incorporates the possibility that the rising post-glacial sea formed a Bridlington Bay initially more deeply recessed than at present by eroding the low-lying water-laid deposits here more rapidly than the boulder clay further south.

From Barmston southwards, coastal erosion has beheaded several valleys draining inland. Some of their ends have in the past been used as anchorages. Two such, near Tunstall and Withernsea, are labelled 'Twoo small crekes for landing of fysher boote' on a map of c.1560. Another, the Stream Dike, which now drains Hornsea Mere seawards, was formerly called Hornsea Beck and had near its mouth a small port of that name, first mentioned c.1228; a pier there, recorded in 1558, is marked on the 1560 map. In 1609 it was said to have lost 38 houses since 1546, with more losses to follow if the pier were not rebuilt or other defence provided. A distinct, abandoned high shoreline shows that the mere was originally much larger and drained inland along a well-marked valley, until the sea, by breaching the eastern rim of its containing hollow and thus providing a lower and more direct outlet, reduced its level. Other meres, occupying similar beheaded valleys, have been lost completely, for example Withernsea, Out Newton and the pool at Sand-le-Mere (Map B); the latter is shown as a lake draining inland on maps from Saxton's of 1577 to Blaeu's of 1622.

Map B also shows Sheppard's location of lost settlements. Hartburn, near Earl's Dike, and Hyde (landing place), east of Skipsea, may be cited as examples of early recorded losses, both having disappeared by about 1400. Later losses include Owthorne, just north of Withernsea, where the church was gone by 1822, and Kilnsea, where the church collapsed down the cliff in 1830. The development of coastal sites for residence and leisure at Hornsea and Withernsea after the arrival of the railway (1854-64), and later elsewhere along the clifftops, has meant that buildings continue to be threatened by the sea; this, along with the loss of high-quality farmland, has made apparent the cost and difficulty of finding a generally satisfactory solution to the problem of coastal erosion.

The regular joining of sea and Humber across the narrow wedge of land south of Easington c.1900-10, and again in 1953 and 1978, illustrates the penultimate stage of a further effect here of coastal retreat - the withdrawal northwestwards of this tip of Holderness, a process important in the evolution of Spurn Point (see pages 8 and 9).

Bibliography on page 140

COASTAL EROSION OF HOLDERNESS

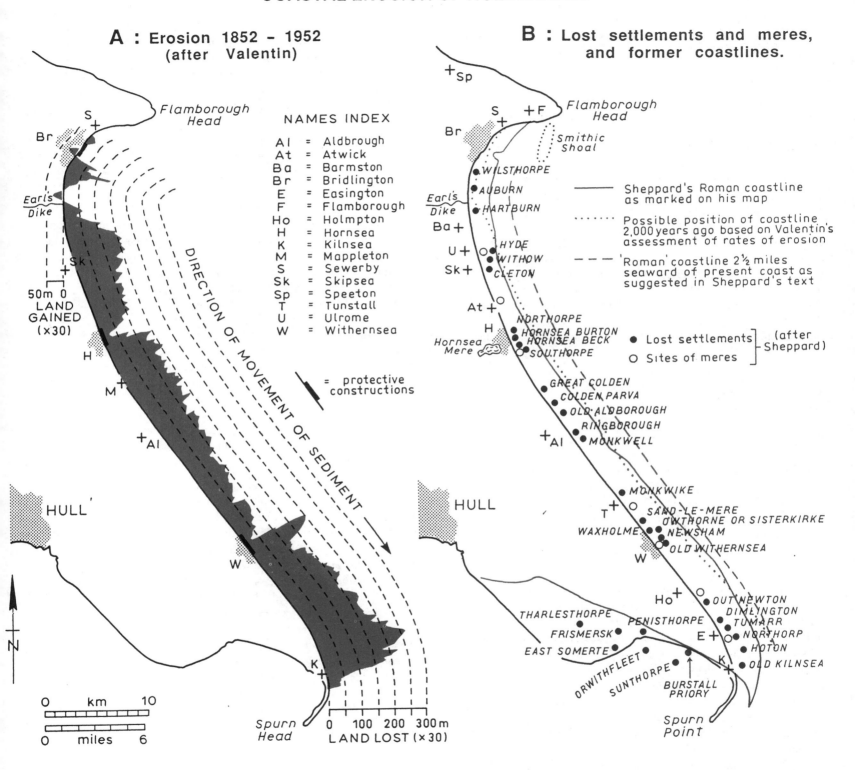

A : Erosion 1852 – 1952
(after Valentin)

B : Lost settlements and meres, and former coastlines.

Flamborough Head

NAMES INDEX

Al = Aldbrough
At = Atwick
Ba = Barmston
Br = Bridlington
E = Easington
F = Flamborough
Ho = Holmpton
H = Hornsea
K = Kilnsea
M = Mappleton
S = Sewerby
Sk = Skipsea
Sp = Speeton
T = Tunstall
U = Ulrome
W = Withernsea

Earls Dike

50m 0
LAND GAINED (×30)

DIRECTION OF MOVEMENT OF SEDIMENT

= protective constructions

HULL

N

0   km   10

0   miles   6

Spurn Head

0 100 200 300m
LAND LOST (×30)

Sp

Flamborough Head

Br

Smithic Shoal

Earls Dike

Ba

WILSTHORPE
AUBURN
HARTBURN

U
HYDE
WITHOW
Sk
CLETON

At

Sheppard's Roman coastline as marked on his map

Possible position of coastline 2,000 years ago based on Valentin's assessment of rates of erosion

'Roman' coastline 2½ miles seaward of present coast as suggested in Sheppard's text

NORTHORPE
H   HORNSEA BURTON
HORNSEA BECK
Hornsea Mere   SOUTHORPE

● Lost settlements ⎫ (after
○ Sites of meres   ⎭ Sheppard)

GREAT COLDEN
COLDEN PARVA
OLD ALDBOROUGH
RINGBOROUGH
Al   MONKWELL

MONKWIKE
T   SAND-LE-MERE
OWTHORNE OR SISTERKIRKE
WAXHOLME   NEWSHAM
W   OLD WITHERNSEA

HULL

Ho   OUT NEWTON
DIMLINGTON
TUMARR
THARLESTHORPE   PENISTHORPE   E   NORTHORP
FRISMERSK   HOTON
EAST SOMERTE   K   OLD KILNSEA
ORWITHFLEET   SUNTHORPE   BURSTALL PRIORY

Spurn Point

7

THE HISTORY OF SPURN POINT

George de Boer

At the southern tip of the Holderness coast lies Spurn Point, a natural spit of sand and shingle extending into the Humber estuary. The history of this feature has been intimately associated with the coastal erosion of Holderness, which not only accounts for its construction, but also makes it susceptible to disintegration as the Holderness coast recedes westwards. The material from which the spit is built is transported southwards along the Holderness shore by waves. However, the spit does not continue the same alignment as the coast, but instead grows southwestwards across the mouth of the Humber, and thus gains shelter from direct attack by the waves that erode the cliffs to the north. The waves that approach its southeast facing shore on balance throw sand and shingle on to or over its long narrow neck, thus building it up rather than washing it away. Some of the material is carried along the shore to the point and stays there so that Spurn grows longer, and some is carried round the point to the river side to form the broader tip. However, although Spurn retreats along with the coast to the north, the withdrawal of the tip of Holderness northwestwards leads progressively to a loss of the shelter on which its existence depends, so that at intervals it is washed away. A variety of evidence indicates an alternation of washing away and regrowth over at least the last few centuries; this course of events is summarised in the maps opposite.

The present spit began to develop c.1600 after its predecessor had been largely washed away. The superimposition of early maps and charts and the successive positions of lighthouses show clearly how this spit grew longer and at the same time retreated westwards at annual rates of 3.1-3.3 m, compared with the 2-2.75 m of southern Holderness (Map A). In December 1849 a wide breach was opened across it, and the 1852 six-inch Ordnance Survey map shows how Spurn was reduced to a string of islets at high water. Further reduction was halted by the closure of breaches and the construction of groynes and revetments. Developments during the period of artificial stabilisation that followed are shown in Map B.

This general pattern of natural development of Spurn c.1600-1852, to which an abundance of evidence testifies, is used in Map C to reconstruct the likely history of earlier spits. The washing away of Ravenser Odd c.1360-70, followed by that of Ravenspurn c.1600, followed again by the artificially averted washing away of Spurn Point c.1850, suggest a periodicity of about 250 years in the development of successive spits. Outlines of Spurn Point near the beginning and end of its period of natural development, when it was little interfered with by human activity, have been used as generalised representations of these earlier spits located in relation to coastlines reconstructed for the relevant dates, assuming for southern Holderness an annual rate of coastal retreat of 2.3 m. Using the dates of stages of development of Spurn Point as likely indicators of the rate of development of these earlier spits, date lines have been drawn from Spurn Point intersecting these proposed outlines of earlier spits, thus suggesting a plausible geographical setting for the main events in the earlier history of Spurn. Thus, that Spurn Point was in 1674 at a stage of development which justified the building of Angell's lighthouse suggests that it is reasonable to suppose that 247 years earlier Ravenspurn could have been at a stage which warranted Reedbarrow's efforts to build a lighthouse in 1427. This reconstruction also provides likely settings for the landings on Ravenspurn of Bolingbroke in 1399 and Edward IV in 1471. The lengthening and later erosion of Spurn Point during 1720-1830 could be similar to the circumstances 500 years earlier in which a likely site for the town of Ravenser Odd appeared soon after 1220 on the spit of that name and suffered severe erosion from about 1330 onwards.

Though the further back in time the more conjectural the reconstruction obviously becomes, the very earliest references to spits here are not out of accord with this framework, which at least provides the kind of geographical setting in which these briefly reported events could have taken place. The oldest of these accounts tells how Wilgils, father of St Willibrord, first bishop of Utrecht, came to 'the promontory encircled by the sea and Humber' and founded a chapel and monastery dedicated to St Andrew. Such a site, possibly on the broader tip of a peninsula with a narrow neck crossed by the tide which would cut it off from the mainland at intervals, might have seemed attractive to a community seeking solitude. It appears to have existed from c.670-770 just as, 1,000 years later, the site of Angell's lighthouse lasted from c.1674-1776; it too was cut off from Holderness when high spring tides crossed the neck of Spurn Point. The details given in *Egil's Saga* of his shipwreck here c.950 resemble conditions at Spurn today when a northerly gale causes heavy seas to break on Spurn and the Stony Binks.

Each of the five spits of this reconstruction seems to have received a name after its appearance, and each name is topographically appropriate. *Cornu vallis* (the horn of the valley) was the name in Wilgils' time, when the valleys in the boulder clay near Kilnsea and Easington would have been long enough, probably at least two miles, to justify this title. The spit on which Egil was wrecked was possibly that later named *Hrafnseyrr* or *Ravenser* (Raven's beach or sand bank), from which Olaf sailed with the remnants of the Scandinavian army defeated at Stamford Bridge in 1066. Later Ravenser became the name of a village near the tip of Holderness, and the next spit to appear was *Ravenser Odd* (the headland near Ravenser), which also became the name of the town established on it. By the time Bolingbroke landed there, the succeeding spit was called *Ravenser Spurn* or *Ravenspurn* (the spur of land near Ravenser). The new name for its successor, *Spurn Point*, is first recorded in 1675.

Bibliography on page 140

THE HISTORY OF SPURN POINT

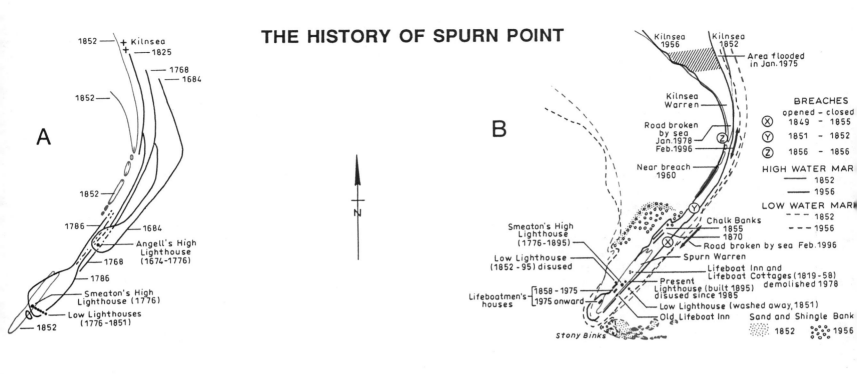

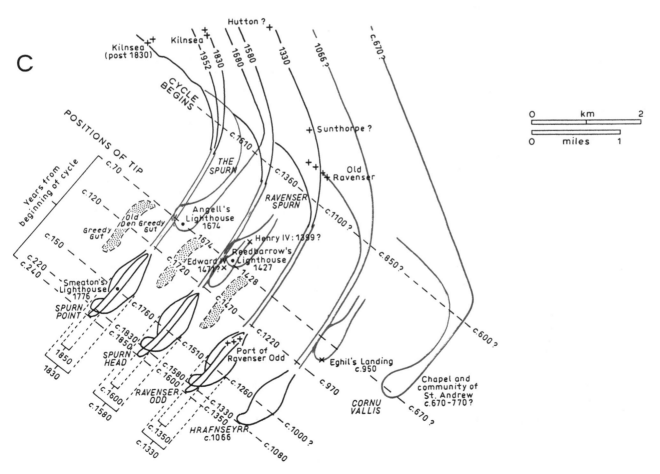

SOILS
Stephen Ellis

The soils of a particular area result from the interaction of a number of factors, namely geology, climate, relief, biota, time and, where present, human activity. Geology is a major control, determining soil characteristics such as size of particles and chemical composition, while climate controls processes such as particle breakdown and leaching, and also exerts an indirect control via its influence on biota. Vegetation influences the type and quality of organic matter added to the soil, while animals can determine the extent to which the organic matter is decomposed, and the nature of aeration resulting from burrowing activity. Relief influences drainage and the stability of soil on slopes, and time determines the extent to which soils are developed. Humans can affect soils both positively and adversely via agricultural, industrial, urban and other activity. The nature and extent of variation of all these factors within an area will therefore determine the physical, chemical and biological characteristics of its soils and the extent to which these vary spatially. Within the East Riding the factors of climate, biota and time do not, on the whole, vary greatly throughout the area at the scale under consideration here, but the remaining factors - geology, relief and human activity - have a marked effect on soil variability, as can be seen by examining the distribution of soil types within each of the four main physiographic regions - the Yorkshire Wolds, Holderness and the Hull valley, the Vale of Pickering and the Vale of York (see pages 2 and 3).

The soils of the Wolds are generally freely drained on account of the permeable chalk bedrock and sloping relief. They are not, however, derived entirely from the breakdown of the bedrock itself; their upper parts comprise silt-rich loess, blown on to the chalk surface under periglacial conditions during the Devensian period (see page 4). This gives them a greater thickness and moisture retention than would otherwise be the case. On the steeper slopes, the soils are often no more than 20 cm thick - these are known as *rendzinas*, the term given to thin soils occurring over chalk or limestone. On the more gently sloping areas, however, the soils are thicker (typically 30-50 cm), and these are known as *brown earths*. Although the rendzinas are often left under pasture or woodland, the brown earths are nowadays extensively cultivated on account of their lower gradients and greater moisture retention. Many soils on the Wolds were probably thicker in the past, but have become shallower due to soil erosion associated with cultivation; consequently soils in footslope or dry valley floor locations have often increased in thickness as a result of having received soil material moved from upslope.

In Holderness and the Hull valley, as on the Wolds, two main types of soil can be recognised. In the flat, more poorly drained areas *gley* soils are found, while on the undulating, more freely drained areas brown earths occur. Gleys are characterised by waterlogging at some position within the soil, either near the surface or at depth, on the basis of which they are known as *surface-water* (*stagnogleys*) or *groundwater*

gleys respectively. Both the brown earths and gleys are generally of a high clay content on account of them being developed in glacial till or post-glacial alluvium, and both are fertile, but historically the gleys were often uncultivated because of their restricted drainage. With the advent of artificial drainage, however, the majority of soils in Holderness and the Hull valley are now under cultivation, and few areas of pasture or woodland remain. In southern Holderness, brown earths occur on the artificially reclaimed deposits around Sunk Island.

The Vale of Pickering presents a similar pattern to Holderness and the Hull valley, with gleys occupying the floor of the Vale and brown earths occurring on the more freely draining margins. Also present in the poorest draining areas are peat soils, where complete saturation of the ground has inhibited the decomposition of organic matter. Again, the soils are mainly fine-grained because of the deposits on which they are developed, and the full potential of their fertility has generally been realised by artificial drainage, as a result of which most of the soils are now cultivated.

In the Vale of York the pattern of soil types is rather more complex than in the previous three areas. Many of the undulating, more freely drained areas possess brown earths. In some of the sandy areas, however, more acidic, nutrient-deficient soils, known as *podzols*, are found. The more poorly drained areas support gleys, while in the southern part of the Vale, large areas of warp occur (see page 4), which support brown earths. *Pelosols* are found only in the northern part of the Vale; these are clay-rich soils which have restricted drainage when wet but are prone to extensive cracking during the summer. With the exception of podzols, most soils in the Vale are fertile, and once again artificial drainage has resulted in widespread cultivation. In the sandier areas this has made the soils susceptible to erosion by strong winds at times during which the surface is not protected by a crop cover.

Although many of the soils of the East Riding are fertile, producing high-quality farmland, they do also present some problems to cultivation. Two of these - drainage and erosion - have already been mentioned, added to which there is the problem of susceptibility to drought. The East Riding is one of the drier regions of England, with a mean annual precipitation of 600-800 mm (compared with 800-1000 mm in more western arable areas), as a result of which irrigation of cropland is often required during the summer months.

Bibliography on page 140

SOILS

VALE OF PICKERING

Malton

THE WOLDS

60 m

Bridlington

HOLDERNESS

YORK

VALE

OF

YORK

Beverley

HULL

SUNK
ISLAND

	Rendzinas

	Pelosols

	Brown earths

	Podzols

	Surface-water gleys

	Ground-water gleys

	Peat

Based on Ordnance Survey
© Crown Copyright

0 km 10
0 miles 6

N

11

THE CHANGING DISTRIBUTION OF REPTILES SINCE THE LATE NINETEENTH CENTURY

B.R. Kirk

Of the six terrestrial native reptiles found in mainland Britain, four have been recorded in the East Riding. These are the adder (*Vipera berus*), grass snake (*Natrix natrix*), common lizard (*Lacerta vivipara*) and slowworm (*Anguis fragilis*). Reports of the occurrence of the other species of lizard - the sand lizard (*Lacerta agilis*) - in the area have been investigated and largely discounted. The other species of British reptile - the smooth snake (*Coronella austriaca*) has never been reported in the area.

By collating observations of reptiles contained in the natural history literature since the latter part of the nineteenth century, it has been possible to detect changes in reptile distribution in the East Riding. Records collected have been plotted for each reptile at tetrad level (2 x 2 km square), and the resulting distributions are shown on the maps opposite.

The last 100 years has seen rapid changes to habitats in the East Riding. Of particular importance have been the destruction and modification of habitats by agricultural practices, such as drainage improvements, ploughing out of grassland and afforestation, together with the expansion of urban centres and increased recreational pressures on the countryside. Changes in the distribution of each of the reptile species have also occurred during this time and appear, to a degree, to be linked with these habitat changes.

A number of records exist of the adder in the East Riding, the majority referring to the late nineteenth and early twentieth century. The Vale of York accounts for most of these records, and sites include Allerthorpe, Riccall and Skipwith Commons, along with the North Cliffe area. Two references to the occurrence of the species on the Wolds also exist from the late nineteenth century. In addition, a record dating from the 1960s has recently come to light for the occurrence of the species in the southern Hull valley.

As shown on the map, during the last 20 years the adder has only been recorded from one of the sites at which it has previously been observed - Allerthorpe Common. Agricultural practices have resulted in degradation of the heathlands of the Vale of York and this has impacted on the distribution of the species. The conversion of the Wolds chalk grassland to arable production may have resulted in the loss of the species from this area. There is also evidence in the literature to suggest heavy persecution of the adder early this century at Skipwith Common and this may have resulted in the absence of the species today at this site, which still retains areas of suitable habitat. Even the Allerthorpe Common site has been greatly reduced in value as a habitat for the adder by large-scale afforestation in the 1960s. Of the four reptile species recorded in the East Riding, the adder has shown the most marked reduction in distribution this century.

The distribution of the grass snake in East Yorkshire is still widespread, although the map indicates that a slight southward contraction has occurred. Examination of the literature reveals an increase in observations of the species since the 1920s. This may represent a genuine increase in distribution or it may reflect previous under-recording. The apparent absence of the grass snake from northern parts of the county is an issue that would warrant further investigation. Today, the grass snake's strongholds are in wetland habitats in the Holderness, Hull valley and Wallingfen areas. In general, the species has remained widespread since at least the 1930s. Its relative success in comparison with the adder reflects its more catholic habitat requirements.

The common lizard has a widespread but localised distribution in the area. Examination of older records suggests that the present distribution is similar to that of earlier this century, although a contraction in range has occurred in the Vale of York. As with the adder, this decline is associated with a loss of heathland habitat. The species also seems to have disappeared from a small number of sites in the western Wolds. With these exceptions, however, it would appear that the distribution of the common lizard has remained relatively stable this century, and populations exist today at locations such as Spurn Point, a number of former gravel pits in Holderness, the Humber bank and the remaining heathlands in the Vale of York. As with the grass snake, the adaptability of this species to a number of habitat types has assisted in maintaining its widespread distribution.

The slowworm appears to have been rare in the East Riding for at least the last 100 years, with early records being confined to a small number of commons in the Vale of York and single records at Filey and Beverley. In fact the two recent records shown on the distribution map both occur in the Hull urban fringe and may represent escaped pets. The majority of older records all date from early this century. Although possibly under-recorded in the area due to its secretive habits, it is still evident that this species has disappeared from a number of its former stations during the last 100 years.

Bibliography on page 140

THE CHANGING DISTRIBUTION OF REPTILES
SINCE THE LATE 19th CENTURY

DISTRIBUTION OF THE ADDER

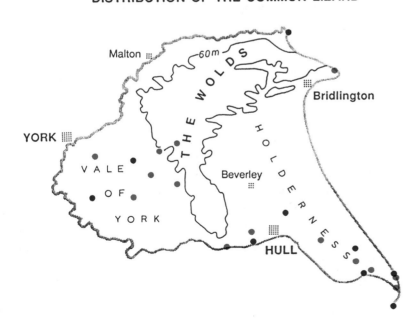

DISTRIBUTION OF THE GRASS SNAKE

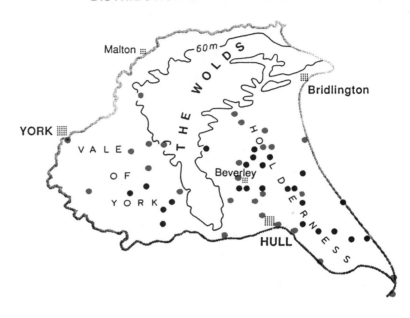

DISTRIBUTION OF THE COMMON LIZARD

DISTRIBUTION OF THE SLOWWORM

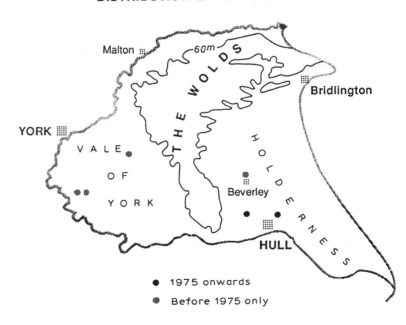

- ● 1975 onwards
- ● Before 1975 only

WILDLIFE CONSERVATION
Richard Middleton

The East Riding's wildlife has been managed and exploited since the earliest days of its colonisation. The woodland, which provided a source of timber for fuel and construction, and fodder for domesticated animals, had been cleared from the Wolds by around 4000 years ago, although on the wetter, less easily cultivated soils of Holderness it persisted into the Iron Age. Animals were also extensively exploited as a source of food. For example, ten fisheries were mentioned on the river Hull and lower Derwent in the Domesday survey, the one at Beverley yielding 7000 eels; indeed, in the early middle ages it was not uncommon for some East Yorkshire tenants to pay their rent in eels. In addition, there were concerted efforts to eradicate animals seen as a physical threat, with bears and wolves largely exterminated from the area by the middle ages, and the persecution of smaller species such as adders, polecats and larger birds of prey continuing until modern times. There is, on the other hand, a long tradition of the preservation of animals for sporting purposes, with over 50 deer parks having been created in the riding before 1700 and the present scattering of small woods throughout the area being due, in no small part, to pheasant shooting and fox hunting interests. Some of the large landowners were also exercising conservation schemes, for landscape and aesthetic reasons, on their own estates from the eighteenth century, but in general the natural world was viewed largely as an unlimited resource to be exploited freely. The idea that species conservation was essential to the maintenance of a stable and well-balanced countryside did not emerge until the late nineteenth century.

Concern for the well-being of birds started to be expressed in the nineteenth century; many species had been shot to extinction in the East Riding, mainly for sport, and some of the naturally rarer species were being over-collected for 'scientific purposes'. By 1870 there had been a series of Wild Bird Protection Acts, but these only afforded protection to certain species during the breeding season and the penalties for non-observation were low. In 1906 Spurn Point was declared a sanctuary by the East Riding County Council, but no provision was made for any enforcement. The following year, the Yorkshire Naturalists' Union (YNU) appealed for funds to support watchers here and also at Hornsea Mere. The importance of Flamborough Head to nesting seabirds was also being recognised, and at Bridlington by-laws were passed which prohibited the shooting of gulls and terns from the town's beaches. In 1945 the YNU established the Spurn Bird Observatory, to study bird migration, at a time when only two other such stations existed in Britain.

The National Parks and Access to the Countryside Act of 1949 made provision for the statutory protection of sites of biological importance. In 1951 Hornsea Mere and Allerthorpe Common were so designated, followed by Flamborough Head the following year and a further seven sites in 1954. East Yorkshire now has almost 50 such Sites of Special Scientific Interest designated for their wildlife value. In the 1950s the need to protect plant as well as animal species was being recognised. This may have been due, at least in part, to the rapid changes being brought about in the countryside as a result of the Agriculture Act of 1947 and the subsequent mechanisation of farming.

Pressure from both naturalists and wildfowlers resulted in the establishment of a safe refuge for wintering wildfowl along the upper reaches of the river Humber. The Humber Wildfowl Refuge was established by an act of Parliament in 1955, and its operation is still overseen by a joint committee of naturalists and wildfowlers.

The Yorkshire Wildlife Trust, founded in 1946, purchased Spurn Point as its first East Yorkshire reserve in 1960, finally affording the site the protection and status that had been sought by conservationists for more than half a century. The organisation now supervises fourteen reserves in East Yorkshire, ranging in size from less than one hectare to almost 250 ha at Skipwith Common and 300 ha at Spurn. The Royal Society for the Protection of Birds operates reserves at Hornsea Mere and Bempton Cliffs. It is at the latter site that the benefits of environmental legislation can be seen to greatest effect, with the variety and number of seabirds nesting on the cliffs being greater now than ever previously recorded. Local organisations are also now playing an important part in conservation; the South Holderness Countryside Society, for example, maintains several nature reserves.

Increased environmental awareness in the 1980s led to a greater involvement of Local Authorities in wildlife conservation. In 1988 Humberside County Council (HCC), after wide consultation, published a list of sites with known wildlife value, which included over 600 sites in East Yorkshire. This was intended to ensure that adequate consideration was given to the natural environment when potentially damaging development was planned. In 1995 HCC published a Wildlife Action Programme, outlining almost 300 known initiatives related to wildlife promotion, conservation and research in the county. In the same year, Hull City Council published a strategy for wildlife conservation in the city, which stressed the importance of maintaining a 'green network' of interconnected sites to facilitate the movement of wild animals and birds.

Recent initiatives have recognised the importance of the wetlands adjacent to the rivers Humber and Derwent, and have resulted in their designation as 'Wetlands of International Importance' under the Ramsar Convention. They have also been given, along with Flamborough Head, the status of Special Protection Area (SPA) under the EC Directive 79/409 on the Conservation of Wild Birds.

There is a greater awareness than ever before of the need to conserve the natural environment. It is unfortunate that this awareness has arisen so late, when much lasting damage has already been done, but efforts are being made not only to preserve what remains but also to create new habitats suitable for colonisation by wild animals and plants.

Bibliography on page 141

WILDLIFE CONSERVATION

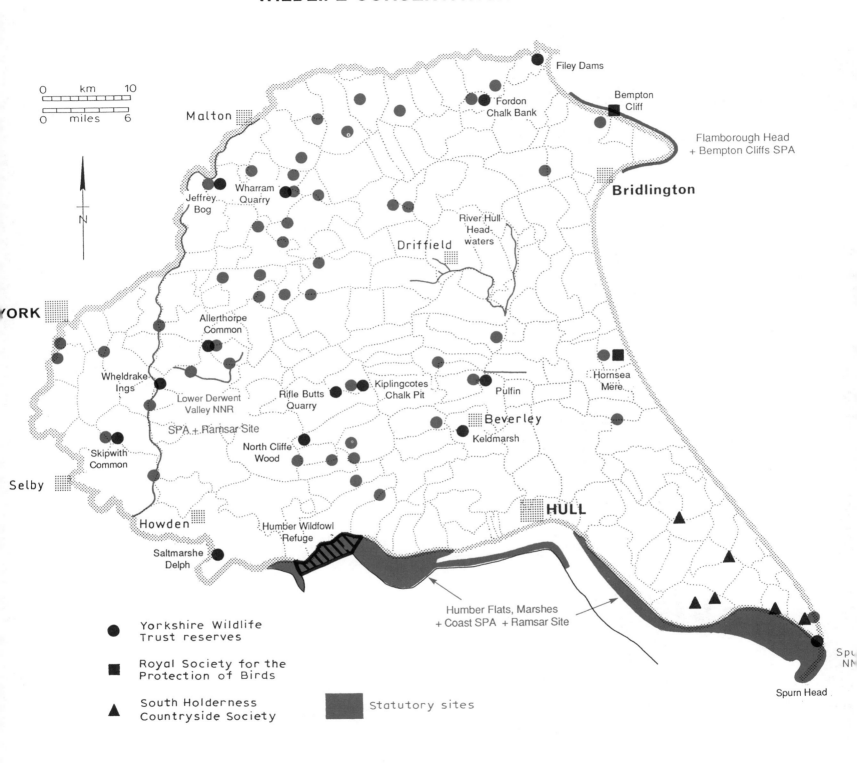

0 km 10

0 miles 6

N

Malton

Filey Dams

Fordon Chalk Bank

Bempton Cliff

Flamborough Head + Bempton Cliffs SPA

Bridlington

Jeffrey Bog

Wharram Quarry

River Hull Head-waters

Driffield

YORK

Allerthorpe Common

Wheldrake Ings

Lower Derwent Valley NNR

SPA + Ramsar Site

Rifle Butts Quarry

Kiplingcotes Chalk Pit

Pulfin

Hornsea Mere

Skipwith Common

Selby

North Cliffe Wood

Beverley

Keldmarsh

Howden

Humber Wildfowl Refuge

HULL

Saltmarshe Delph

Humber Flats, Marshes + Coast SPA + Ramsar Site

Spurn NNR

Spurn Head

● Yorkshire Wildlife Trust reserves

■ Royal Society for the Protection of Birds

▲ South Holderness Countryside Society

Statutory sites

ARCHAEOLOGY

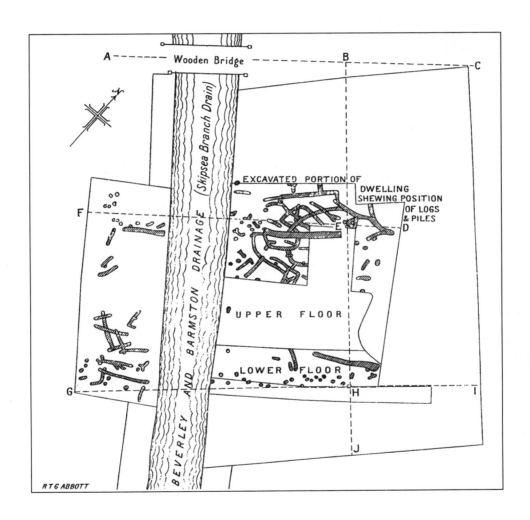

THE EARLIEST INHABITANTS: HUNTER-GATHERER SOCIETIES

Robert Van de Noort

The archaeological record of East Yorkshire is mainly determined by two factors, which in turn influence the distribution maps of presently known archaeological sites as presented in this volume - land use and the past and present activities of archaeologists in the region. Land use determines the survival of prehistoric settlements, burial sites and boundaries. Archaeological sites are most likely to be preserved as earthworks or extant structures on non-arable land. Arable land use, and particularly modern deep-ploughing, accounts for much damage to such sites, although it may increase their visibility as crop marks in aerial reconnaissance, or as scatters of cultural material at the surface. Settlements, both rural and urban, may mask their own predecessors, while some archaeological landscapes have been covered by natural sedimentation processes, only to be rediscovered after extensive drainage and land reclamation. The personal interests of archaeologists account for much of what is known of human activity over the last 12,000 years, and our comprehension of the prehistoric past is therefore not evenly represented in time or space. Archaeological interest has been traditionally focused largely on the Neolithic, Bronze Age and Iron Age earthwork remains on the Yorkshire Wolds, but more recently attention has shifted to the wetlands, with projects in the Vale of York, Holderness and the Vale of Pickering.

Hunting, fishing and gathering of nuts, fruits, root vegetables and other naturally available resources formed the dominant mode of subsistence for most of the prehistoric period. Much of the earliest human activity in the East Riding was destroyed by Devensian ice movements (see pages 4 and 5), with only a few finds associated with the Palaeolithic era being known. Following the retreat of the ice sheet and the rapid climatic amelioration of the early Holocene, forests became re-established in the region. In the low-lying areas - the Vales of Pickering and York, the Hull valley and Holderness - rich plant and animal resources became available for exploitation, and the region is famous for its early Mesolithic sites, dating from around 7500 to 4300 BC.

The most important of these sites is Star Carr in the Vale of Pickering. After the original excavation of 1949-51, the site was thought to be a wooden platform on the edge of a lagoon with associated finds of hunting equipment, including a large collection of antler barbed 'harpoon' points, lithic artefacts, animal bones, 21 stag skulls and a wooden paddle-shaped object. More recent analysis has, however, revealed that the wooden platform is part of a larger occupation site, and assumptions that the site was occupied seasonally only during the winter and early spring are currently being re-assessed. Nearby sites at Seamer Carr (North Riding) and Flixton also date to this period, and a possibly early Mesolithic site at Round Hill in Holderness has recently been discovered.

Elsewhere, evidence for early Mesolithic exploitation occurs as finds of barbed 'harpoon' points. To date seventeen such artefacts have been discovered in Holderness, with a concentration in and around the glacial meltwater gravels at Brandesburton. Thus far none has been found to be associated with a settlement site, and the most recent find, in a kettle-hole at Gransmoor in the Hull valley, was apparently related to a hunting expedition. The barbed points are mostly of bone, rather than of antler as at Star Carr, and on typological grounds they are considered to be younger than those from Star Carr.

Further archaeological evidence of Mesolithic occupation of the East Riding reinforces the importance of the wetland areas for subsistence. Flint implements and scatters of debris from flint-working dated to the later Mesolithic period have been found in the Vale of York, the Hull valley and Holderness, but are mainly absent from the Yorkshire Wolds. While the debate concerning the timing of the northwards migration of fish after the end of the glacial period continues, it is evident that the wetlands attracted both large mammals such as red deer and aurochs, and water-fowl, which may have formed the basis for the subsistence economy. Undoubtedly the coastal resources would have been exploited, and coastal shell middens from elsewhere have illustrated the importance of shellfish in late Mesolithic subsistence. Unfortunately, the Post-glacial rise in sea level has masked any evidence of settlement along the East Riding coast at this time.

Towards the end of the Mesolithic period, and during the earliest stages of the succeeding archaeological period - the Neolithic - hunting, gathering of fruits and root vegetables, and fishing remained an important aspect of the subsistence economy, but the arrival or adoption of new customs and subsistence practices is illustrated in the palaeoecological record by forest clearance and a wider distribution throughout the East Riding of archaeological remains attributed to this date.

Bibliography on page 141

THE EARLIEST INHABITANTS:
HUNTER-GATHERER SOCIETIES

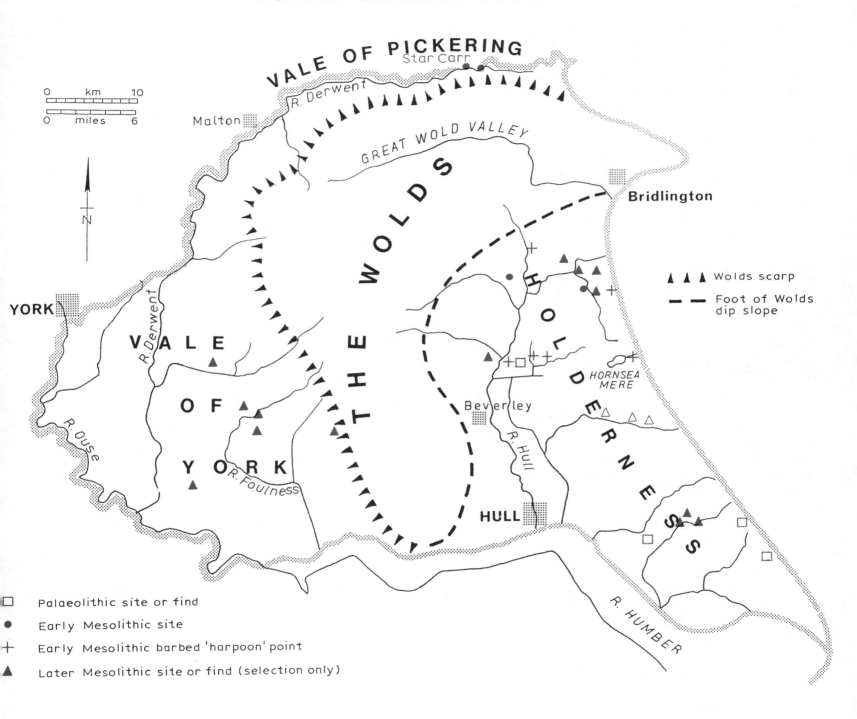

VALE OF PICKERING

Star Carr

R. Derwent

Malton

GREAT WOLD VALLEY

Bridlington

T H E   W O L D S

H O L D E R N E S S

0   km   10

0   miles   6

N

YORK

R. Derwent

V A L E

O F

Y O R K

R. Ouse

R. Foulness

HORNSEA MERE

Beverley

R. Hull

HULL

R. HUMBER

▲▲▲▲ Wolds scarp

--- Foot of Wolds dip slope

□ Palaeolithic site or find

● Early Mesolithic site

+ Early Mesolithic barbed 'harpoon' point

▲ Later Mesolithic site or find (selection only)

EARLY AGRICULTURALISTS: THE NEOLITHIC PERIOD

Robert Van de Noort

The archaeology of early agriculture in the East Riding has provided little direct evidence of farming activities; rather, we know a great deal more about the ritual and mortuary practices of the early agriculturalists. The period of these earliest farmers is commonly referred to as the Neolithic era. In the perception of archaeologists three decades ago, the Neolithic was characterised by the use of polished stone axes and adzes, the production of pottery, a sedentary lifestyle and a subsistence based on farming rather than hunting and gathering. These were all major innovations in themselves and the resulting assumption was that this new lifestyle was related to processes of colonisation by farming communities. However, theories of the introduction of agriculture by colonists from the continent are no longer considered valid. It is accepted that certain products, such as seed corn and domesticated animals, and skills, such as the production of pottery and polished tools, originated from the continent, but the conversion of the dominant mode of subsistence from hunting and gathering to farming is now thought to have extended over several centuries, with pioneer farming communities originating from the continent and hunter-gatherers existing side by side. Indeed, both modes of subsistence may have been used by the same people. Recent DNA analysis of skeletons indicates that as little as ten per cent of our ancestry is related to the early continental farming communities, the remainder relating largely to the indigenous hunter-gatherers.

Direct evidence for the earliest farming activities comes mainly from the analysis of fossil pollen grains. A reduction in tree pollen, resulting from either the cutting of leaf fodder for cattle or the clearance of forest in order to provide areas for grazing and cereal cultivation, provides the best known evidence. Research from various sites in Holderness indicates that the first clearances, the so-called 'elm decline', occurred around 3900 BC, but evidence for extensive arable agriculture, including the presence of cereal pollen, is lacking. Consequently, it is assumed that the early agriculturalists in the region were mainly pastoralists, with cereal production being of limited importance, possibly confined to religious and mortuary practices. Not until much later, around 1000 BC, was large-scale forest clearance undertaken throughout the region, with arable rather than pastoral farming becoming the dominant mode of subsistence.

While the pollen evidence is derived largely from natural wetland deposits in the Holderness lowlands, the vast majority of Neolithic ritual and mortuary sites are situated on the higher, drier ground of the Yorkshire Wolds. The earliest sites attributed to this period are rectangular mortuary enclosures, culminating in the construction of monumental rectangular shaped burial mounds, known as long barrows. These monuments housed mainly chambers for the deposition of human remains, and the input of labour needed for construction, extending over long periods or occurring in a series of building phases, is considered an important element in the making of societies and endorsement of their socio-political grouping. The long barrows at Kilham and West Heslerton are examples of such monuments. Similarly, round barrows of this period developed over time, the barrow itself being the final stage of a building project that could have lasted several centuries. The occurrence of monuments of the early Neolithic period within the same cultural landscape as that of later monuments, indicates that their importance did not end with the completion of construction.

In the later Neolithic period, from around 2500 BC, the construction and modification of the earlier ritual and mortuary monuments ceased, and new types of monuments appeared. Round barrows were built for individuals rather than groups, and sometimes contained grave goods including Beaker pottery as an indication of high status, and henges and cursuses were constructed, sometimes resulting in elaborate ritual landscapes. One such landscape is centred around the Rudston Monolith, the tallest prehistoric standing stone in Great Britain. It is a Jurassic gritstone and must therefore have been transported a distance of at least ten miles to its site on the chalk of the Yorkshire Wolds. Three cursuses, or narrow enclosures best described as processional avenues, focus on the monolith and a fourth runs below it, along the Great Wold Valley. Two great barrows and two henges, or circular ceremonial sites, also occur within this landscape. In all, four great barrows are known - Willy Howe and Newton Barrow on the floor of the Great Wold Valley, South Side Barrow to the south of the Gypsey Race, and Duggleby Howe at the west end of the Great Wold Valley. These are huge mounds, over 30 m in diameter, which add to the variety of monuments in this period.

In contrast to ritual and mortuary sites, Neolithic occupation sites have been identified as concentrations of flint and broken pottery, but no excavations of such settlements have taken place in the East Riding. The material culture of the Neolithic is represented by pottery of the Grimston, Towthorpe and Ebbsfleet styles, with Peterborough Ware, Grooved Ware and Beakers dominating the pottery assemblage of the later Neolithic period. The concentration of occupation debris of this period is greatest on the Wolds, but substantial evidence for occupation has also been found in the Vale of York and Holderness. In addition, polished flint and stone axes, and smaller flint tools such as arrowheads and knives, have been found in abundance both on the Wolds and in the Hull valley and Holderness.

Bibliography on page 141

EARLY AGRICULTURALISTS: THE NEOLITHIC PERIOD

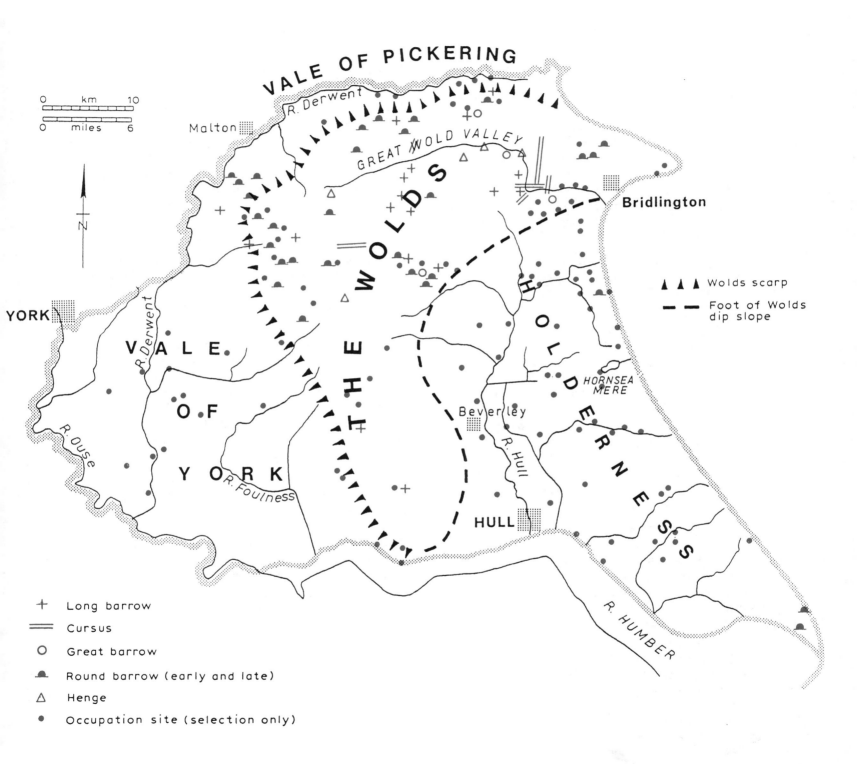

VALE OF PICKERING

R. Derwent

Malton

GREAT WOLD VALLEY

Bridlington

THE WOLDS

YORK

R. Derwent

VALE

OF

YORK

R. Ouse

R. Foulness

HOLDERNESS

HORNSEA MERE

Beverley

R. Hull

HULL

R. HUMBER

Wolds scarp

Foot of Wolds
dip slope

0   km   10
0   miles   6

N

+   Long barrow

=   Cursus

O   Great barrow

🝰   Round barrow (early and late)

△   Henge

•   Occupation site (selection only)

21

THE AGRARIAN SOCIETY OF THE METAL AGES

Robert Van de Noort

Agrarian societies had been established by the later Neolithic period, and the integration of continental pioneer farmers and indigenous hunter-gatherers in the region would have been complete by around 2500 BC. In the later Neolithic period the first archaeological indications of differential wealth or status within communities appear, in the shape of central, individual graves in round barrows furnished with specific grave goods. It is possible that the expression of status through monumental graves and material culture reflects a crisis within or between communities, and this expression of differentiation continues throughout the Bronze and Iron Ages, covering the period from around 1500 BC to the conquest of the region by the Romans. From about 1000 BC, new archaeological sites such as hillforts and linear earthworks were constructed, not only providing archaeologists with settlements to excavate, but also indicating changes in the organisation of society.

Palaeoenvironmental studies indicate that forest clearance was well underway by 1000 BC. All trees appear to have been affected, not only elm and lime as during the early Neolithic 'elm-decline' (see page 20). This phase of clearance is commonly associated with the widespread introduction of arable farming, in particular on the Yorkshire Wolds, although pastoralism remained important; indeed, it was probably still the dominant mode of subsistence.

Archaeological evidence for occupation in the earlier Bronze Age is largely limited to the distribution of round barrows, many of which were excavated in the nineteenth century by W. Greenwell and J.R. Mortimer. The continued use of this mortuary form into the earlier Bronze Age is indicative of a persistence of structures and perceptions within the region, regardless of the introduction of the first bronze tools. A completely different type of site attributable to this period is the Humber foreshore at North Ferriby, where over the years the remains of at least three timber boats have been discovered.

For the period after 1000 BC, the archaeological evidence is greatly varied. Hillforts were an innovation in the area, and on the Wolds they have been identified, for example, at Grimthorpe, Devil's Hill, Staple Howe and Thwing. All are roughly circular in form and are defended by ramparts, which in the case of Grimthorpe and Thwing included timber box structures and a deep external ditch. At Grimthorpe all interior features have been destroyed by cultivation, but a lengthy excavation campaign at Thwing found an inner ditch and a central wooden structure, measuring 25 m across. A large number of finds and further features indicate a settlement with regional political and possibly religious functions, supported by an affluent material culture. Other settlement sites have been identified on the Wolds and in Holderness, some with palisades, others consisting of individual or small groups of round houses. Another type of archaeological site are the so-called 'lake-dwellings' in northern Holderness, although recent

investigation at West Furze and Round Hill has provided alternative explanations for these sites. West Furze has now been re-interpreted as a trackway, which crosses the elongated mere complex in this area, and there is evidence for an elaborate entrance on the east side of the trackway, suggesting some sort of symbolic boundary. Radiocarbon assay of a wooden pile from the site at Round Hill suggests an Early Mesolithic date rather than a Bronze Age date for the wooden structures.

In the early Iron Age, many of the hillforts remained in use, although larger, nucleated settlements were also becoming apparent. The settlement at Wetwang Slack, for example, consisted of over 80 circular huts and round houses within a large field system which comprised fields, tracks, lanes and enclosures. Settlements dating to this period have been found throughout the East Riding, although they avoid the low-lying wetland areas.

A relatively small percentage of round barrows in the East Riding can be attributed to the period around 1000 to 500 BC, and the majority of burial sites attributed to this phase have urns containing the cremated remains of the deceased, often interred secondarily in the barrows. In the last phases of the Bronze Age and into the early Iron Age, these characteristics continue, but human remains have also been recorded at settlement sites.

Many linear earthworks are considered to date to the period after 1000 BC, although their long term use and incorporation of earlier monuments such as burial mounds indicate that their significance far outlived their original function, namely delineation of the landscape, probably with respect to political territories. Danes Dike, a massive earth-and-ditch feature enclosing the Flamborough headland, may be considered the most important example of a linear earthwork in the East Riding, although its age remains a matter of debate.

A final archaeological category requiring mention is metalwork. A large number of stray bronze finds indicate the extent of exploitation of the landscape in the East Riding throughout this period. Bronzes are found as grave goods in the earlier Bronze Age, but in the later Bronze Age and the Iron Age the largest concentration of bronzes, and particularly bronze weapons, comes from the wetlands in the Vale of Pickering, the Hull valley and Holderness.

Bibliography on page 141

THE AGRARIAN SOCIETY OF THE METAL AGES

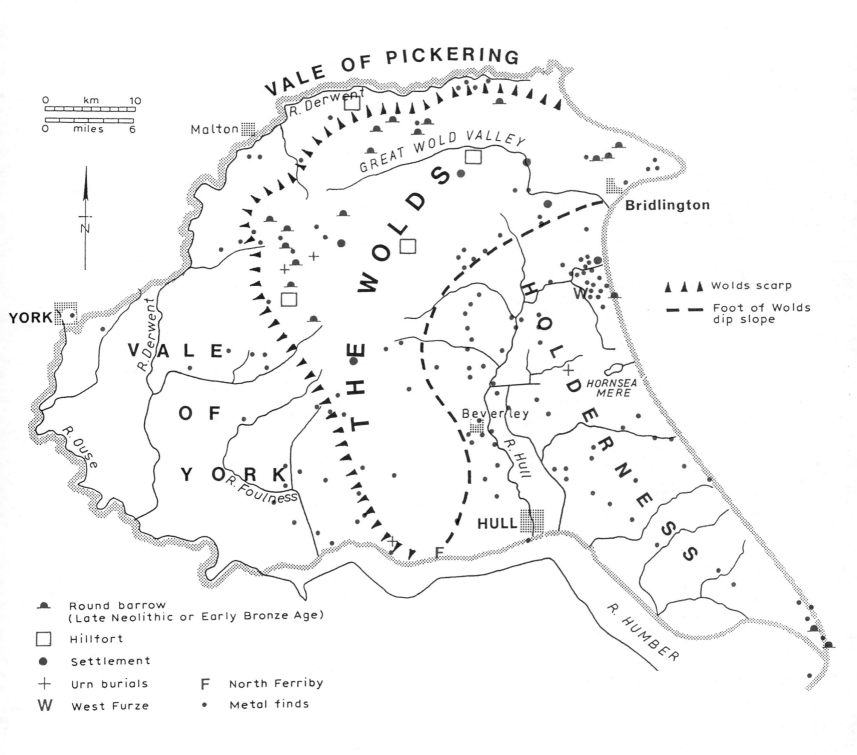

VALE OF PICKERING

R. Derwent

Malton

GREAT WOLD VALLEY

Bridlington

T H E   W O L D S

YORK

R. Derwent

R. Ouse

V A L E

O F

Y O R K

R. Foulness

H O L D E R N E S S

HORNSEA MERE

W

Beverley

R. Hull

HULL

F

R. HUMBER

▲▲▲ Wolds scarp

– – – Foot of Wolds dip slope

0   km   10

0   miles   6

N

Round barrow
(Late Neolithic or Early Bronze Age)

☐ Hillfort

● Settlement

+ Urn burials

W West Furze

F North Ferriby

• Metal finds

23

THE ARRAS CULTURE

Robert Van de Noort

Around 500 BC, there are indications of a climatic amelioration, and an associated expansion of settlement and exploitation of the lowlands of the Vale of York and Holderness. This period of expansion may have been short-lived, however, with the lowlands being partially inundated following marine transgression, resulting in a generally more competitive and more stratified society by the fourth and third centuries BC.

From the fourth century BC onwards, something like a distinct cultural identity becomes visible in East Yorkshire. This is commonly referred to as the Arras culture or tradition, and is characterised by the construction of burial mounds surrounded by square-plan ditches, rather than the circular-ditched barrows of the Neolithic and Bronze Age. Research into these square-ditched barrows was undertaken in the nineteenth and early twentieth century by the barrow diggers Boynton, Mortimer and Greenwell, when many of the mounds were still visible as earthworks, and more recently as a result of large-scale mineral extraction and new discoveries from aerial reconnaissance. In contrast, the archaeological investigation of settlement and industrial sites of this period only commenced in the last three decades.

The distribution of squared-ditched barrows is largely confined to East Yorkshire, with a few additional examples known from North Yorkshire, and these features are unique in the British Isles. The number of known square-ditched cemeteries in the area is still increasing, mainly because of ongoing aerial photographic work, but currently over 350 cemeteries have been identified, of which a representative selection is mapped. The distinct burial tradition appears to have evolved from the fourth century BC, when isolated square-ditched barrows were constructed, to a common mortuary rite in the second century BC, with some cemeteries including hundreds of barrows. The bodies were usually, but not exclusively, placed in the grave in a crouched position. Grave goods included weapons (most commonly swords), vessels and often a joint of meat (pig or sheep). Burial dress included brooches, bracelets and necklaces.

Among the most spectacular finds from the Arras culture burials are the remains of vehicles. These have been identified at, for example, Wetwang Slack, Garton Slack, Garton Station, Kirkburn, Danes Graves and possibly at Hornsea. While the discoveries of wheels in the grave used to be interpreted as those of 'chariots', current thinking is more inclined to describe the vehicles as carts. The majority of these finds have been associated with female graves, although a recently excavated cart burial at Wetwang Slack evidently related to a male warrior, with grave goods including a sword, shield and seven spears. The two wheels are commonly found removed from the cart, being placed on the floor of the grave beneath the deceased or stacked against the wall.

The cart burials and the square-plan ditches surrounding the barrows have previously been related to La Tène traditions in the Champagne, Ardennes and central Rhineland regions. However, the East Yorkshire Arras culture is no longer considered to be the result of any large-scale invasion or influx from the continent. Settlement research, for example at Wetwang Slack and North Cave, and particularly the analysis of domestic pottery, has made a strong claim for the continuity of occupation in the region, from well before the fourth century BC to the Roman period. These settlements were characterised by round houses, 7-10 m in diameter and probably with a conical roof, which were enclosed by rectangular ditches and linked by droveways in the later Iron Age. Alternative explanations for the continental customs in Iron Age East Yorkshire include effects of 'acculturation' following cross-Channel trade, or the presence of a small group of immigrants which had a disproportionate influence on the mortuary practices of the native elite, which were later copied by the population at large.

Among the most important archaeological discoveries from this period is the Hasholme Boat, which was found in 1984 and subsequently excavated. It was situated in Wallingfen, an area of former wetland with extensive creek systems, in the Vale of York. The excavation identified a 12.6 m long logboat, with a girth of over 5 m, which was constructed from a single tree, the felling date of which has been dendrochronologically dated at 322-277 BC. The boat was propelled by up to 20 paddlers, and its final cargo included timbers and prime joints of beef. The vessel is thought to have played a role in the transport of iron ore and products, and possibly firewood, to and from the Wallingfen area; recent archaeological research has identified several iron-working and manufacturing sites of the Iron Age period.

In the late pre-Roman Iron Age, the effects of the expanding Roman empire become visible archaeologically in East Yorkshire. The site of Redcliff, immediately to the west of North Ferriby on the river Humber, dates mainly to the mid-first century AD and therefore pre-dates the Roman conquest of the region, but the material culture of the site is dominated by Roman imports. This site has been described as a 'port of trade', where exchange of goods took place with the then Roman site of Old Winteringham on the south bank of the Humber.

After the Roman conquest of the region, the new political organisation and division of England closely followed the late pre-Roman Iron Age tribal territories. The region of East Yorkshire formed in its entirety the *civitates* of the Parisi, with its probable capital at Brough, or *Petuaria*. It is therefore most likely that during the Iron Age, the people of the Arras culture increasingly saw themselves as belonging to the tribe of the Parisi.

Bibliography on page 141

THE ARRAS CULTURE

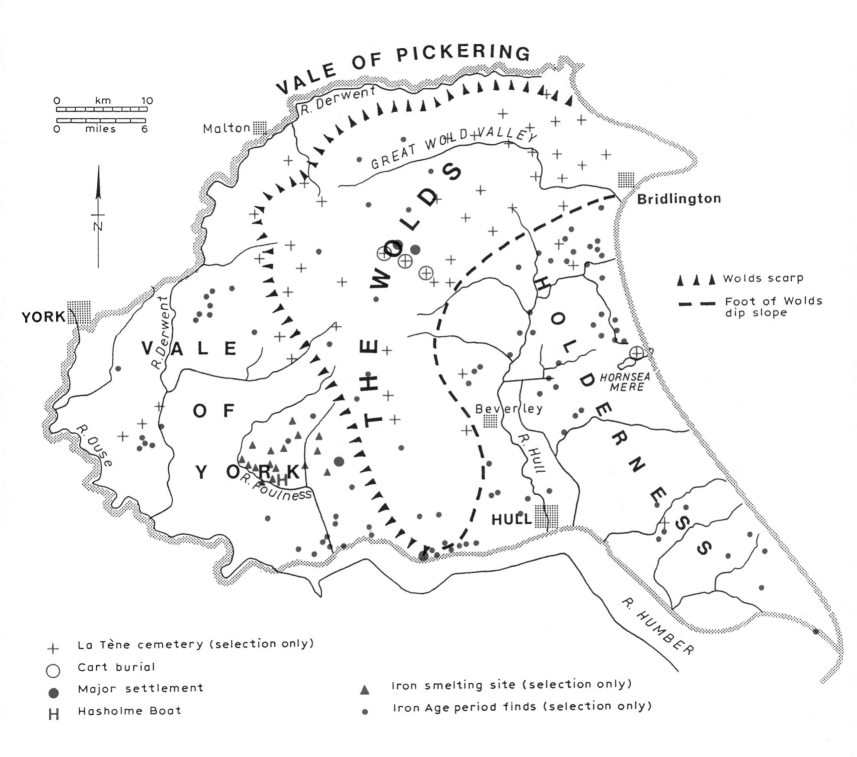

0 km 10

0 miles 6

N

VALE OF PICKERING

R. Derwent

Malton

GREAT WOLD VALLEY

Bridlington

THE WOLDS

YORK

R. Derwent

R. Ouse

VALE

OF

YORK

R. Foulness

H

HOLDERNESS

HORNSEA MERE

Beverley

R. Hull

HULL

R. HUMBER

Wolds scarp

Foot of Wolds dip slope

+   La Tène cemetery (selection only)

○   Cart burial

●   Major settlement

H   Hasholme Boat

▲   Iron smelting site (selection only)

•   Iron Age period finds (selection only)

THE ROMAN AND EARLY MEDIEVAL PERIODS

Robert Van de Noort

The Roman conquest of the East Yorkshire region commenced in the AD 70s, probably during the governorship of Petillius Cerialis or shortly thereafter. A process of political and cultural acculturation or 'Romanisation' between the Roman military and native Parisi resulted in what is commonly referred to as a 'Romano-British' society. Environmental evidence suggests that marine regression allowed occupation and exploitation of the lowlands of the Vale and York and Holderness, until a major fourth century transgression resulted in widespread flooding.

Archaeological evidence for the conquest of the region comes mainly in the form of remains of fortresses and forts, and Roman roads. At Brough (*Petuaria*), an early bridgehead was established which included a fort and port, and forts at Hayton, Malton and possibly Stamford Bridge are all associated with the conquest of the territory of the Parisi. The fortress at York (*Eburacum*) was established by AD 75, and became the temporary home of legion IX Hispana. By AD 95, the sites at Hayton and Stamford Bridge had lost their military significance, and by AD 130 the military role of Malton also appears to have been reduced. Only York retained its military position, and during the Roman period its civilian functions increased; it became the provincial capital and eventually headquarters of the *Dux Britanniarum* in the early fourth century.

The main roads in Roman East Yorkshire were of military origin. The extension of Ermine Street on the Humber north bank, from Brough to York, was built in the AD 70s, linking York with Lincoln and London. The roads to Malton and Stamford Bridge are also of first century date, while others may have been constructed later.

The main settlement in Roman East Yorkshire was Brough (*Petuaria*), which is now generally considered to have been the *civitas* capital of the Parisi. It is possible that it replaced the late pre-Roman Iron Age site at Redcliff as the region's civic and trade centre shortly after AD 125. Its location on the Humber and on the main road from Lincoln to York is seemingly ideal for such functions. Our understanding of other towns in Roman East Yorkshire is very limited. Recent research at the Roman Small Town at Shiptonthorpe provides an insight into an alternative urban economy of the third century. It is likely that a large number of late pre-Roman Iron Age nucleated villages would have continued to be occupied into the Roman period, while marine regression provided opportunities for the location of new settlements in the Vale of York (e.g. Faxfleet) and Holderness (e.g. Kilnsea and possibly Hull).

One particular element of the settlement system were *villae*. These were the rural seats of the tribal elite, but their role as agricultural centres is unclear. The concentration of *villa* sites in the area around *Petuaria* reinforces the view that the tribal elite was based in the country, rather than the *civitas* capital, and that their power base was agricultural production. However, the remarkable mosaics found in some *villae*, for example at Brantingham and Rudston, also indicate their importance within the Roman political structure.

Although agricultural production undoubtedly dominated the regional economy, a large number of pottery and tile kilns from Roman East Yorkshire have been recorded. More than 40 Romano-British pottery kilns have been identified from the area around Holme-upon-Spalding Moor, and a major pottery production centre was located at Crambeck in North Yorkshire. Smaller numbers of kilns are also known from elsewhere in the region.

In the second half of the fourth century, a series of coastal signal stations was constructed between Huntcliff, in North Yorkshire, and Filey, most likely in an attempt to protect the region from coastal raids, the first of which is recorded to have taken place in AD 367. Most authors on Roman East Yorkshire have postulated a continuation of the line of signal stations from Flamborough Head to Spurn Point, with possibly three stations in between, although there is no archaeological evidence for such a line of defence because of coastal erosion.

The construction of the signal stations marks the beginning of the end of Roman Britain, which formally terminated in AD 410, when emperor Honorius withdrew the military defence of the province. There is a general lack of archaeological information on fifth century Romano-British activity in East Yorkshire, due at least in part to a rise in sea level in the late and post-Roman period, which may have resulted in large-scale abandonment of settlements and industrial production sites in the Vale of York and Holderness. Some evidence exists, however, for the continued occupation of *villa* and settlement sites on the Wolds.

The presence of Saxons from the continent has been demonstrated archaeologically, but it is not always clear whether this dates to the fifth century or to some later period. Anglo-Saxon settlements have been identified at several sites, including York, Rudston, West Heslerton and Driffield, the latter possibly developing into a royal centre by the early eighth century. Early Anglo-Saxon cemeteries consisted of inhumation burials or cremations, and are more widespread than the known settlements. Furthermore, secondary interments in round barrows of Neolithic and Bronze Age date, as well as in cemeteries of the Arras culture, are common on the Wolds. Additional archaeological research will be necessary in order to increase our understanding of East Yorkshire in the Anglo-Saxon period. In particular, the location of Anglo-Saxon and Danelaw settlements on the site of Domesday-period villages must be considered a real possibility, in the light of research at Wharram Percy and elsewhere.

Bibliography on page 141

THE ROMAN AND EARLY MEDIEVAL PERIODS

VALE OF PICKERING

R. Derwent

GREAT WOLD VALLEY

THE WOLDS

Malton

EBURACUM
YORK

VALE

OF

YORK

R. Derwent

R. Ouse

R. Foulness

PETUARIA

Bridlington

H
O
L
D
E
R
N
E
S
S

HORNSEA
MERE

Beverley

R. Hull

HULL ?

R. HUMBER

▲▲▲ Wolds scarp

Foot of Wolds
dip slope

0   km   10
0   miles   6

N

Legend

▣ Fortress/Civitas	○ Building debris
□ Fort	▷ Early Anglo-Saxon settlement
● Settlement	+ Early Anglo-Saxon cemetery
— Road	• Roman period finds (selection only)
P Pottery or Tile kiln	
▲ Villa	⬆ Temple

27

POPULATION AND
SETTLEMENT

DOMESDAY VILLS

J.J.N. Palmer

It is customary to preface discussions of the places named in Domesday Book with a warning that William the Conqueror's great survey of 1086 can be an unreliable or misleading guide to settlement. There are many reasons for this, but one is of fundamental importance.[1] The basic unit of the Domesday Inquest was the manor, a unit of ownership, not of settlement. Manor and settlement might coincide, but we can rarely be certain that this was the case. Settlements might contain several manors, and manors might include many settlements. The Domesday scribe often named only the vill in which the administrative centre of a manor lay, thereby concealing the existence of other places of habitation which belonged to that manor. If the manor was large, its central vill might then appear to be surrounded by many square miles of empty countryside. The large manors can therefore represent a special problem; but even manors of modest size are problematic, for Domesday Book rarely gives any indication of the nature of settlement within the manor, even where there are good reasons for believing that manor and vill were coterminous. A single-manor vill of, say, two dozen households might represent a nucleated village, a handful of hamlets, a scatter of individual farms, or some combination of these three settlement forms; Domesday Book does not allow us to distinguish between them. It can therefore be an uncertain guide to the broad distribution of settlement, and no guide at all to the different forms that settlement might take.[2]

For all its deficiencies, however, Domesday Book is overwhelmingly the most important guide to early medieval settlement we possess, and for some areas its limitations are modest. Fortunately, the East Riding is one of these areas, largely because the compilers of the Yorkshire Domesday usually named the separate components of the larger manors. The significance of Domesday Book for the East Riding can best be conveyed by some statistics. Before 1086, the map of the riding is almost a blank. Only four places are named in sources older than that date, and only two dozen more by later copies of documents purporting to be earlier than 1086. To this meagre total, Domesday Book adds 413 new names, thereby providing the first documentary record of 94 per cent of all places in the riding then known to exist.[3] In the East Riding, as elsewhere, the recorded history of most settlements begins in 1086.

Although the history of most settlements begins with Domesday Book, the pattern recorded there reveals that the riding was already an 'old country' by that date, for the great majority of places that have ever existed in the riding were already settled. Domesday Book names 88 per cent of the townships recorded in the early fourteenth century, near the peak of the medieval expansion of settlement, and 87 per cent of those mapped in the mid-nineteenth century, together with many others which disappeared after 1086. More settlements were lost than were founded in later centuries.

The main discrepancies between the settlement pattern in Domesday and that recorded at later dates can mostly be accounted for by the action of the North Sea and the Humber, or by urban growth. Apart from the changes along the east coast,[4] around Spurn, and at Sunk Island, a number of townships appear to have grown up after 1086 in the marshland areas, the most significant concentrations being along the river Hull, and in the Wallingfen area of the southern Vale of York.[5] One other apparent concentration between Stamford Bridge and Newton-upon-Derwent may, in fact, be an illusion created by Domesday's method of recording manorial statistics.[6] As for towns, Hull, Hedon, and Brough are, of course, 'new towns' of the later medieval period. With these modest exceptions, however, the settlement of the East Riding was virtually complete by 1086.

Notes and bibliography on page 141

DOMESDAY VILLS

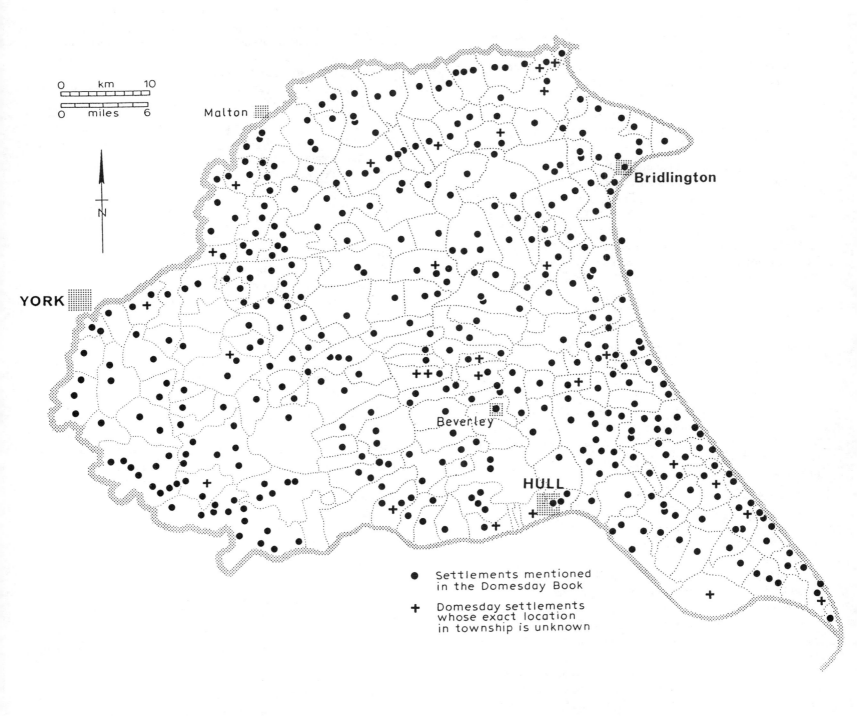

Malton

YORK

Bridlington

Beverley

HULL

● Settlements mentioned
in the Domesday Book

+ Domesday settlements
whose exact location
in township is unknown

CASTLES AND MOATED SITES

Alison Williams

Whatever the origin of the castle, a subject which has generated considerable debate, defensive strongholds combining domestic residences of aristocratic status first appear in the East Riding following the Norman conquest. William and his leading barons constructed castles here as defensive and administrative centres to dominate the local population. Strategic locations were chosen amid the marshes of Holderness, along the river Derwent and on the slopes of the Wolds.

Within the East Riding, all but one of the castles belong to this early period when construction typically consisted of an earthen mound or motte, encircled by a ditch and surmounted by a timber tower, with or without a defended bailey at ground level. The scale of these timber castles varied enormously from Drogo de la Beuvrière's massive motte and bailey castle at Skipsea, to the small, isolated watch-tower mottes, such as Giant's Hill, Thorganby, which overlooked the Derwent. Only Wressle castle represents the later tradition of stone-built castles. Built c.1380 by Sir Thomas Percy, this crenellated palace with tall corner towers combined grand domestic buildings with a military look and was surrounded by a water-filled moat.

At Aughton, the motte and bailey castle must have been redundant at the time when the manor house and moat were built partially within the bailey. A date range from the twelfth to fifteenth centuries for the construction of moated sites is generally accepted, with a peak occurring between 1250 and 1350. Construction dates are known for few sites, although the existence of a moat may usefully be referred to in documents. At Baynard castle, Cottingham the moats are first recorded in a manorial extent of 1276, although a castle was mentioned here c.1170-80.

There are now some 185 known moated sites within the East Riding, an increase of 60 sites on those listed by Jean Le Patourel 25 years ago.[1] Whilst some moats survive as water-filled features or with dry ditches, many others have disappeared beneath modern developments or have silted up and been eradicated by the plough. These sites are usually only visible as crop or soil marks from the air. Many of the possible moated sites have been recognised in this way and there remains the potential for further lost sites to be revealed. That said, the distribution map probably reflects the general medieval pattern. The majority of the moated sites are located below the 60 metre contour, close to a ready water supply on the low-lying Quaternary deposits. The distribution clearly illustrates the importance to the moat-builders of an impermeable and easily worked sub-soil; on the chalk uplands, banks and walls were employed in place of moats.

Few other physical characteristics can be said to typify the moated sites of the East Riding, which demonstrate a multiplicity of forms. Generally, a wide, water-filled ditch surrounded a square, rectangular or D-shaped island; however, this could be a single, double or more complex enclosure. At Baynard castle, the remains of one moat lie within those of another; in 1282 the manor house was described as 'well-constructed with double moats and enclosed by a wall'. At Skeffling two separate moats are linked by a feeder channel, whereas at Scorborough unlinked moats lie so close together that they must surely have been associated. In contrast to these complex arrangements, there are moats which only partially enclose a site, such as the three-sided moat at Low Catton mentioned in an extent of 1258.

The majority of the moated sites are associated with manorial holdings, both lay and ecclesiastical, located within, or on the edge of, a known medieval settlement where they surrounded the manor house and associated domestic structures. Of the smaller category of sub-manorial moated sites, a higher proportion occur away from settlement and are generally taken to have enclosed farmhouses attached to freehold estates. In the East Riding, few such sites appear to be associated with the colonising of marginal land, or assarting, and the origins of many remain obscure. Ecclesiastical moated properties, which included monastic granges, religious houses and hospitals, were also frequently sited away from settlement. Not all moats surrounded buildings. Apparently empty moated enclosures could contain gardens and orchards, as on the bishop of Durham's estate at Howden. Medieval deer park lodges could be moated too, to keep the deer out.[2] The only known moated site to have had an industrial function was at North Grange, Wawne, one of several moated granges belonging to Meaux abbey. When excavated, this moat was found to have enclosed a number of tile kilns dating to the mid-thirteenth century.[3]

Some moated buildings were very large and grand, and frequently acquired the label of 'castle'. At Burstwick castle, the moat around the royal manorial residence was dug in c.1291, when the house was enlarged to include great and little halls and two chapels. A number of the wealthier lords obtained royal licences to fortify their properties, and several of the moated manor houses were provided with crenellation, stone walls and towers. The Percy family was granted permission to crenellate their moated manor at Leconfield castle in 1308 and at Riccall, where the licence was dated 1350; here a fifteenth-century, three-storeyed brick tower survives.

In common with such fortification, moats had more to do with giving an impression of, rather than actually providing, any great measure of defence. Access to the moated island could be restricted by timber drawbridges such as the fourteenth-century example excavated at Hall Garth, Beverley[4], but permanent bridges and causeways were far more common. It seems likely, therefore, that moat construction was prompted more by the desire of owners to enhance their status and conform to a fashion than by practical functions such as defence, or the use of the moat as a drain, sewer or fishpond. The tradition of moat-building eventually declined and few moats were dug after the fourteenth century, although the moated site on Sunk Island is a post-medieval creation.[5]

Notes and bibliography on page 142

CASTLES AND MOATED SITES

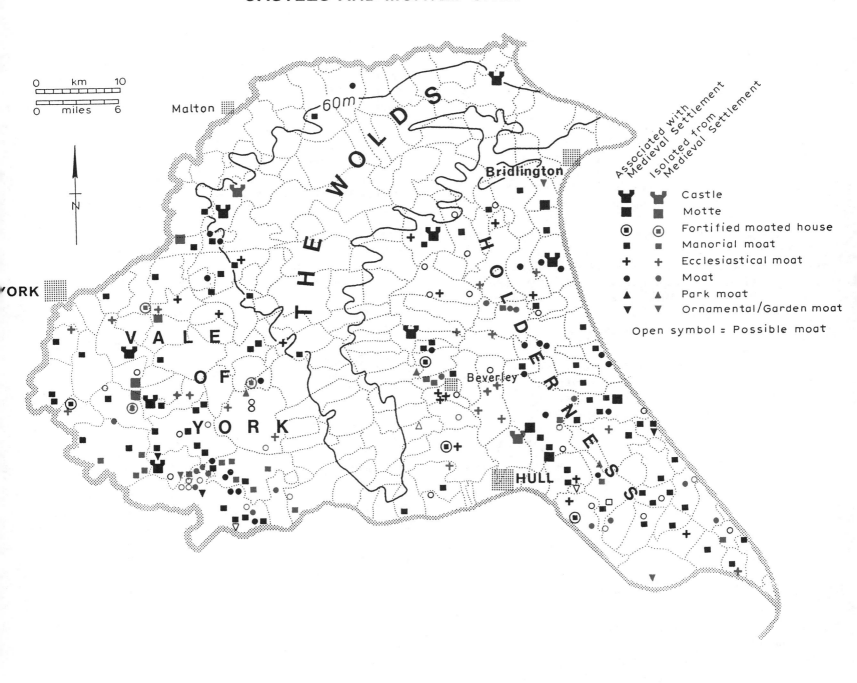

Malton

60m

Bridlington

THE WOLDS

YORK

VALE

OF

YORK

HOLDERNESS

Beverley

HULL

	Associated with Medieval Settlement	Isolated from Medieval Settlement
Castle		
Motte		
Fortified moated house		
Manorial moat		
Ecclesiastical moat		
Moat		
Park moat		
Ornamental/Garden moat		

Open symbol = Possible moat

0   km   10

0   miles   6

N

MEDIEVAL HULL
D.H. Evans

As one of England's principal waterways, the Humber forms an access route to the sea for almost all of Yorkshire and a large part of the East Midlands. As such, there was a clear role for a port which could be established close to the mouth of the river, but which also enjoyed a safe, deep harbour that was not prone to silting.

The precise nature of early settlement at the confluence of the rivers Hull and Humber is still uncertain. Iron Age and Roman farmsteads and riverside settlements are known on the slightly higher ground in the northern and eastern suburbs of the modern city, and by Domesday a number of new hamlets had been established slightly further downstream; however, the land adjoining the mouth of the Hull appears to have been unsuitable for settlement, as the river still had two outlets (the Auld Hull and Sayer Creek, presumably separated by a tract of badly drained marsh). At some point during the twelfth and thirteenth centuries, the river was artificially channelled into Sayer Creek, and it is around this time that the settlement of Wyke was to emerge, on land owned by Meaux abbey, in a position which was ideally suited for exporting the abbey's wool clip. Evidence has been found from a number of excavations within the Old Town for intensive human activity beginning here c.1260.

At the end of the thirteenth century, King Edward I was looking for a suitable port to serve as a supply base for his forthcoming campaigns against Scotland. He acquired the vill of Wyke and the grange of Myton from the monks of Meaux for an undisclosed sum in 1293. Edward's newly purchased lands became the site of a new town - the King's Town or Kingston-upon-Hull. It was an ambitious foundation which enclosed a much larger area than that which seems to have been occupied by its predecessor; the older streets in the town are characterised by sinuous lines which mirror those of the river Hull and various smaller watercourses, whereas the Edwardian streets are laid out on more of a gridiron pattern. The early history of the King's Town proved to be anything but a success; even after 20 years, many of the new leases had not been taken up. In 1317 the borough took the drastic step of reducing the rents of many of the newly-founded plots to one-third of their value. Thereafter, the growth of the town began to take place.

A series of royal rentals help to chart this growth. At the time of acquisition (1293), the town comprised around 60 households.[1] The 1347 rental shows a significant increase in size, as 166 tenements were recorded. The 1377 Poll Tax returns record 1,557 adult taxpayers, which suggests a population of over 3,000; this was the 26th highest return for an English provincial town.[2] Thereafter, it is difficult to find any reliable data by which to estimate any changes in the fifteenth and sixteenth centuries.[3] However, an indication that the fortunes of the town still remained buoyant may be provided by the Subsidy payments of 1525, which were the 21st highest of the provincial towns.[4]

Construction of a defensive circuit around three sides of the town began in 1321-4. It initially comprised a great ditch and bank, topped with a palisade, and linking four freestanding gates; however, by the late 1330s, work had begun on replacing sections of the palisade in brick, and this was to continue until 1406. By the close of the middle ages, the defences incorporated some 30 interval towers and a number of posterns. There was also a D-shaped battery facing onto the Humber, and a chain tower on the foreland.

Hull's economy was firmly based on its role as a leading port, with a large coastal and continental trade. The latter connections were principally with the Low Countries, the Baltic, and with northern and western France. It functioned as the principal customs port for the whole Yorkshire coast during the fourteenth century, and for the southern Yorkshire and north Lincolnshire coasts during the fifteenth century.

Comparatively little manufacturing was carried out in the town. A certain amount of cloth was made here, but the bulk of locally finished textiles came from Beverley.[5] Similarly, small numbers of leather-workers and metal-workers are recorded in Hull's medieval documents, but at no time does the total for these craftsmen rise into double figures. The bulk of the population within the walled circuit seems to have been engaged in retail and service industries. Outside the walls, a brick and tile making industry developed, with the de la Pole tilery in Trippett, and the King's Tilery on the west side of the town. Records for the latter survive for the period 1302-1425; in most of the years for which the output was recorded, it made between 92,000 and 105,000 bricks or tiles per year. Brick was used extensively in almost all of the town's major public buildings and works. Other industries located outside the walls were milling and lime-burning.

The town was served by a massive church (Holy Trinity, possibly established in 1285), a chapel of Hessle parish. A second major church (St Mary the Virgin, Lowgate) is first mentioned in 1327. This was also a chapel-of-ease, dependent upon North Ferriby parish. Three major monasteries were founded during the thirteenth and fourteenth centuries - the Carmelite friary (1289), the Augustinian or Austin friary (1316/17), and the Carthusian priory (1378). There are also records of seven hospitals, nine maisons dieu, and a bedehouse, an indication of the economic prosperity of the town.[6]

Notes and bibliography on page 142

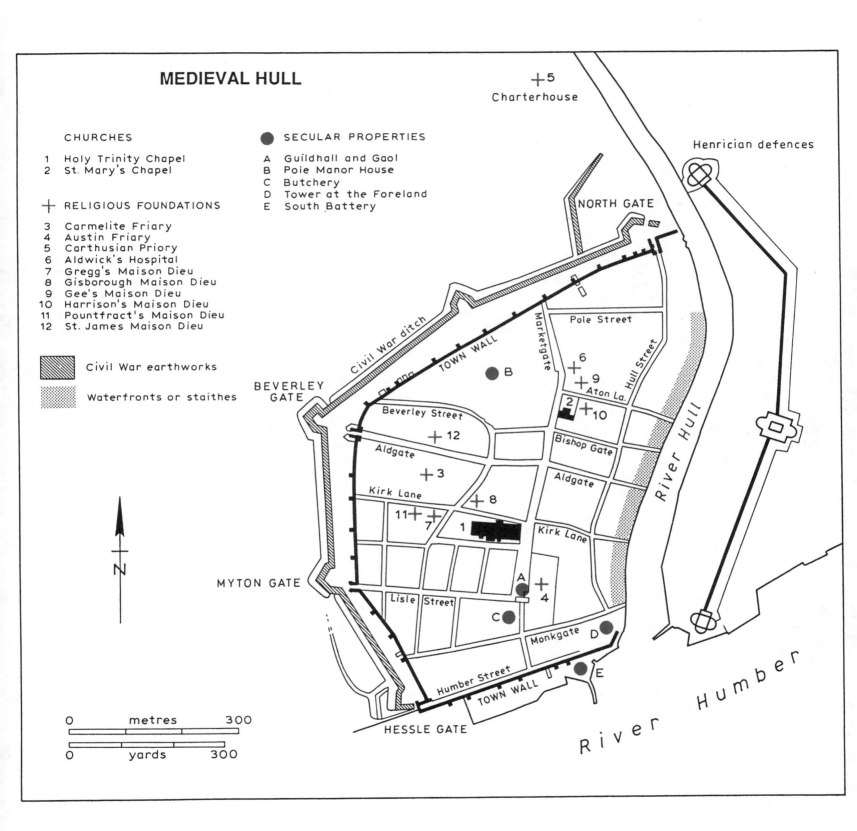

MEDIEVAL HULL

CHURCHES

1 Holy Trinity Chapel
2 St. Mary's Chapel

+ **RELIGIOUS FOUNDATIONS**

3 Carmelite Friary
4 Austin Friary
5 Carthusian Priory
6 Aldwick's Hospital
7 Gregg's Maison Dieu
8 Gisborough Maison Dieu
9 Gee's Maison Dieu
10 Harrison's Maison Dieu
11 Pountfract's Maison Dieu
12 St. James Maison Dieu

Civil War earthworks

Waterfronts or staithes

● **SECULAR PROPERTIES**

A Guildhall and Gaol
B Pole Manor House
C Butchery
D Tower at the Foreland
E South Battery

+5
Charterhouse

Henrician defences

NORTH GATE

BEVERLEY GATE

Civil War ditch

TOWN WALL

Marketgate

Pole Street

6
9
Aton La.

2
10

Beverley Street

12

Aldgate

Bishop Gate

3

Aldgate

Kirk Lane

8

11
7

1

Kirk Lane

B

River Hull

MYTON GATE

A
4

Lisle Street

C

Monkgate
D

E

Humber Street

TOWN WALL

HESSLE GATE

River Humber

N

0   metres   300

0   yards   300

THE GEOGRAPHICAL GROWTH OF HULL
M. Trevor Wild

Most English industrial towns mushroomed in the eighteenth and nineteenth centuries from small market towns or swollen villages. Some, however, including Hull, developed around a substantial historic core, which had important effects on shaping urban growth. The 'Old Town', positioned where the river Hull joins the Humber, was first laid out, in grid form, following its acquisition by Edward I in 1293. Medieval Hull was sufficiently important to be enclosed by urban fortifications on the northern, western and Humber sides. Later defences were built on the far bank of the river Hull to protect the 'Old Harbour'. These structures were later demolished to make way for the 'Town Docks' (Queen's 1778, Humber 1809, Prince's 1829, Railway 1846 and Victoria 1850) and adjoining buildings. However, they did restrict Hull's physical growth for several centuries even though, by 1770, the town had become England's twelfth largest urban centre, with a population of 15,000. Until the opening of Queen's Dock ushered in the Industrial Revolution in Hull, urban expansion had been almost entirely compressed inside the inadequate space bounded by the medieval walls and the river.

The Industrial Revolution brought an emphatic surge in port traffic in Hull, a rapid expansion in manufacturing and a sharp acceleration in population growth. By the 1850s, shipping tonnage had increased by nearly 20 times (63,795 tons in 1772 to 1,207,236 tons in 1856), and the population had reached 86,000. The removal of the wall and its gateways, the reclamation of marshland beyond and the willingness of landowners to sell land for suburban development had facilitated the first significant extension of Hull since its charter. Map A, using Craggs' map of 1817 and Goodwill and Lawson's 1856 plan, shows the principal directions of growth - westwards along the Humber bank and Hessle Road, northwestwards to Spring Bank and Beverley Road, and northwards as an industrial zone through Wincolmlee and alongside the river Hull.

The late eighteenth and early nineteenth centuries saw 'intensive' urban growth, with high housing densities, congested industrial concentrations, and very little open space. The built-up area of mid-nineteenth century Hull, with a population density of 161 persons per acre, contained many crowded slums. The most insanitary were in the courts and alleys of the 'Old Town', but there were also slum quarters in North Myton, South Myton and Drypool. Very different was the spacious housing which accommodated Hull's growing middle-class population. Typically this was built as villa-type residences lining the thoroughfares leading out from the city.

After the 1850s, urban development became more extensive (Map B). During 1851-1911 the population increased by 211 per cent to 278,000, one-quarter of this increase coming from boundary extensions. This demographic growth, however, was easily eclipsed by the fourfold increase in the built-up area between 1856 and 1914,

reflecting the introduction in 1854 of by-law controls on residential development, and further regulations in 1893, which substantially reduced the densities of new working-class housing. Increasing quantities of land used for railways and the provision of four large municipal parks were additional factors.

A notable feature was the emergence of two prominent industrial zones, mainly comprising engineering, paint, leather, textile and oil-seed factories and small shipyards. Concentration of industry alongside the navigable river Hull had already been noticeable in the early nineteenth century. By 1914 this zone had spread northwards two miles beyond Wincolmlee. The other industrial axis followed the new docks along the Humber shoreline, ultimately from St Andrew's Dock in the west to King George Dock in the east (Map C).

Geographical expansion of Hull accelerated markedly after the First World War, the built-area spreading from eight square miles in 1914 to seventeen in 1939 and 25 in 1988, despite population decline from a peak of 314,000 in 1931 to 245,000 in 1991. This paradox of 'extensive' urban growth yet demographic stagnation and decline is characteristic of most British cities at this time. The demographic trend stems partly from falling birth rates, but more from population shifts to dormitory settlements in the surrounding countryside. The huge spread of cities such as Hull after 1918 followed certain institutional changes, most notably the 1919 'Addison' Housing Act, with its commitment to public supply of new working-class housing. Built in accordance with early principles of urban planning, council housing in low-density peripheral estates, with new schools and playing fields, became a familiar feature in the urban landscape. The majority of Hull's suburban council homes were built within eleven estates (Map C), mostly containing between 1,000 and 3,000 dwellings. However, the two most recent estates - Orchard Park (3,500 dwellings) and the giant Bransholme 'satellite' (9,240) - were built on a much larger scale to re-house people from Hull's massive slum clearance programme of the 1960s and 70s. The low-density principle was discarded here, and high-rise flats and other multi-dwelling structures dominated.

Hull has an unbalanced geography of post-1918 municipal and private suburbia. Two-thirds of the former is situated east of the river Hull (in 'East Hull'), whose remoter position has meant a cheaper and readier supply of development land, whereas three-quarters of the latter is in 'West Hull', where owner occupiers were attracted by better air quality and accessibility. Today all of West Hull, apart from some vacant land adjoining the river Hull, is built up. Only in East Hull, principally in the northern part, is there potential for much further suburban growth, and already the largest site here is taken for the Kingswood extension, a large new residential project promoted by housing association and private capital.

Bibliography on page 142

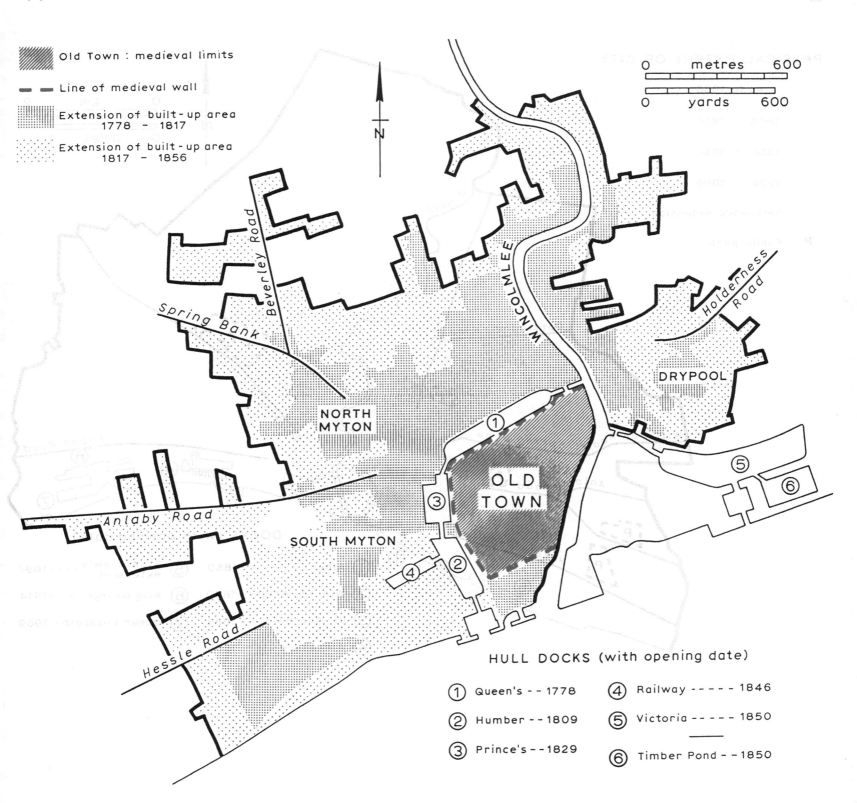

A

THE PHYSICAL GROWTH OF HULL : 1778-1856

Old Town : medieval limits

Line of medieval wall

Extension of built-up area
1778 – 1817

Extension of built-up area
1817 – 1856

N

metres 600

yards 600

Beverley Road

Spring Bank

WINCOLMLEE

Holderness Road

DRYPOOL

NORTH
MYTON

Anlaby Road

SOUTH MYTON

OLD
TOWN

Hessle Road

HULL DOCKS (with opening date)

① Queen's -- 1778   ④ Railway ----- 1846

② Humber -- 1809   ⑤ Victoria ----- 1850

③ Prince's -- 1829

⑥ Timber Pond -- 1850

B

THE PHYSICAL GROWTH OF HULL : 1856-1995

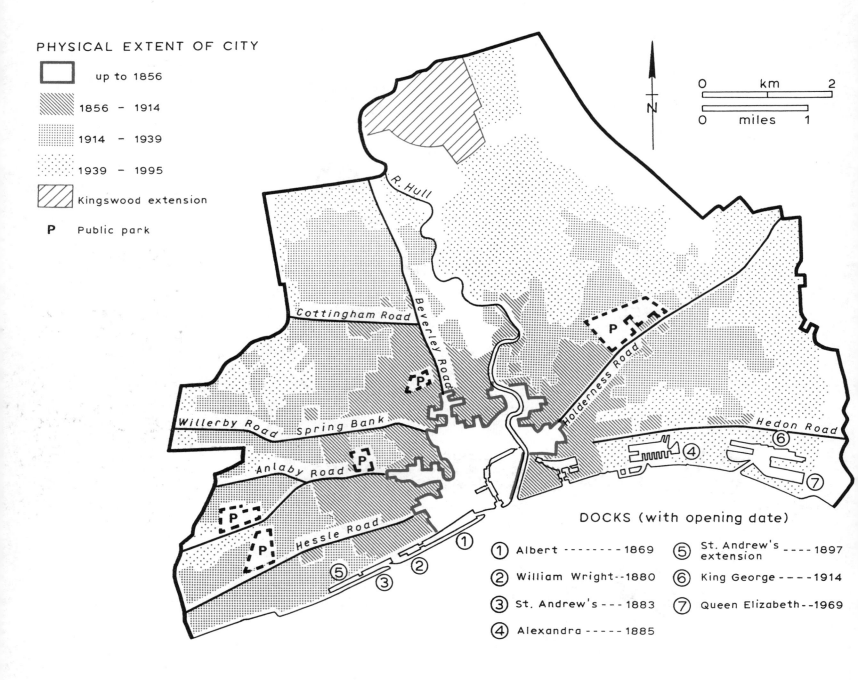

PHYSICAL EXTENT OF CITY

up to 1856

1856 – 1914

1914 – 1939

1939 – 1995

Kingswood extension

P   Public park

R. Hull

Cottingham Road

Beverley Road

Willerby Road

Spring Bank

Anlaby Road

Hessle Road

Holderness Road

Hedon Road

N

| 0 | km | 2 |

| 0 | miles | 1 |

DOCKS (with opening date)

① Albert -------- 1869
② William Wright--1880
③ St. Andrew's ---- 1883
④ Alexandra ----- 1885
⑤ St. Andrew's extension ---- 1897
⑥ King George ---- 1914
⑦ Queen Elizabeth--1969

C THE GEOGRAPHICAL DEVELOPMENT AND FUNCTIONAL AREAS OF HULL

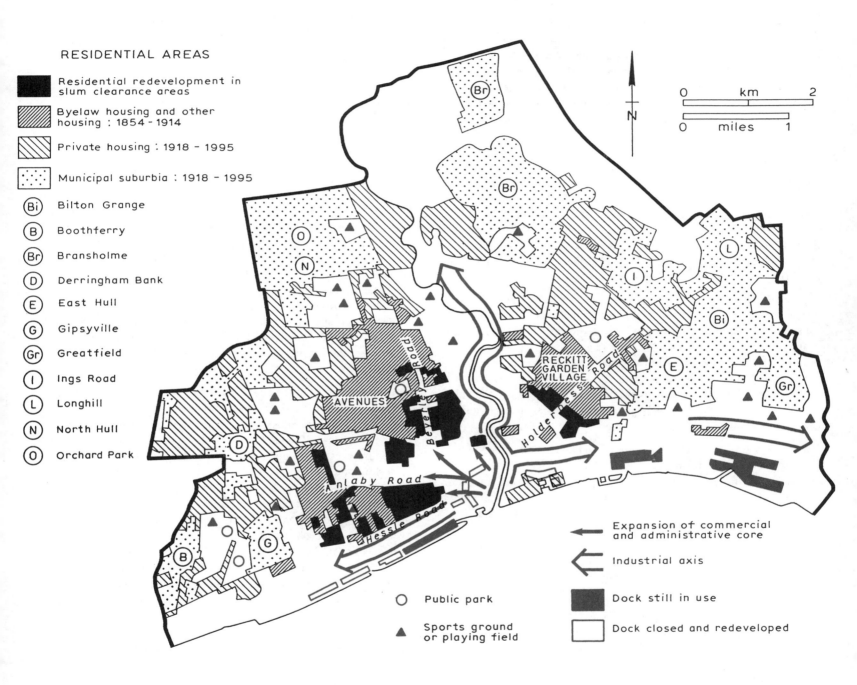

MEDIEVAL BEVERLEY

D.H. Evans

The physical location of Beverley, in the shelter of the dip slope of the Wolds escarpment, and on the only reasonably dry crossing-point in this part of the Hull valley (prior to its draining in the eighteenth century), made it a natural choice for early settlement. Human activity in the area is attested from the Neolithic onwards, and there was clearly at least one Roman farmstead at the northern end of the future town.[1] However, the first significant settlement is represented by the foundation of the monastery of *Inderauuda* by St John of Beverley in the opening years of the eighth century. This religious house is traditionally held to have been destroyed in a Danish raid of 866, and archaeological excavations have demonstrated that the site was certainly abandoned in the mid-ninth century.[2] It was refounded in the early tenth century as a college of secular canons. Presumably, some sort of extra-mural secular settlement was already developing around the collegiate church by this date, but our present state of knowledge suggests that Beverley was essentially a Norman foundation, dating to the early years following the Conquest.

The new Norman town had two principal foci - a large market at its northern end, and the Minster, a long way to the south. To these was subsequently added a third element - a waterhead to the south and east of the Minster, formed around the Beck (a canalised watercourse linking the town to the river Hull). Water was to play a major part in the evolution of the town; not only did the numerous watercourses flowing through it influence the types of crafts and industries which grew up here, but they effectively dictated the elongated shape of the town, and the sinuous pattern of its streets.

Excavations in the southern part of the town have demonstrated that many of the tenement boundaries discernible today had been established by the end of the eleventh century. The burgage plots were mostly long narrow strips of land, laid out at right-angles to the main streets, although considerable variations in their length show that the plots were not contemporary in origin, and indicate that some boundaries may have respected pre-existing features. Nevertheless, some evidence for formal planning is discernible within certain parts of the medieval town, which in turn suggests seigniorial control in the laying out of plots.

The economic success of the town was based on a number of factors. Firstly, it served not only as a major market for the area, but also as the only large port in the Hull valley, before it was eclipsed by the emergence of Hull in the later thirteenth century. Secondly, Beverley established itself as a centre for wool processing and textile manufacture during the twelfth century, with raw wool and Beverley cloths rapidly becoming the town's leading export. Thirdly, large parts of Beverley overlay extensive deposits of alluvial clays which were suitable for ceramic manufacture and, hence, pottery, brick and tile making became major industries in the economy of the town. Clay roof tiles were produced in the Grovehill and Beckside area from the mid-twelfth century, and bricks from the later thirteenth century onwards. Another major industry was tanning and leather working; evidence for this has been found from the early twelfth century onwards. Last, but not least, a regular source of income was provided by pilgrims visiting the shrine of St John of Beverley.

Rapid growth during the twelfth century led to the construction of two parish churches. St Mary's, which appears to have been built in the second quarter of the twelfth century, served the secular community developing at the northern end of the town; whilst St Nicholas, first mentioned c.1160, ministered to the needs of the boatmen and craftsmen in the Beckside and Grovehill area. The growing status and wealth of the town in the twelfth and thirteenth centuries is also reflected in the construction of new defences, and in the establishment of friaries and other religious institutions. A defensive circuit of walls was never constructed around Beverley, but a large town ditch (the Bar Dyke) was excavated along its western and northern sides, and is first mentioned in 1169. A series of gates (or Bars) controlled the main routes in and out of the town. The major religious houses were the Dominican and Franciscan friaries, and the preceptory of the Knights Hospitallers, all of which were founded on peripheral land in the thirteenth century. The same century also witnessed the construction of the hospitals of St Giles and St Nicholas, to be followed in the fourteenth and fifteenth centuries by additional hospitals and leper houses.

The precise impact of the Black Death on the town is uncertain, but it seems to have coincided with the period at which it was at its most prosperous. The Lay Subsidy returns for 1334 place Beverley among the top 20 towns in England in terms of taxable wealth. By 1377 it was the tenth largest provincial town in the realm, and the second largest in Yorkshire; the Poll Tax returns for that year record 2,663 tax-payers, which suggests a total population of over 5,000.[3] Thereafter, the fortunes of the town began to waver somewhat, as the wool trade declined and property values slumped during the fifteenth century. An event which had probably as great an impact on the town's economy as the decline of the local textile industry was the Dissolution. Yet, even this was not cataclysmic, for in 1552 the population was said to be at least 5,000 (much the same as in 1377), and a study of St Mary's parish records suggests that the figures continued to rise during the subsequent decades.[4] In economic terms, however, Beverley failed to keep pace with the growth of more successful rivals, such as Hull, and hence by the sixteenth century it had slipped out of the ranking of the top 40 English provincial towns.[5]

Notes and bibliography on page 142

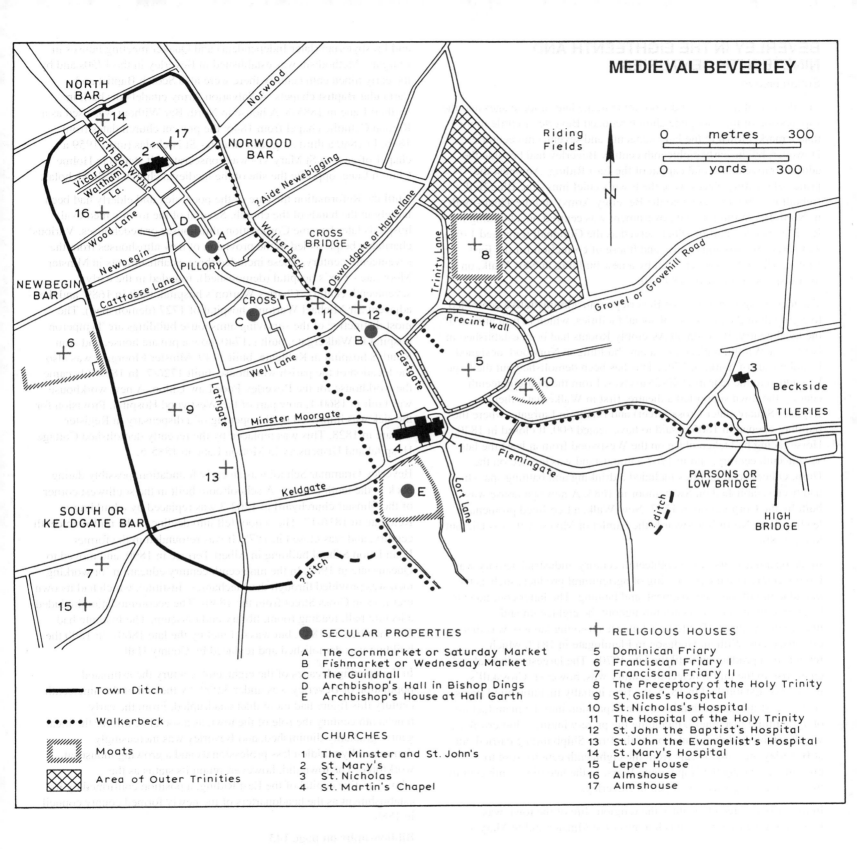

MEDIEVAL BEVERLEY

Riding
Fields

0 metres 300

0 yards 300

N

NORTH BAR
+14

2 +17 NORWOOD BAR
Norwood

Vicar La.
Waltham La.
North Bar Within

16 +

Wood Lane

D
A

Newbegin
PILLORY

NEWBEGIN BAR

Cattfosse Lane

CROSS
C

6 +

Well Lane

Walkerbeck

?Aldi Newebigging

CROSS BRIDGE

Oswaldgate or Hayrerlane

Trinity Lane

+8

Precint wall

11 12
B

Eastgate

5 +

10 +

Grovel or Grovehill Road

3

Beckside
TILERIES

Lathgate

9 +

Minster Moorgate

4
1

Flemingate

PARSONS OR
LOW BRIDGE

?ditch

HIGH
BRIDGE

13 +

Keldgate

E

Lort Lane

SOUTH OR
KELDGATE BAR

7 +

?ditch

15 +

● SECULAR PROPERTIES

A The Cornmarket or Saturday Market
B Fishmarket or Wednesday Market
C The Guildhall
D Archbishop's Hall in Bishop Dings
E Archbishop's House at Hall Garth

CHURCHES

1 The Minster and St. John's
2 St. Mary's
3 St. Nicholas
4 St. Martin's Chapel

+ RELIGIOUS HOUSES

5 Dominican Friary
6 Franciscan Friary I
7 Franciscan Friary II
8 The Preceptory of the Holy Trinity
9 St. Giles's Hospital
10 St. Nicholas's Hospital
11 The Hospital of the Holy Trinity
12 St. John the Baptist's Hospital
13 St. John the Evangelist's Hospital
14 St. Mary's Hospital
15 Leper House
16 Almshouse
17 Almshouse

──── Town Ditch

••••• Walkerbeck

▨ Moats

▧ Area of Outer Trinities

BEVERLEY IN THE EIGHTEENTH AND NINETEENTH CENTURIES

Susan Neave

The decline of the cloth and wool trade in the later middle ages and the suppression of the collegiate church reduced Beverley to little more than a market town in the later sixteenth and seventeenth centuries. However, by the early eighteenth century Beverley had become the administrative and social capital of the East Riding. Amongst the principal meeting places were the town's chief inns - the Blue Bell (rebuilt in 1796 and renamed the Beverley Arms) and the Tiger - both in North Bar Within. Local government was centred on a building in Register Square, part of which served as the Guildhall (enlarged 1762) and part as the sessions house and house of correction for the East Riding. The latter was replaced by a new building in New Walk, on the outskirts of the town, 1805-10.

The increasing importance of Beverley as an administrative centre led to a growth in the provision of social facilities, which in turn attracted the local gentry. By 1745 an Assembly Rooms had been established in North Bar Within, replaced by a new building in Norwood, designed by John Carr of York, in 1762. This has been demolished but the large hall added to the rear in 1840-2 survives. From the mid-eighteenth century the town supported a theatre, first in Walkergate, then in Register Square (later Cross Street) and finally in Lairgate, where the building opened in 1805 is said to have seated 600. It closed in 1840. Horse racing had taken place on the Westwood from at least the late seventeenth century, and in 1767 a grandstand was erected on the Hurn. Other social facilties included a drinking and bathing spa which had been established on Swinemoor in 1684. A new spa house was built by the Corporation in 1747. New Walk, a tree-lined promenade leading from North Bar towards the hamlet of Molescroft, was laid out in the 1780s.

In the opening years of the eighteenth century, industrial activity was largely centred on the processing of agricultural products such as the manufacture of malt and oatmeal, and tanning. The latter continued to be an important local industry throughout the eighteenth and nineteenth centuries. The town's longest surviving tannery was that established by William Hodgson in Flemingate in 1812, which remained in production until the late 1970s. The largest industrial enterprise in the mid-nineteenth century was, however, Crosskill's ironworks. Established in 1825, the firm initially manufactured items such as cast iron lamps but it was the expansion into the manufacture of agricultural machinery, including the prize-winning 'clod-crusher', which established the reputation of the firm. Shipbuilding carried out at Beverley on a small scale from the eighteenth century rose to prominence during the Napoleonic Wars. In the late nineteenth century iron shipbuilding was developed in Beverley.

In the early eighteenth century the religious life of the town was focused on the two Anglican churches - the Minster and St Mary's -

and Presbyterian (later Independent) and Quaker meeting houses in Lairgate. Methodism was established in Beverley in the 1750s and by the early nineteenth century there were also Scotch Baptist and Particular Baptist chapels. A Salvation Army citadel was built in Wilbert Lane in 1885-6. A house in North Bar Without was used as a Roman Catholic chapel from 1846; the present church dates from 1898. In 1880 a third Anglican church - St Nicholas (until 1959 a chapel-of-ease to St Mary's) - was consecrated. It stands in Holme Church Lane, opposite the site of the medieval church of St Nicholas.

Until the Reformation the care of the poor, sick and elderly had been largely in the hands of the church. Several of the town's medieval hospitals later became Corporation almshouses or bedehouses. Various charitable bequests led to the provision of new almshouses from the seventeenth century. These included three establishments in Minster Moorgate - Fox's hospital (demolished), founded in the early seventeenth century, Charles Warton's hospital, built in 1689, and the adjacent Sir Michael Warton's hospital of 1727 (demolished). The most distinctive of the surviving almshouse buildings are Tymperon hospital in Walkergate, built c.1740, now a private house, and Ann Routh's hospital in Keldgate, built 1749. Minster Moorgate was also the location of the parish workhouse, built 1726-7. In 1838 it became the workhouse for the Beverley Poor Law Union. A new workhouse was built in 1860-1, now part of the Westwood Hospital. Provision for the sick was improved by the opening of a dispensary in Register Square in 1828. This was replaced by the recently demolished Cottage Hospital and Dispensary in Morton Lane in 1885-6.

Beverley Grammar School was an early foundation, possibly dating back to the tenth century. A schoolroom built in the southwest corner of the Minster churchyard in 1702-3 was replaced by a building in Keldgate in 1816-17. The school fell into decline in the mid-nineteenth century, and was closed in 1878. It was refounded in the former Foundation School building in Albert Terrace in 1890, and moved to Queensgate in 1902. In the nineteenth century education for working men was provided through the Mechanics' Institute, which had its own premises in Cross Street from the 1840s. The accommodation included a lecture hall, reading room, library and museum. The Institute had 360 members in 1847, but was defunct by the late 1860s. In 1890 the building was demolished and replaced by County Hall.

In the opening decades of the eighteenth century the estimated population of Beverley was under 3,000; by the end of the nineteenth century this figure had more than quadrupled. From the early nineteenth century the role of the town as a social centre for the local gentry gradually diminished, and Beverley was increasingly dominated by middle-class professionals and a growing industrial workforce. The town did, however, retain its status as the administrative capital of the East Riding, a position confirmed by its establishment as the headquarters of the newly formed county council in 1889.

Bibliography on page 143

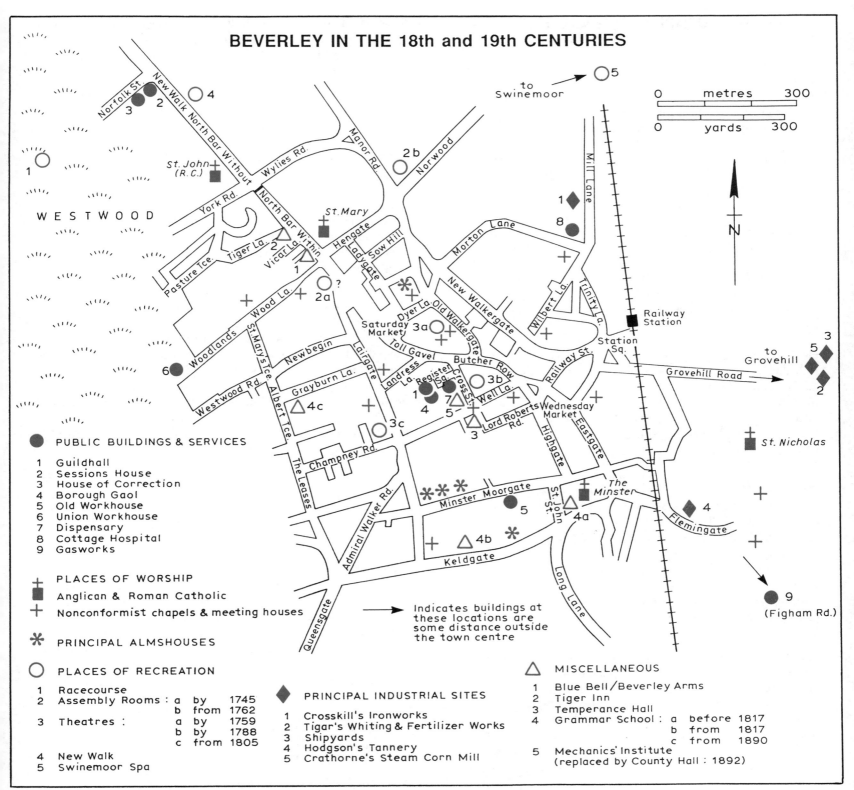

BEVERLEY IN THE 18th and 19th CENTURIES

WESTWOOD

St. John (R.C.)

to Swinemoor ○ 5

0 metres 300
0 yards 300

N

Mill Lane

○ 4

Norfolk St.
3 ● ● 2

New Walk
North Bar Without

Wylies Rd.

Manor Rd.

Norwood

○ 2b

1 ◆
Morton Lane

8 ●

○ 1

York Rd.
North Bar Within

St. Mary

Hengate
Ladygate
Sow Hill

New Walkergate

Wilbert La.
Trinity La.

Railway Station ■
Station Sq.

Pasture Tce.
Tiger La.
Vicar La.
△ 2
△ 1

Wood La.
○ 2a ?

Woodlands

✳
Dyer La.
Old Walkergate
Saturday Market
3a ○
+

St. Mary's Tce.
Albert Tce.

Newbegin
Laitgate
Landress La.
Toll Gavel

Grayburn La.

Butcher Row
Cross St.
Well La.

Railway St.

3 ◆
5 ◆
to Grovehill
Grovehill Road
2 ◆

6 ●

Westwood Rd.

△ 4c

Register Sq.
1 ●
7 △
4
5
△ 3
Lord Roberts Rd.

Wednesday Market

St. Nicholas ■ +

○ 3c

Eastgate

Champney Rd.

The Leases

Admiral Walker Rd.

✳ ✳ ✳
Minster Moorgate
5 ●

Highgate
St. John St.

The Minster
△ 4a

◆ 4
Flemingate

+

△ 4b
✳

+

Keldgate

Long Lane

Queensgate

Indicates buildings at
these locations are
some distance outside
the town centre

● 9
(Figham Rd.)

● PUBLIC BUILDINGS & SERVICES

1 Guildhall
2 Sessions House
3 House of Correction
4 Borough Gaol
5 Old Workhouse
6 Union Workhouse
7 Dispensary
8 Cottage Hospital
9 Gasworks

✝ PLACES OF WORSHIP
■ Anglican & Roman Catholic
+ Nonconformist chapels & meeting houses

✳ PRINCIPAL ALMSHOUSES

○ PLACES OF RECREATION

1 Racecourse
2 Assembly Rooms : a by   1745
                   b from   1762
3 Theatres :   a by   1759
                   b by   1788
                   c from   1805
4 New Walk
5 Swinemoor Spa

◆ PRINCIPAL INDUSTRIAL SITES

1 Crosskill's Ironworks
2 Tigar's Whiting & Fertilizer Works
3 Shipyards
4 Hodgson's Tannery
5 Crathorne's Steam Corn Mill

△ MISCELLANEOUS

1 Blue Bell/Beverley Arms
2 Tiger Inn
3 Temperance Hall
4 Grammar School : a before 1817
                   b from   1817
                   c from   1890
5 Mechanics' Institute
(replaced by County Hall : 1892)

BASED ON 1996 STREET PLAN

43

POPULATION DENSITY: 1672 AND 1743

David and Susan Neave

Accurate population figures do not exist for most settlements before the first national census of 1801. Estimates of population can, however, be made from a number of sources, primarily drawn up for taxation or ecclesiastical purposes. Some of the standard sources for estimating population change in the early modern period, for example the diocesan returns of 1563 and 1603, and the protestation returns of 1641/2, do not exist for the East Riding.[1] There are, however, hearth tax returns of the 1670s and archiepiscopal visitation returns of the mid-eighteenth century, and these have been used to compile population density maps.

Hearth tax returns list, by township, all households liable to pay the tax on hearths which was levied between 1662 and 1689. Returns survive in the Public Record Office for all or part of the East Riding for 1670, 1672 and 1673.[2] The 1672 returns have been used as they provide the fullest and most legible lists of both tax-paying and exempt householders. Archbishop Herring, in 1743, and Archbishop Drummond, in 1764, issued printed forms to the clergy of the diocese of York requiring answers to a number of questions, including the number of families in the parish. Returns were made for most East Riding parishes, and except for a handful of larger parishes where the number of families given is obviously an estimate, the figures seem trustworthy. Occasionally the incumbent gives the number of inhabitants as well as families. The 1743 returns, which are in print, have been used.[3] Any gaps have been filled by reference to the 1764 returns.[4] In a few cases there are no returns for either year.

There is plenty of evidence to show that 'household' as used in the hearth tax returns and 'family' as used in the visitation returns are comparable units, and provide an acceptable basis on which to study population change. The data are mapped by township in 1672, and by ecclesiastical parish in 1743, except where the incumbents make separate returns for townships. Although this makes the earlier map of greater individual use, it does have an obvious disadvantage for comparison between the two. Fortunately there are many single-township parishes in the East Riding. The larger multi-township parishes are most common in mid-Holderness and the southern Vale of York.

The 1672 map shows that the most sparsely populated areas are the high Wolds and the Vale of Pickering, and the most populous townships are to the north and west of Hull, in north and south Holderness, and along the river Ouse. Population density is at its highest in the towns of Hull (1,369 households), Beverley (620), Bridlington (352) and Hedon (117), and the fishing village of Filey (77). The last two are no more populous than many villages but they cover a small acreage - Hedon only 321 acres and Filey 833 acres.

By 1743 there were two additional townships with a density of over 75 people per 1000 acres - Pocklington, a thriving market town and Sculcoates, to the north of Hull. In 1672 Sculcoates, a small township of 738 acres, had only fifteen taxed households. This had risen to 88 'little and poor' families by 1743, an early phase in the suburban development of Hull.

Such population rise is not typical, for a general comparison of the two maps shows an overall reduction in population density. The emptiness of the high Wolds and the Vale of Pickering is even more evident in 1743. In the early eighteenth century Daniel Defoe commented that the middle of the East Riding 'is very thin of towns, and consequently of people, being overspread with Woulds' and the incumbent of Weaverthorpe noted on his visitation return in 1764 how 'thinly are our would (sic) villages peopled'.[5] Throughout the East Riding far more townships and parishes show a decline than show a rise in population. The marked decrease in the population of the rural East Riding (18.9 per cent) evidenced by the 1672 and 1743 returns occurs in other English counties.[6]

Nationally, it was a period of limited and fluctuating population growth, interspersed with significant periods of population stagnation and decline. At the same time, towns and cities were growing. It has been calculated that between 1670 and 1750 the total number of people living in English towns with a population of 5,000 or more rose from 680,000 to 1,220,000, an increase of almost 80 per cent.[7] High urban mortality meant that most of the population rise was achieved by migration from the countryside. The 'pull' of the towns was clearly of significance to rural depopulation; nevertheless it was the 'push' factors that principally accounted for settlement contraction in the East Riding.

There is much evidence to show that the direct actions of landowners in reducing the number of tenants was the major factor. The enlargement of the deer park at Londesborough by Lord Burlington caused the depopulation of Easthorpe in the early eighteenth century, and at Scampston the village was partly destroyed when grounds of the hall were laid out. Enclosure of the open fields contributed to the halving of the populations of the villages of Birdsall and Burnby. At Warter the 85 households in 1673 were reduced to 58 families in 1743, largely by the engrossment of farm holdings. Sir Joseph Pennington of Warter Hall gradually bought out the other freeholders in the parish, demolished empty or decayed housing and divided the land between remaining tenants. In 1730 Sir Marmaduke Constable was advocating a reduction in the number of cottages at Everingham, in the Vale of York, and here the 57 households listed in 1672 had fallen to 27 in 1743. Similarly at Watton, in the Hull valley, where the village contracted from 71 households in 1673 to 34 families by 1743, contemporary map evidence shows that this was brought about by the almost total removal of one street, and by halving the number of houses in another.[8] Many other examples could be cited.

Notes and bibliography on page 143

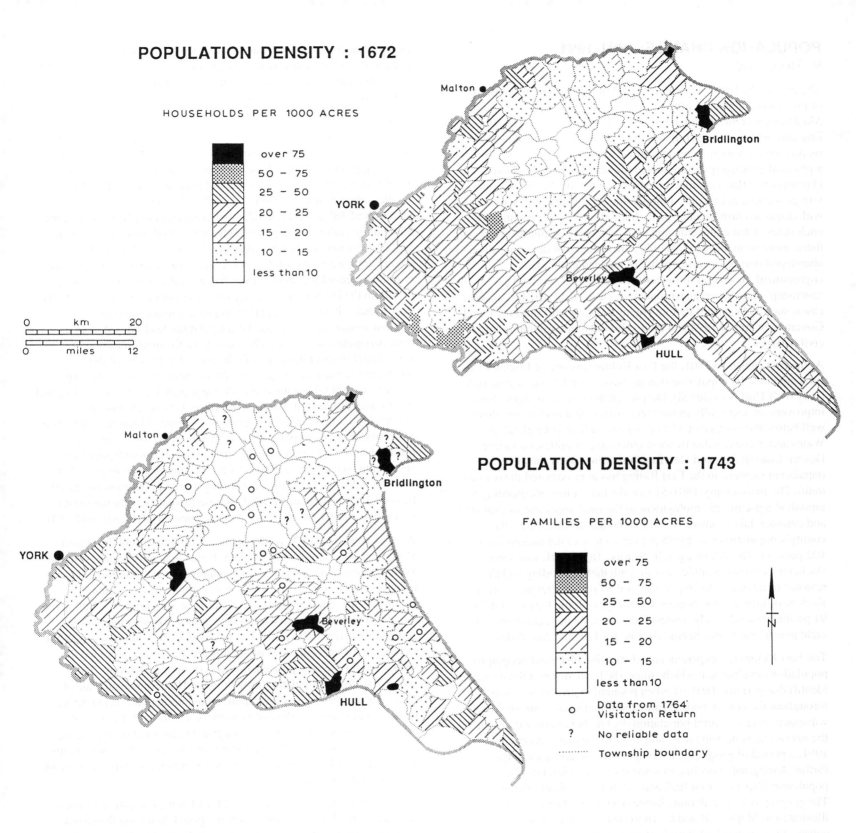

POPULATION DENSITY : 1672

HOUSEHOLDS PER 1000 ACRES

over 75
50 - 75
25 - 50
20 - 25
15 - 20
10 - 15
less than 10

Malton

Bridlington

YORK

Beverley

HULL

0   km   20
0   miles   12

POPULATION DENSITY : 1743

FAMILIES PER 1000 ACRES

over 75
50 - 75
25 - 50
20 - 25
15 - 20
10 - 15
less than 10

○   Data from 1764
    Visitation Return

?   No reliable data

....   Township boundary

N

Malton

Bridlington

YORK

Beverley

HULL

POPULATION CHANGE: 1801-1991

M. Trevor Wild

The area of the former East Riding of Yorkshire contains a microcosm of provincial England. Forming part of the northern limits of Halford Mackinder's environmental and cultural concept of 'Lowland England' and the 'English Plain', it has a major industrial port, several market towns, various seaside resorts, some 50 miles of coastline, and a physical geography differentiated into chalk wolds, lowland claylands and flat reclaimed marshlands. Outside the urban centres, village settlement prevails, although the rural landscape is also dotted with dispersed farmsteads, mostly built after the parliamentary enclosures of the eighteenth and early nineteenth centuries. Here and there, more so in the 'High Wolds', are the sites of deserted villages, abandoned during an earlier phase of enclosures and land engrossment. In several instances their territories survived as 'township' areas (even anachronistic ecclesiastical parishes in some cases, such as Wharram Percy, Argam and Cowlam) until the Local Government Act of 1894 and their subsequent incorporation into new civil parishes.

At the first census in 1801, the East Riding was one of England's most rural counties. Its population density was under 100 per square mile, (only 69 if Hull is excluded). Despite great progress in agricultural improvement, especially in land reclamation and enclosures, this was well below the average of 152 per square mile over England and Wales and was exceeded by most other rural counties, including Devon, Lincolnshire and Herefordshire. Since 1801, however, population increase in the East Riding has approximated the national trend. The half-century 1801-51 saw the fastest rise. Responding to growth in agricultural employment in the rural areas and to industrial and commercial expansion in Hull and other urban centres, the county's population rose by 98 per cent, close to the nationwide rate of 102 per cent. The following half-century, 1851-1901, saw some slackening of demographic growth, with the East Riding and the national trend easing to 76 per cent and 81 per cent respectively. It slackened further in the twentieth century, with the long period 1901-91 producing a relatively modest increase of 43 per cent in the county, eight percentage points behind the rate for England and Wales.

The East Riding has experienced a distinctive historical geography of population development which, since 1801, divides into three clearly identifiable periods: 1801-61 when population growth was widespread throughout the county both in rural and urban areas; 1861-1931 which witnessed extensive rural population decline but continued growth in the towns and suburban areas; and 1931 to the most recent census in 1991, a period of geographical complexity, including the imprints of further demographic decline in some rural localities, but also population dispersal from Hull and extensive rural suburbanisation. The geography of population change over each of these periods is illustrated in Maps A, B and C. These maps are based upon a consistent framework of statistical areas in the form of the post-1894 civil parishes[1] (henceforth, parishes), urban local authorities and, for Haltemprice to the immediate west of Hull, ward districts. However, to facilitate comparison with other material in this atlas, the boundaries of the historic ecclesiastical parishes are drawn (as dotted lines).

1801-1861

During this period the population of the county more than doubled, from 110,614 to 238,034. Over half of this increase came from the rapid expansion of Hull, whose number of inhabitants soared from 29,965 to 99,196. There was also rapid population growth in the smaller urban centres, Norton and Driffield setting the pace with increases of 385 per cent and 226 per cent respectively. However, the dominating feature in Map A is widespread rural population growth. Indeed, only nine of the rural parishes, less than 5 per cent of the county area, went against this trend; all the rest experienced increases, two-thirds recording gains of over 50 per cent and almost one-third, mostly in the High Wolds, having increases above 100 per cent. In the East Riding, therefore, the parliamentary enclosures and the implementation of capitalised farming did not lead immediately to rural depopulation. This was because, until the mechanisation of agricultural production in the middle and later decades of the nineteenth century, farming in this predominantly cereal-growing county was still labour intensive. Consequently farm work was in good supply and, although it was poorly paid and often seasonal, its availability curbed rural out-migration at a time of high rural birthrate and 'natural' demographic increase. When, in the 1850s and 60s, mechanisation did begin to make strong inroads, rural depopulation soon set in (see graphs and bar charts). Having risen from 56,311 in 1801 to 98,961 in 1851, the East Riding's rural population increased by only 2.3 per cent during 1851-61, and thereafter, with the single exception of 1901-11, declined in every intercensal decade until 1931.

As evidenced in Map A, rural population growth during the period 1801-61 was geographically uneven. It was generally strongest in the Wolds, where many parishes saw a doubling or even trebling of numbers. More so than elsewhere in the county, parliamentary enclosures had encouraged intensification of agriculture, including the transformation of extensive tracts of common pastures into labour-demanding cereal cultivation. The large population increases in Wold villages in the early decades of the nineteenth century provided the workforce for the new post-enclosure system of agriculture. The somewhat slower population growth in the Holderness and Vale of York sub-regions reflects their more mixed agricultural economies, which could operate with smaller workforces. In the Vale of York there are also indications that out-migration, attracted by expanding urban centres such as York and Goole, and towns further away in the industrial West Riding, was already occurring on a significant scale by the middle of the period.

In detail, Map A illustrates that rural East Riding contained a variety of local trends. Parishes with very rapid population growth existed alongside others with slower increases, and occasionally one with a static or even declining trend. Such marked local differences owed much to variations in landholding structure and settlement control, with a fundamental distinction between 'open' and 'close' parishes. In the former, land and property would be owned by several small landowners and proprietors who, because of their own labour requirements and the prospect of profits from speculative cottage construction, encouraged incomers to settle and augment local population growth. In 'close' parishes and villages, however, land and property belonged predominantly to influential 'gentry' or aristocratic families who actively resisted the settlement of newcomers, partly because of their potential burden upon the rates (often the 'owner' of a 'close' parish was the sole ratepayer) and partly on account of the landowners' desire to exclude all except key servants and estate workers from what were deliberately designed as pure versions of the English village. Unskilled agricultural labour for the tenant farms of 'close' parishes was brought in from 'open' villages and the nearest market town. Characteristic examples of 'open' parishes and villages in the East Riding are Langtoft on the Wolds, Rillington in the Vale of Pickering and North Frodingham in Holderness. During 1801-61 their populations grew by 149 per cent, 133 per cent and 129 per cent respectively. These were much larger increases than those in 'close' parishes such as Sledmere (49 per cent), Wintringham (1 per cent) and Burton Constable (13 per cent) in corresponding locations. Indeed, all of the nine parishes which recorded population decline in this period were of the 'close' type, including, for example, Thornton (-18 per cent) in the Vale of York and Halsham (-1 per cent) in southern Holderness.

1861-1931
The population of the county doubled again between 1861 and 1931, rising from 238,000 to 483,000. During this period, however, there were two contrasting processes at work - a continuing accumulation of people within most urban areas, spilling over into adjoining suburban parishes in the case of Hull, and, reversing the build-up of the preceding period, long term depopulation in the rural areas (Map B). These processes were inter-connected through heavy rural to urban migration. By 1931, as much as 79 per cent of the East Riding population lived in urban areas, including the 314,000 inhabitants of the city of Hull. Demographic trends amongst the various urban centres, however, did vary considerably. Hull, assisted by boundary extensions, recorded a 216 per cent growth, not quite as fast as before but nonetheless impressive. Quite soon after the opening of railways to Bridlington (in 1846), Filey (1847), Withernsea (1854) and Hornsea (1864), these four coastal resorts also experienced rapid population growth. Filey, once a quiet fishing village, saw a doubling of inhabitants during 1861-1931, whilst numbers trebled in Bridlington and quadrupled in Hornsea. Withernsea, growing from little more than a hamlet, could, however, claim the most spectacular pace of growth, its population multiplying from just 202 to over 4,000. None of the inland urban centres matched these trends. Those that were favoured by a more balanced local economy, namely Driffield and Norton with

their manufacturing industries and Beverley with its additional 'shire town' functions, experienced reasonably healthy gains of between 25 and 50 per cent, but others, such as Pocklington (-1 per cent), Howden (-15 per cent) and Market Weighton (-20 per cent), virtually wholly dependent upon agriculture, suffered population decline. The latter were decaying market towns which had failed to broaden their economic functions beyond agricultural supply industries and providing services for surrounding farming communities. Like the large majority of villages and rural parishes, these small urban centres were highly vulnerable to the 'Great Agricultural Depression' which first swept the cereal-growing counties of England in the 1870s, abruptly ending the prosperous 'high farming' era. Initiated by a series of wet summers and then sustained by strengthening competition from overseas, especially North America and Australia, this depression continued with little relief until the 'plough-up' campaigns of the late 1930s and the Second World War. The East Riding, with its emphasis on arable farming, suffered badly, losing 49 per cent of its wheat and 21 per cent of its barley acreage. In total 92,000 acres of crop land were 'grassed down', left to waste or sold for military airfields or suburban development.

Agricultural depression, however, was not the only reason for rural decay and depopulation during this period. The middle decades of the nineteenth century had seen important advances in the mechanisation of cereal farming, particularly the adoption of drilling, winnowing and threshing machines which were being widely used in the East Riding by the 1860s. Machines such as these reduced agricultural jobs for the county's large pool of unskilled farm labourers. Much of this rural population, therefore, was forced by technological change to migrate and seek work in the nearest towns, especially the growing town of Hull. Later in the century many emigrated to the United States, Canada or Australia, the very countries that were providing the greatest competition for East Riding farmers. Not all rural migrants, however, were agricultural labourers and their families. The Agricultural Depression was also accompanied by an unrelenting decline in rural trades and crafts. Census data confirm this trend in the early twentieth century. During the period 1911-31 the number of blacksmiths in East Riding rural districts fell from 555 to 320, whilst those of boot and shoemakers, innkeepers and carpenters dwindled by 35, 32 and 16 per cent respectively. Decline in these occupations had a debilitating effect on village communities, undermining their organic self-sufficiency and reducing local entrepreneurship. In part this was itself a consequence of population decline and shrinking numbers of customers, but it also owed much to the increasing capitalisation of these activities and associated shifts from village workshop to urban factory.

All except 8 per cent of the East Riding's rural area endured population losses during 1861-1931. However, the pace of population decline varied considerably across the county, more so within the sub-regions than between them. Very noticeable in Map C is the tendency for the heavily depopulating parishes, those suffering declines of over 25 per cent, to form distinct local clusters. Some reflected the geography of the Agricultural Depression, which was most severe in the wheat and barley lands of the High Wolds, the Hull valley and northern Holderness. Other clusters corresponded with the remotest parts of the county, notably the Derwent 'warplands' in the Vale of York and the western Wolds between Market Weighton and Norton. Even in these localities, however, some places experienced only moderate depopulation. With very few exceptions these are 'close' parishes where large landowners retained their key employees. For example, Sledmere, a classic 'close' parish in the heart of the Wolds, experienced a modest 5 per cent population decline over the whole period, whereas the nearby 'open' parish of Langtoft suffered a much heavier 32 per cent reduction. The small minority of rural parishes which went against the declining population trend during this period are almost invariably situated either close to the county's various urban centres, particularly Hull, Beverley and Bridlington, or in the extreme west of the county, adjoining York and Selby. In these locations a 'suburbanising' effect was already emerging by 1931.

1931-1991
Population growth in the East Riding, dampened by a falling birth rate, slowed markedly during this period with numbers increasing by only 14 per cent from 483,000 to 550,000. A major feature is the exodus of people from Hull, whose population fell from a peak of 314,000 in 1931 to 245,000 in 1991. Another important feature, however, is the demographic expansion of all other urban centres, ranging from 12 per cent in Beverley, whose closely drawn boundary excludes much of the town's recent residential expansion, to 252 per cent in Market Weighton, whose limits are wide enough to contain all of its post-1931 development. Depressed agricultural conditions continued up to the Second World War and there was no let-up in the depletion of agricultural employment and decline of rural trades and crafts. The 1931 census did, however, mark the end of the long period of rural depopulation, and the dawn of a new phase of rural population growth that has progressed to the present day. The pattern of population change over 1931-91 is, therefore, markedly different from that of the preceding period. There is a much diminished occurrence of rural depopulation; the only extensive areas where this continued were the northern and central Wolds, which remain predominantly agricultural and are beyond the reach of suburbanising influences from Hull or any other expanding urban centre. Elsewhere, in the Vale of York and Holderness, only odd 'patches' of rural depopulation persist.

Around 60 per cent of the county's area has experienced population growth since 1931. The dominating process here is the wide dispersal of people, principally from the city of Hull but also, on a lesser scale, from certain of the smaller urban centres. The 'Hull effect' positively covers about one-third of the county. Before 1931, population growth in the vicinity of Hull had been confined to the adjoining 'suburban' wards of Haltemprice District and parishes situated within a dozen miles from the city boundary. Since then, however, it has spread out, eastwards into southern Holderness, northwards towards Driffield, and westwards following the communications axis of the Hull-Leeds railway, the A63 trunk road and, since its completion in 1976, the M62 motorway. In Map C, this latter zone of strong population growth merges with another locale of rural suburbanisation in the Vale of York which is associated with employment expansion at Drax power station in the 1960s and more recently the Selby coalfield across the river Ouse and the county boundary. Further north the zone meets the suburbanising influence of York.

The positive influence of proximity to Hull and other urban centres is counteracted in detail in many places. Particularly significant is the tendency for surviving 'close' parishes, still under landowner control, to resist residential expansion, although some, after the selling off of tied cottages, have undergone major social change. For example, the parish of Dalton Holme with its picturesque village of South Dalton, near Beverley and within commuting range of Hull, has seen its population dwindle from 365 in 1931 to just 186 in 1991. In contrast, 'open' parishes, not subject to landowner control and containing larger villages from the outset, tended to attract new residential development and population growth; several in fact had already recorded a demographic upturn at the 1931 census. Later, after the Second World War, 'open' parishes experienced a more vigorous wave of rural suburbanisation which, guided by county planning policy, focused on the larger and more viable villages, especially those advantaged by modern infrastructure and adequate local services. In 1979 the new county of Humberside strengthened this trend in its first County Structure Plan, a key feature of which was the concentration of new rural housing development within designated growth villages. There is a clear connection through time between the historical 'open' villages, the suburbanising villages of the 1950s and 60s, and these 'selected' settlements. Two contrasting parishes, adjoining each other in the Vale of York, illustrate this. Holme-upon-Spalding Moor, designated as a 'selected settlement' in 1979, was an 'open' parish. With 1,624 inhabitants in 1931, it had already contained a large community before the onset of suburbanisation. By 1991, the village, despite its remoteness, had grown substantially and the parish population had risen to 3,006, most of this increase coming after the introduction of the County Structure Plan. The experience of the neighbouring parish of Cliffe, a 'close' parish and not a 'selected settlement', has been very different. Cliffe had just 157 inhabitants in 1931, fewer than in 1801, and by 1991 its population was only 107.

Note and bibliography on page 143

POPULATION CHANGE : 1801-1861

A

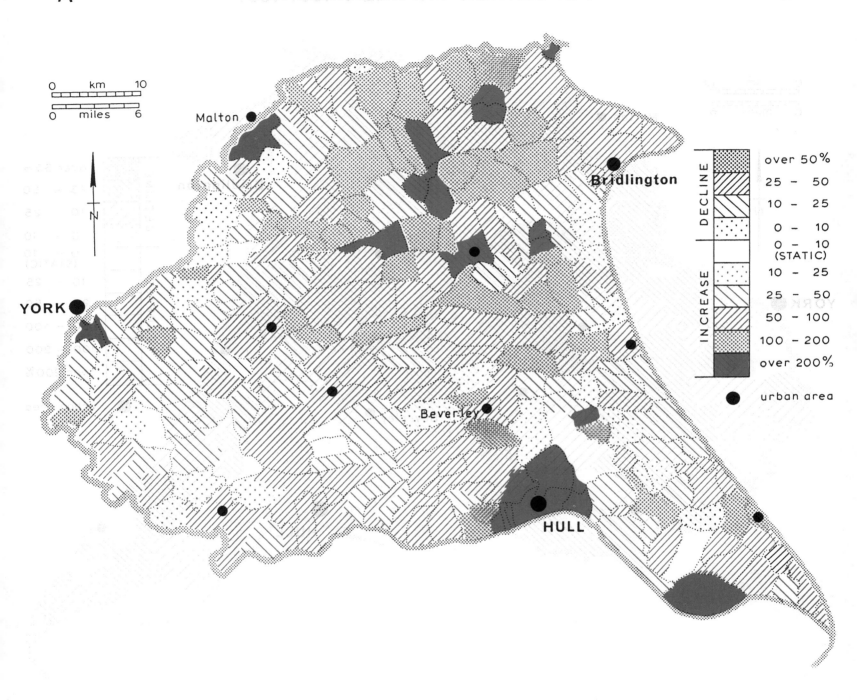

km 0 — 10
miles 0 — 6

N

Malton ●

Bridlington ●

YORK ●

Beverley ●

HULL ●

DECLINE
over 50%
25 — 50
10 — 25
0 — 10

INCREASE
0 — 10 (STATIC)
10 — 25
25 — 50
50 — 100
100 — 200
over 200%

● urban area

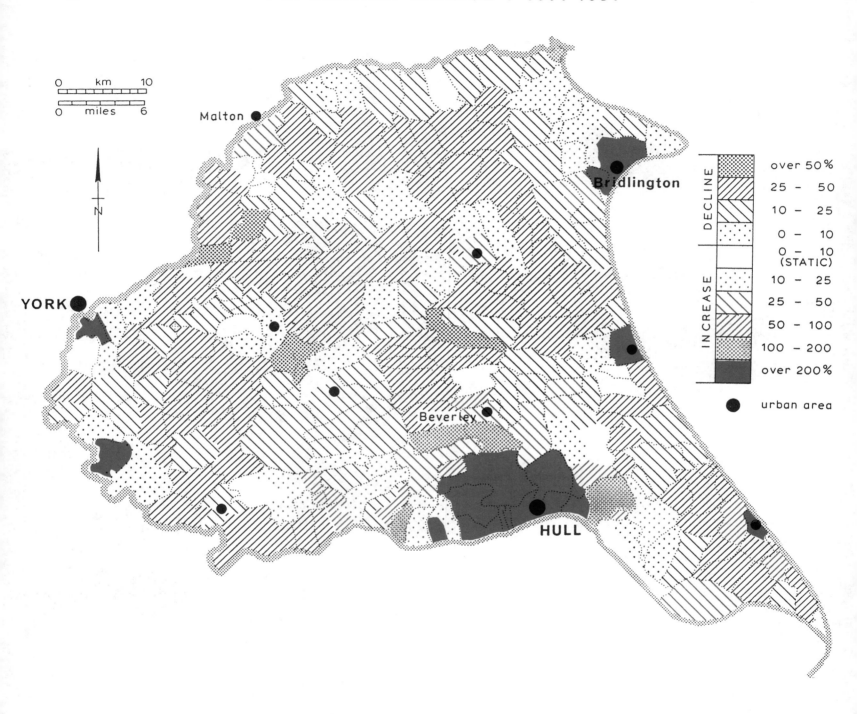

B   POPULATION CHANGE : 1861-1931

DECLINE	over 50%
	25 - 50
	10 - 25
	0 - 10
	0 - 10 (STATIC)
INCREASE	10 - 25
	25 - 50
	50 - 100
	100 - 200
	over 200%

● urban area

Malton ●

Bridlington

YORK ●

Beverley

HULL

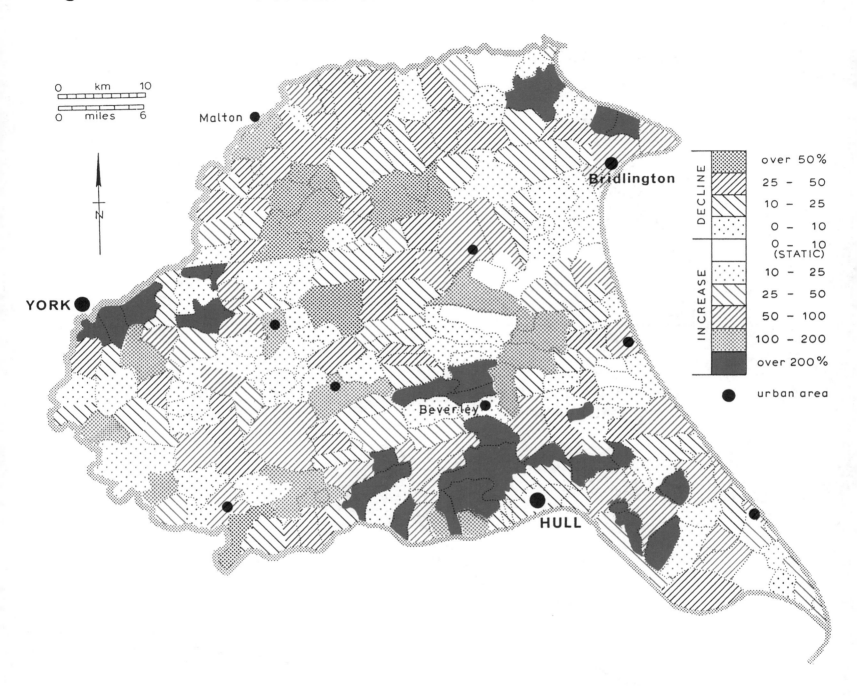

C POPULATION CHANGE : 1931-1991

0   km   10

0   miles   6

N

Malton ●

Bridlington ●

YORK ●

Beverley ●

HULL ●

DECLINE
over 50%
25 - 50
10 - 25
0 - 10

0 - 10 (STATIC)

INCREASE
10 - 25
25 - 50
50 - 100
100 - 200
over 200%

● urban area

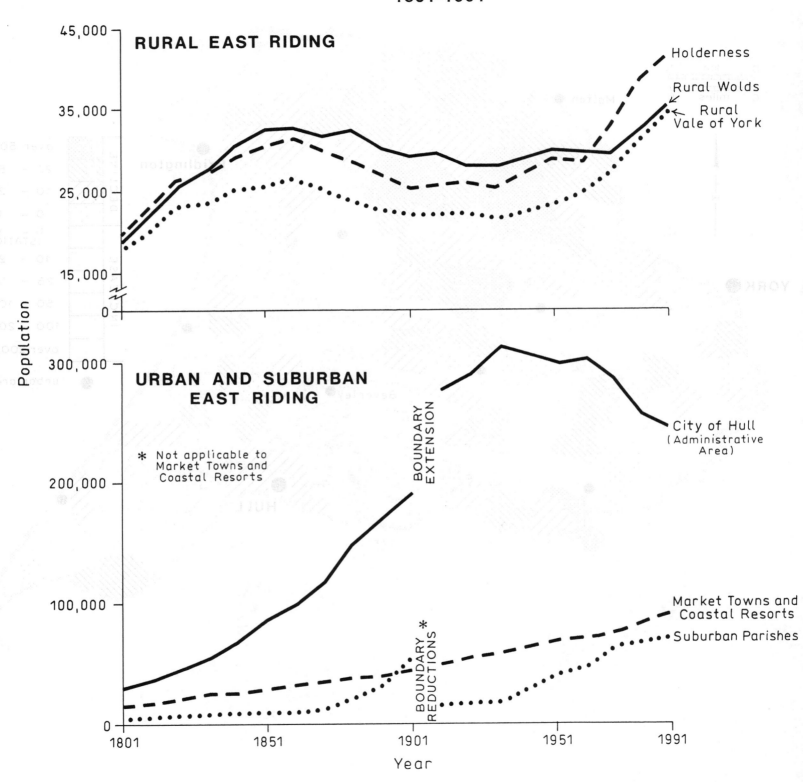

POPULATION CHANGE IN RURAL AND URBAN EAST RIDING:
1801-1991

RURAL EAST RIDING

Holderness
Rural Wolds
Rural Vale of York

URBAN AND SUBURBAN EAST RIDING

* Not applicable to Market Towns and Coastal Resorts

City of Hull (Administrative Area)

BOUNDARY EXTENSION

BOUNDARY REDUCTIONS *

Market Towns and Coastal Resorts

Suburban Parishes

Population

Year

POPULATION CHANGE PER INTERCENSAL DECADE
IN RURAL AND URBAN EAST RIDING

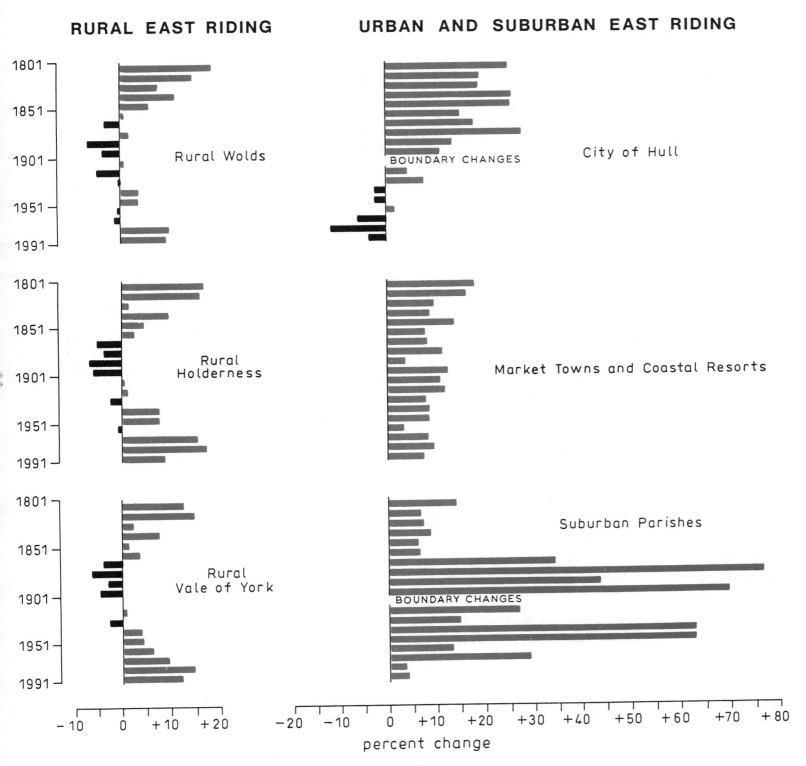

RURAL EAST RIDING

URBAN AND SUBURBAN EAST RIDING

Rural Wolds

City of Hull

BOUNDARY CHANGES

Rural Holderness

Market Towns and Coastal Resorts

Rural Vale of York

Suburban Parishes

BOUNDARY CHANGES

percent change

DESERTED SETTLEMENTS
Susan Neave

The sites of around 130 deserted settlements have been located in the East Riding, and more could almost certainly be added to the list.[1] The identification of many of these sites is due to the pioneering work of Maurice Beresford in the 1950s. The results of Beresford's research on the depopulated settlements of the East Riding were initially published in gazetteer form in the second part of a four-part study, 'The Lost Villages of Yorkshire', 1951-5; a revised gazetteer was published in 1971.[2] The map produced here is based on the revised gazetteer, with further modifications in the light of more recent work by local archaeologists, historians and members of the Medieval Settlement Research Group.

The criterion which Beresford adopted was that sites should have 'either good documentary evidence for their existence at some point in time, or good evidence from fieldwork and air photographs'.[3] Settlements lost to the North Sea and the Humber estuary have not been mapped.

Depopulation of settlements took place throughout, and far beyond, the medieval period. The reasons for the desertion of individual settlements are not always clear, especially in the middle ages when documentary material is limited. The epidemic of 1349-51 known as the Black Death decimated the population of the East Riding, but there is no evidence to support the traditional view that large numbers of villages became depopulated as a direct result of the pestilence. It does, however, seem certain that the reduction in population led to a gradual movement away from marginal lands as the pressure on better quality land eased.

Economic changes from the late fourteenth century onwards played a major part in the desertion of settlements. The enclosure of arable land and conversion to sheep pasture, which caused much unrest in the fifteenth century, continued to result in depopulation in the East Riding as late as the seventeenth century. The township of Eastburn, in Kirkburn parish, was acquired by John Heron of Beverley between 1664 and 1666. In a tithe case brought before the church courts in 1682 it was reported that 'the town of Eastburn aforesaid did anciently consist of several messuages and cottages ... about twelve years ago the said messuages and other dwelling houses were totally demolished by the aforesaid Mr Heron except two little cottages ... and all grounds belonging the township are converted into meadow and pasture'.[4] At the end of the seventeenth century Eastburn was described as sheep walk. The well-preserved village site lies southwest of Eastburn Farm.

There are numerous examples of post-medieval desertions in the East Riding. A distinction has been made between those settlements deserted before the mid-seventeenth century and those which documentary evidence shows still had five or more houses in 1660. A number of settlements which fall into the latter group had substantial populations in the middle ages and had shrunk considerably by the seventeenth century. Nevertheless, map evidence, where available, suggests that the houses which remained in the mid-seventeenth century continued to represent a nucleated settlement. A map of the now-deserted village of Wauldby, dated 1653, shows a group of buildings, including six houses and a chapel, clustered around a large pond. Five households were assessed in the hearth tax returns of 1672. A more substantial village was to be found at Neswick, in Bainton parish, in 1672, when 25 households were assessed for the hearth tax. There are now only two farms in the township. Some of the finest depopulated settlement sites in the East Riding represent late desertions, for example Cottam, in Langtoft parish, which still had nine houses and extensive open fields at the beginning of the eighteenth century.

Emparking resulted in some settlement depopulation in the eighteenth century. The hamlet of Easthorpe in Londesborough parish was finally swept way in the 1730s as part of the extensions to Lord Burlington's deer park. More commonly a village was only partially removed at emparking, as at Howsham, or was replaced immediately by a new village, and these have not been included on the map. An exception is Sledmere, where the old village was cleared away some years before a new estate village was created.

Sometimes there is little or nothing to see at a deserted village site, but often the earthworks of streets, crofts and houses are clearly visible. Many sites are especially impressive from the air. The majority of deserted village sites are on private land, although some are accessible via public footpaths. The East Riding is, however, fortunate in having within its historic boundaries the most famous deserted village site in England - Wharram Percy - now under the care of English Heritage and open to the public. The village was abandoned gradually over two centuries, final depopulation taking place around 1500 when several households were evicted and the arable land and house sites were converted to pasture for sheep farming. The site was excavated by Beresford, Hurst and others over a 40-year period. Situated high on the Yorkshire Wolds, its ruined church nestling at the bottom of a steep-sided valley, Wharram Percy must surely be one of the most evocative deserted village sites in the whole of the country.

Notes and bibliography on page 143

DESERTED SETTLEMENTS

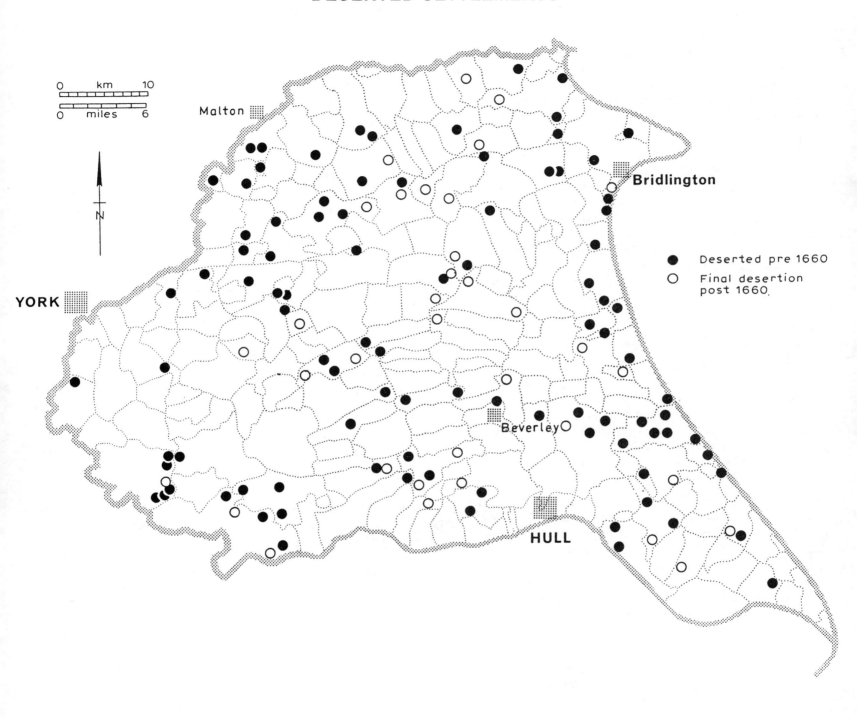

Malton

YORK

Bridlington

Deserted pre 1660

Final desertion post 1660

Beverley

HULL

VERNACULAR BUILDING MATERIALS

David and Susan Neave

The map opposite shows the general distribution of building materials (excluding brick, tile and slate) as observed in standing traditional or vernacular buildings - that is pre-Victorian farmhouses, cottages and associated buildings in rural areas and pre-eighteenth century urban buildings. In the case of cobble stone any use as a walling material has been plotted (including churches).[1]

There is little good building stone in the East Riding, with the exception of the limestones and sandstones from the Jurassic belt on the western edge of the Wolds (see page 5), but even these are rarely of the quality to produce ashlar or fine carved detail. The stone varies from the cream or grey oolitic limestone of the South Cave-Newbald area through the grey Coral Rag from North Grimston to the rich iron-coloured sandstones at Howsham. The oolitic limestone was used at Beverley Minster before the mid-thirteenth century and in other local churches throughout the middle ages. Numerous limestone farmhouses and cottages dating from the seventeenth to nineteenth centuries are found in a narrow band of villages from Elloughton to Goodmanham, but it is in the villages in the northwest of the riding that stone is used most extensively. Here a good-quality light-grey limestone was quarried at Acklam until the mid-nineteenth century.

As H.E. Strickland reported in 1812 'the old buildings of the wolds are in general composed of chalk stone'.[2] The plentiful chalkstone usually weathers badly when not protected by whitewash or render, but the stone quarried in the northeast Wolds is remarkably hard-wearing as evidenced by the 1674 lighthouse at Flamborough and a former dovecote of 1670 at Bessingby. Throughout the northern Wolds there are many examples of chalk walling with an outer facing of brick.

Along the east coast from Kilnsea to Hunmanby, cobble stones - rounded boulders from the glacial deposits - were collected from the beach for centuries and used extensively for building. They range greatly in both geology and colour but the most durable and widely used are of dark basalt. The stones were used for churches in Holderness from the thirteenth century, being carried as far inland as Preston, Long Riston and North Frodingham. Use for houses and farm buildings was more restricted and generally confined to the coastal settlements, where examples of cobble cottages from the seventeenth century remain.[3]

The use of imported stone is not plotted but this was usually confined to ecclesiastical and important secular buildings in the middle ages, and public and commercial buildings in the nineteenth and twentieth centuries. The most widely used was the white Magnesian Limestone from Tadcaster which was transported by water for use in Beverley Minster and all the major churches of the East Riding, as well as Wressle castle. Closer at hand was the fine white limestone quarried at Hildenley, in the North Riding, two miles west of Malton.[4] Hildenley stone from Kirkham priory was reused locally in farmhouses and cottages after the dissolution. Reused monastic stone is also found at Bridlington and Warter.

Timber was never plentiful in the East Riding and today there are few timber-framed buildings. The main areas of woodland recorded in Domesday Book were to the south and southwest of Beverley and to the south and southeast of York. It is in the latter area, between the rivers Ouse and Derwent, where there was a royal forest until the early thirteenth century, that box-framed buildings are most numerous. Box-framed houses were more likely to be built in the Vale of York, Hull valley and Holderness than on the upland areas of the Wolds and Jurassic hills and the few remaining buildings still bear this out. Surviving examples, along with archaeological and documentary evidence, suggest that cruck-framed buildings were more common on the upland areas, although good examples have been demolished in the last 25 years in Holderness and the Hull valley. Almost all of the surviving cruck-framed buildings are close to the North Riding where such structures are much more numerous. As vernacular buildings are examined more closely, a few more timber-framed buildings will be identified in the East Riding, particularly in the towns. There are half-a-dozen known timber-framed buildings in Beverley and one in Hull, but others are suspected from exterior evidence.[5]

Mud, the most readily available and most widely used building material in the East Riding before the eighteenth century, has not been plotted as only two standing examples of mud-walled buildings are known. These are at Beeford and Roos, both in Holderness. Documentary and literary evidence for mud-walled buildings is extensive. In 1797, for example, the majority of the houses at Leconfield in the Hull valley were of mud and thatch, and Captain Edward Anderson in his poem *The Sailor*, commenting on buildings at Kilham in the eighteenth century, noted that 'the walls were mostly clay, and thatched with straw'.[6]

Thatch was the universal roofing material in the East Riding before the mid-eighteenth century.[7] Wheat or rye straw was generally used, with reed a possibility in the low-lying areas of the Vale of York, Holderness and the Hull valley. Postcard views of East Riding villages at the beginning of this century often show the odd thatched farmhouse or cottage, but nothing now remains with the exception of the great fifteenth-century tithe barn at Easington and a restored early eighteenth-century farmhouse at Howsham. The nineteenth-century estate cottages at Warter were not thatched until *c*.1930. Thatch was usually replaced by pantile which, with brick, became the dominant building materials of the East Riding from the late eighteenth century.

Notes on page 144

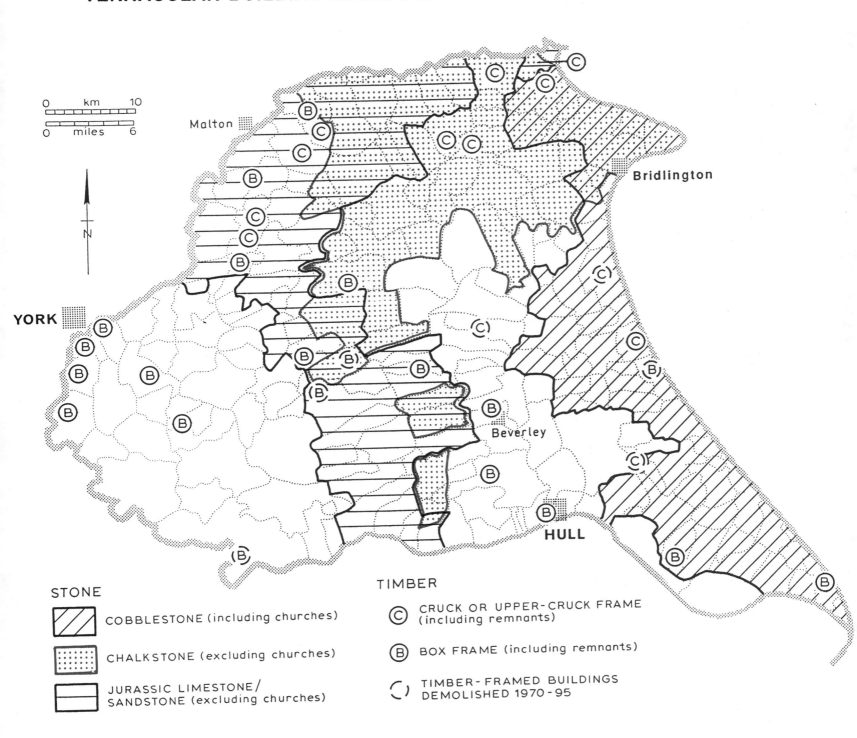

VERNACULAR BUILDING MATERIALS : USE IN STANDING STRUCTURES

0 km 10

0 miles 6

N

Malton

Bridlington

YORK

Beverley

HULL

STONE

COBBLESTONE (including churches)

CHALKSTONE (excluding churches)

JURASSIC LIMESTONE/
SANDSTONE (excluding churches)

TIMBER

(C) CRUCK OR UPPER-CRUCK FRAME
(including remnants)

(B) BOX FRAME (including remnants)

( ) TIMBER-FRAMED BUILDINGS
DEMOLISHED 1970-95

LANDOWNERSHIP AND LAND USE

MEDIEVAL PARKS
Susan Neave

Documentary evidence has been found for some 50 medieval parks in the East Riding, with indications that several more existed.[1] Parks mapped are those which existed before 1700, but the majority of these were established by 1500. The map shows a concentration of parks in the southern half of the riding, in the low-lying areas such as Holderness and the Vale of York, where woodland is recorded in the early middle ages. A number of parks lay within the boundaries of the former Ouse and Derwent forest, which was disafforested sometime in the thirteenth century. The earliest parks recorded are those at Burstwick in Holderness, and Etton near Beverley, both mentioned in the twelfth century, but the major period of emparking appears to have been in the following two centuries, when many licences to empark were granted. The most important and best documented parks were those created by the great landowners. These include deer parks at Catton, Leconfield, Wressle and Newsholme, on the estates of the earls of Northumberland, at Burstwick, a royal manor, at Beverley and Bishop Burton, both manors owned by the archbishops of York, and at Howden, which belonged to the bishops of Durham.

In contrast to the landscaped parks of the eighteenth and nineteenth centuries, which were usually designed to provide an attractive setting for a country house, the parks created in the middle ages were simply private enclosures, often situated some distance from a castle or manor house, in which to keep deer. They varied considerably in size. Some covered areas of less than 50 acres, and could have supported only a small herd of deer, whilst the largest East Riding park, owned by the archbishops of York at Beverley, was over 2000 acres in extent. Only the larger parks provided the opportunity for hunting.

In many parks herds of both red deer, native to England, and fallow deer, thought to have been introduced by the Normans, were maintained. Venison was a highly prized commodity. In the 1570s William Harrison wrote of deer as 'that vain commodity which bringeth no manner of gain or profit to the owner, since they commonly give away their flesh, never taking penny for the same, because venison in England is neither bought nor sold by the right owner, but maintained only for his pleasure'.[2]

Deer required a varied habitat, and most parks probably comprised a mixture of open grassland (a grassy clearing known as a laund or lawn), woodland and coppice. The management of woodland was an important aspect of the economy of the medieval park. Deer parks were commonly enclosed by a ditch surrounded by an earthen bank, topped by an oak pallisade or pale. The park keeper had to ensure that the pale was kept in good repair, to prevent the deer escaping and to secure the park from poachers. On some of the larger estates a 'palester' was employed to carry out this task. A well-managed park would yield sufficient timber to keep the pale in good repair, but there are many examples of parks where poor management meant that wood from elsewhere had to be used. When the Crown surveyed the forfeited parks of the earls of Northumberland in the mid-sixteenth century they found that at Newsholme park in Howdenshire the pale was 'clean wasted' and no timber was available to repair it. The fence may have been damaged by the natural elements, or by poachers, but almost certainly some of the wood had been stolen for firewood or building work. The manorial court at neighbouring Wressle, where the earls of Northumberland held more emparked land, laid down a by-law stating that 'none [shall] bear wood nor pale boards ... from the great park nor little park'.[3]

Numerous cases of poaching and trespass in East Riding deer parks are recorded. Sometimes these were straightforward cases of common poaching, but more often they are indicative of grievances connected with emparking or of feuds amongst the local gentry. At Beverley, where the burgesses were aggrieved at the loss of common rights caused by emparking, there are many references in the archbishops' registers from the mid-thirteenth century onwards to cases of trespass and poaching within the hunting park. The usual penalty for this offence was excommunication.

As the middle ages drew to a close the popularity of parks declined, and only a handful of new parks were created in the East Riding in the fifteenth and sixteenth centuries. Changes in the ownership of church and monastic lands following the Reformation led to the abandonment of many parks, but economic factors and changes in fashion also played a part. Parks were expensive to maintain, and landowners increasingly found it more profitable to lease out their parkland. In the eighteenth century a new wave of emparking spread across the country, with landowners creating the picturesque landscaped parks which remain such a feature of the English countryside. These, however, bore little resemblance to the deer parks created by the medieval landowners.

Using maps and other documentary evidence it has been possible to determine the boundaries of many of the East Riding's medieval parks, but few have left much impression on the modern landscape. A notable exception is at Bishop Burton, where there are large stretches of an impressive boundary bank. This marked the perimeter of the archiepiscopal deer park.

Notes and bibliography on page 144

MEDIEVAL PARKS

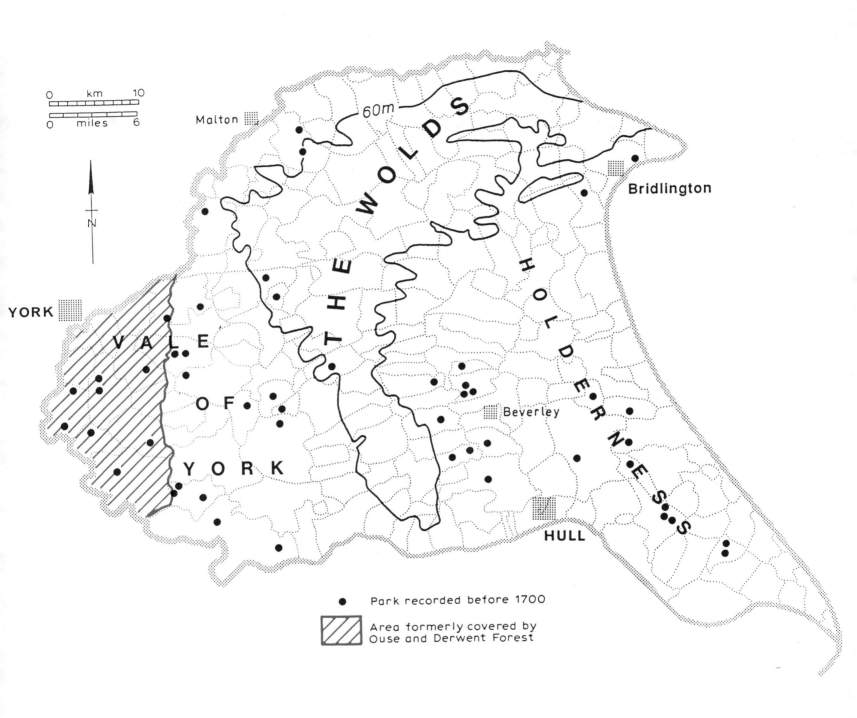

Malton

60m

THE WOLDS

Bridlington

YORK

VALE

OF

YORK

HOLDERNESS

Beverley

HULL

● Park recorded before 1700

/// Area formerly covered by
     Ouse and Derwent Forest

0   km   10
0   miles   6

N

LANDOWNERSHIP AND PARISH TYPE, *c.*1830

Janice E. Crowther

Classification of parishes into 'open' and 'close' dates from at least the early nineteenth century,[1] and gives a useful insight into the structure of social and economic life in the countryside. 'Close' or 'estate' villages, often recognisable by their attractive architecture and regular layout, were usually dominated by a single landowner. Such villages often had a school endowed by the landlord, and although the parish church might have been kept in good order by him, he was frequently instrumental in preventing the building of a nonconformist chapel, and expected his tenants to be industrious, sober and deferential. In a classic 'close' township a landlord deliberately kept the population low by limiting the number of cottages, thus controlling the numbers of wage-dependent families, who would gain settlement and claim relief from the poor-rates when they could no longer work. Such a landowner might draw most of his labour from neighbouring 'open' villages, where there were many property owners, numerous humble cottages to rent and a high population. 'Open' villages usually contained several public houses and dissenting chapels, and often had a reputation as centres of unruliness and radicalism.

Any attempt to classify townships into 'open' and 'close' must begin with the ownership structure; the Land Tax returns, which provide uniquely detailed evidence of the ownership of property over a 50-year period,[2] have here been used to construct a map of the East Riding *c.*1830. Other sources could also be consulted to give a more detailed picture. For example, directories list nonconformist chapels, public houses, shops, craftsmen and rural industries, while census reports indicate population, numbers of inhabited houses and cottages, and occupational structure. In the map opposite, Warter qualifies as a 'close' township because of its ownership structure. More research would answer such questions as how many cottages there were in the village, and whether or not the labour supply was sufficient to supply the estate's needs. South Dalton, in many ways the archetypal estate village, does not qualify as 'close' on ownership, because in 1830 Lord Hotham paid only 79 per cent of the tax and there were five owners of land.[3]

The Land Tax in the East Riding was collected on a township basis, which is how the map has been arranged. A similar classification to that used by Stewart Bennett for Lincolnshire has been adopted, counting how many people owned land in each township, and whether the property was concentrated into only a few hands.[4] 'Close' townships are divided into three types - those with a single owner, those with fewer than five owners and where the largest paid more than 85 per cent of the tax, and those where only one of those criteria applied. 'Open' townships are represented by two types - those with over 40 landowners and where the largest paid less than 25 per cent of the tax, and those where only one of those criteria applied. Townships which have been left blank on the map are in an intermediate category, neither 'open' nor 'close'.

H.E. Strickland wrote in 1812, 'Landed property is less divided in the East Riding than in other parts of the Country', and he described the Wolds in particular as being 'occupied ... in very large tracts'.[5] Many high Wolds townships were characterised by concentrated landownership.[6] By a deliberate policy of purchasing land whenever it came on the market, and by judicious marriages, a gentry family such as the Sykes might gain enormous influence locally. Other long-established landowners such as the Boyntons were content to dominate only the immediate area around their manor house.[7] Unlike the Wolds, Holderness had relatively few 'close' townships. 'Open' townships were quite numerous in the neighbourhood of Patrington, Aldbrough and Hornsea, and also on the southern and western side of the Wolds.

In the first half of the nineteenth century the population of 'open' townships grew quite rapidly, but so too did that of many 'close' townships. Londesborough was owned by the Duke of Devonshire and only one other proprietor in 1830. Its population was 183 in 1801 and 293 in 1851. Millington had 33 proprietors in 1830, and none owned more than 25 per cent of the land. The population rose from 183 in 1801 to 289 in 1851, more or less the same as Londesborough. However, Boynton, a 'close' village, and Burton Fleming, an 'open' one, provide a contrasting picture. Boynton's population grew very little in the nineteenth century, whereas Burton Fleming grew by two and a half times between 1801 and 1851.[8] In a study of the Wolds, B.A. Holderness identified a total of 68 'close' townships (out of a total of 157) and found that between 1801 and 1841, their population grew by an average 32 per cent, whilst the growth for all 157 was 61.2 per cent.[9]

In order to produce the information in the map, the data on owners only have been selected from the Land Tax returns, for a single year. However, the returns have far more to offer. They list occupiers as well as owners, and thus may be used to assess the degree of owner-occupancy in the riding. Because they are available for a 50-year period, they may also be used to study change over time, both in terms of numbers of owners and of occupiers, and the proportionate share of the taxes paid by those groups.[10] The actual acreage was not specified, and the valuation of property on which the tax was based hardly changed over a century or more, therefore any attempt to convert tax paid into an acreage equivalent is fraught with problems.[11] However, historians interested in gentry families can use the returns to follow their fortunes, and family historians might also find them a valuable source. If they are used as only a broad guide to individuals' relationship to the land, the Land Tax returns can provide invaluable information on landownership during a period of rapid change.

Notes on page 144

LANDOWNERSHIP AND PARISH TYPE : *c.* 1830

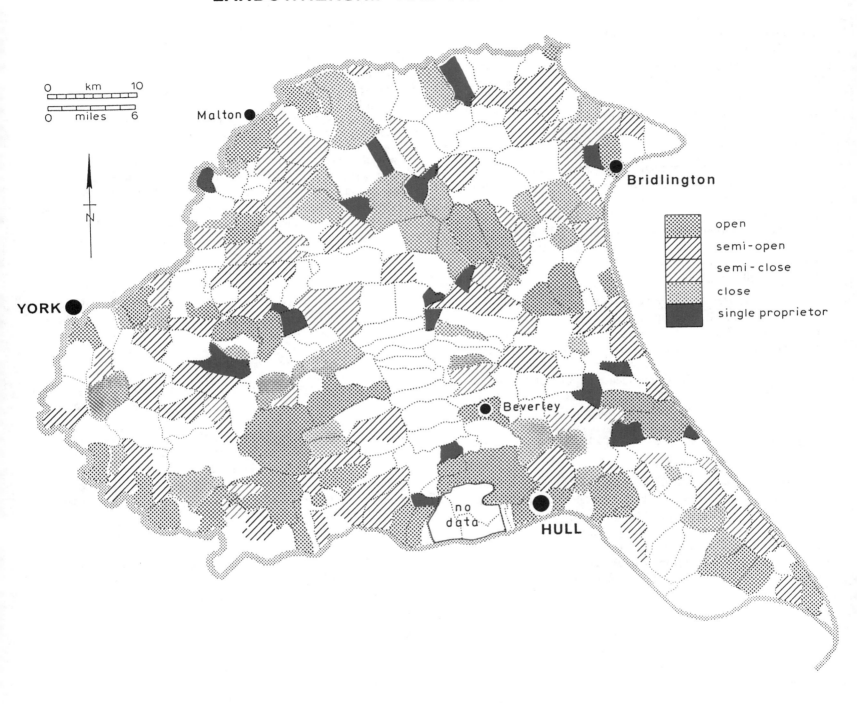

0 km 10

0 miles 6

N

Malton

Bridlington

YORK

Beverley

no data

HULL

open

semi-open

semi-close

close

single proprietor

SEATS OF THE GENTRY
David Neave

The importance of landownership in the social and landscape history of the East Riding is evident from a number of the maps in this atlas. The location of the seats of the gentry is of particular significance because of the impact of a resident landowner on the local community. In a nineteenth-century estate village, religious and political freedom could be restricted, and leisure pursuits controlled, but this might be balanced by improved accommodation and better educational and employment opportunities.

The map opposite plots the location of gentry seats in the late seventeenth century and the late nineteenth century. The information for the earlier period is from the hearth tax returns for 1672, which provide information on house size based on the number of hearths, and a list of the East Riding gentry compiled c.1685.[1] The 1873 information is based on the Parliamentary Paper *Return of Owners of Land, 1873*, published 1875 and a list of principal seats in the East Riding in Kelly's *Directory* of 1872.[2]

In the late seventeenth century there was a concentration of gentry houses in and around Beverley, with other clusters along the western edge of the Wolds and to the south and east of York. Beverley, then just emerging as the administrative and social centre of the East Riding, had nine resident gentry, and to the south of the town was Beverley Parks, the newly-built residence of Michael Warton, the wealthiest of the riding's landowners. The Wartons had their origins as Hull merchants, as did the Gees of Bishop Burton. York merchants had similarly established themselves on country estates near to the city - Sir Henry Thompson at Escrick, Tobias Jenkins at Grimston and Sir John Hewley at Bell Hall, Naburn.

The Wolds had almost no resident gentry. There was a sprinkling of gentry houses in Holderness, including Burton Constable Hall, the seat of Viscount Dunbar, which had 40 hearths - the largest house in the East Riding. Most of the large country houses in the riding in 1672, including Burton Constable, had been built in the late Elizabethan-Jacobean period. Other examples are Burton Agnes (32 hearths), Howsham (24), Boynton (23), Londesborough (21) and Bishop Burton (20).

In the late nineteenth century the majority of East Riding gentry lived in houses built between 1750 and 1830, the high point in English country house building. These included Sledmere, the only country house on the high Wolds, largely built 1783-1800 by Sir Christopher Sykes, and South Dalton, built 1771-6 for Sir Charles Hotham. The Hothams moved to South Dalton after the hall at Scorborough, where they had lived since the middle ages, had been destroyed by fire in 1705-6. This move from the Hull valley to the eastern edge of the Wolds may have been part of the general movement of gentry residences from the lowlands to more upland areas, a pattern which has been observed elsewhere.[3]

In the East Riding, the preference was for the western edge of the Wolds. This area provided a healthier and more picturesque setting than Holderness or the low-lying Vale of York. Here in 1873 were clustered the houses of the peers - Lord Londesborough, Lord Muncaster, Lord Halifax and Lord Middleton. The proximity to York would always have been important, more so in the eighteenth century when the county capital was the social and administrative centre of the north of England. It is noticeable that amongst the few landed gentry who retained their seats in the less fashionable lowlands were the riding's leading Roman Catholic families.

The decline in minor gentry houses in the Vale of York and Holderness by 1873 is particularly marked. Of seventeen 'ancient' halls and manor houses recorded in the Holme Beacon division of Harthill wapentake, eleven had gone by 1850, mostly removed in the eighteenth and early nineteenth centuries. These included Hayton Hall, demolished 1805, and the Elizabethan hall of the Vavasours at Spaldington, demolished 1838.[4] Elsewhere a number of the greater houses of the late seventeenth century had also gone. Risby Hall and Beverley Parks were demolished in the late eighteenth century and Londesborough Hall was taken down in 1818-19. When Lord Albert Denison (later Lord Londesborough) bought the estate in 1849 there was only a shooting lodge at Londesborough. It was enlarged in 1875 and 1898 to house the many guests, including royalty, who came for the shooting parties.[5]

Some of the country houses in 1873 were new. Christopher Sykes built Brantinghamthorpe, 1868-83, for the purpose of entertaining the Prince of Wales. It was designed by George Devey, one of the leading country house architects, who also worked at High Hall, Bishop Burton in 1870. Another country house specialist, William Burn, designed Ganton Hall (1866-8), and the Hull architect Cuthbert Brodrick was responsible for Yokefleet Hall (1868-74). At the same time, many older houses were being refurbished and greatly extended, including Birdsall House (1871-5), Hotham Hall (1871), South Dalton Hall (1872-7) and Warter Priory (1872). Although country house building was largely halted from the late 1870s by the agricultural depression, landowners continued to improve their homes. Warter Priory was further extended in 1885-95 by its new owner, Charles Wilson, the shipping magnate, and in the 1890s the Lords Halifax virtually rebuilt Garrowby Hall.

In the twentieth century, particularly after the Second World War, the process was reversed. A reduction in size of country houses, by the successful removal of nineteenth-century additions (for example, at Everingham and Houghton), or demolition has been the pattern. The first major loss was Red Hall, Winestead, demolished 1936, soon to be followed by Sunderlandwick Hall (c.1947), High Hall, Bishop Burton (1951), Kilnwick Hall (1951-2), Welton House (1952), Neswick Hall (1954), and more recently Warter Priory (1972).

Notes and bibliography on page 144

SEATS OF THE GENTRY : 1672/85 and 1873

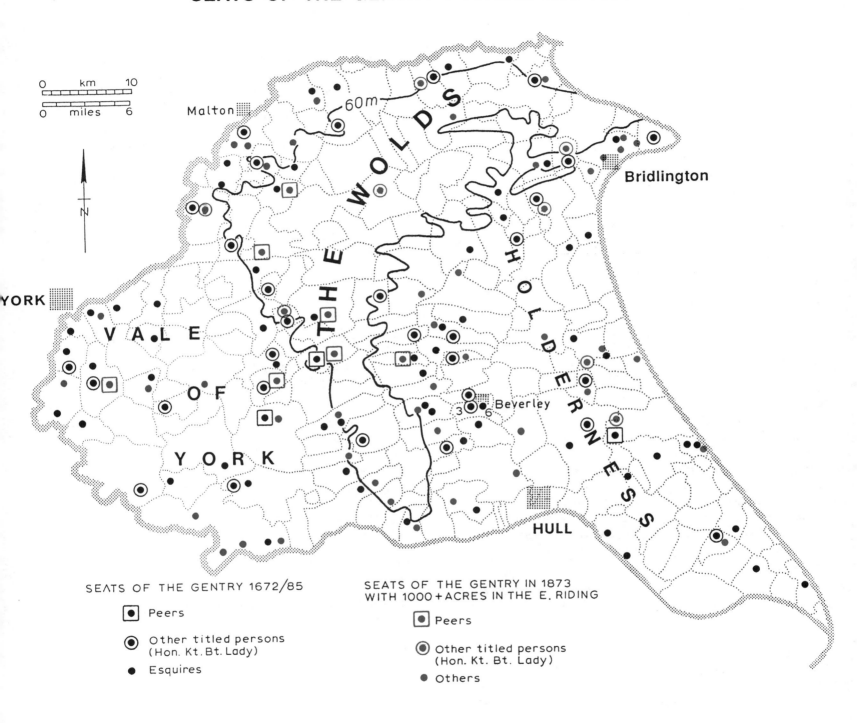

0 km 10

0 miles 6

N

Malton

60m

THE WOLDS

HOLDERNESS

Bridlington

YORK

VALE

OF

YORK

3 6 Beverley

HULL

SEATS OF THE GENTRY 1672/85

☐ Peers

◉ Other titled persons
(Hon. Kt. Bt. Lady)

• Esquires

SEATS OF THE GENTRY IN 1873
WITH 1000+ACRES IN THE E. RIDING

☐ Peers

◉ Other titled persons
(Hon. Kt. Bt. Lady)

• Others

THE INCIDENCE AND CHRONOLOGY OF PARLIAMENTARY ENCLOSURE

Janice E. Crowther

In the East Riding the parliamentary enclosure period spanned well over a century; the earliest act of enclosure (Scagglethorpe) was passed in 1725, and the last (Skipwith) in 1901. At the opening of the eighteenth century approximately 40-50 per cent of the riding was still being farmed under the open-field system. Many farmers and landowners were content to continue in the old style, but others wished to farm more efficiently by using new crops and techniques, and they found the communal nature of open-field farming increasingly restrictive. An act of parliament was required for an enclosure if there was not total agreement among all interested parties. The initiative to obtain an act usually came from the larger landowners, who may have seen enclosure as an opportunity to raise rents. Meetings were held to gauge the degree of support,[1] an attorney was employed to deal with the application to parliament, and local MPs were called upon to shepherd the bill through all its stages. Sometimes there was opposition, but it rarely came from humble cottagers, who lacked the means to present expensive counter-petitions to parliament.

Once the act was passed, commissioners and surveyors were employed to re-allot the land into compact holdings that could be farmed independently without reference to neighbours. The commissioners' decisions were recorded in the enclosure award, a legally binding document with three copies. The period between an act and award could be lengthy, sometimes over a decade. However, the new owners were usually able to take over their plots within a year or two of the commissioners starting work. It was then that the transformation of the landscape began. In the new fields which had been staked out by the surveyors, there were ditches to be dug, fences to be erected and hedges to be planted within a stipulated period. Farmhouses were built outside the village for the first time, and new roads were constructed. Sometimes several neighbouring villages were enclosed at about the same time: Skipsea, Ulrome, Beeford and Atwick in northern Holderness were all enclosed in the 1760s, and the impact locally must have been very striking.

The East Riding may be divided into three broad geographical regions - the Wolds, Holderness including the Hull valley, and the Vale of York. The history of enclosure on the Wolds is the simplest to describe. It has been estimated that almost 70 per cent was enclosed by act. The large rectangular fields, broad straight roads with wide grass verges, and Georgian farmhouses surrounded by shelter belts remain as a legacy of the work of enclosure commissioners and surveyors. The pattern of enclosure in Holderness and the Hull valley is more complex. Much of the area (approximately 60 per cent) was already enclosed when the parliamentary enclosure period began, and any attempt to work out the exact chronology of early enclosure in this district is doomed to failure, since it was rarely well documented. The field patterns of old and new enclosure in Holderness show a diversity which is not apparent on the Wolds,[2] and the winding roads of some parts of Holderness follow the balks of the long-gone open fields. In the Vale of York even less of the land was affected by parliamentary enclosure. Only about a quarter of that district was enclosed by act, many parishes having lost their open fields well before the eighteenth century. Much of the parliamentary enclosure which did take place was of large common pastures, such as Wallingfen and Holme Moor.

The map opposite shows the incidence and broad chronology of parliamentary enclosure over the riding. It also depicts enclosures initiated by formal agreement,[3] which were accompanied by a written award legalising the changes. The map does not attempt to show the proportion of land which was enclosed by award. A density map would show considerable variations from one district to another.[4] Parishes and townships unaffected by act (or agreement) and award are left unshaded. Many of those were enclosed in the sixteenth and seventeenth centuries.[5] The map and the bar chart show that much of the parliamentary enclosure in the riding (47 per cent of all acts passed) took place before 1780.[6] Some districts, notably on the eastern and western slopes of the Wolds, were principally enclosed in the 1760s and 70s. On the high Wolds, enclosure tended to be in the middle period (1780-1819) and was probably linked to the high corn prices which could be obtained during the French and Napoleonic wars, 1793-1815.[7] As the map shows, there were several quite late enclosures in the Vale of York, especially in the southwest corner. Most of them involved only a few hundred acres, the bulk of the land having been enclosed well before the parliamentary enclosure period.

A parliamentary enclosure generated numerous documents. Anyone interested in the enclosure of their parish should consult the act in conjunction with the award, which includes details of the commissioners' decisions concerning roads, rights of way, ditches, hedges, stone pits and so on. The enclosure plan is often the first accurate map of a parish or township and is thus an invaluable record. Other documents may include formal claims to land (which the commissioners required from landowners), objections from rivals, requests for particular plots, correspondence and lists of costs. Those that have survived for a few East Riding enclosures make fascinating reading.

Notes and bibliography on page 145

THE INCIDENCE AND CHRONOLOGY OF PARLIAMENTARY ENCLOSURE

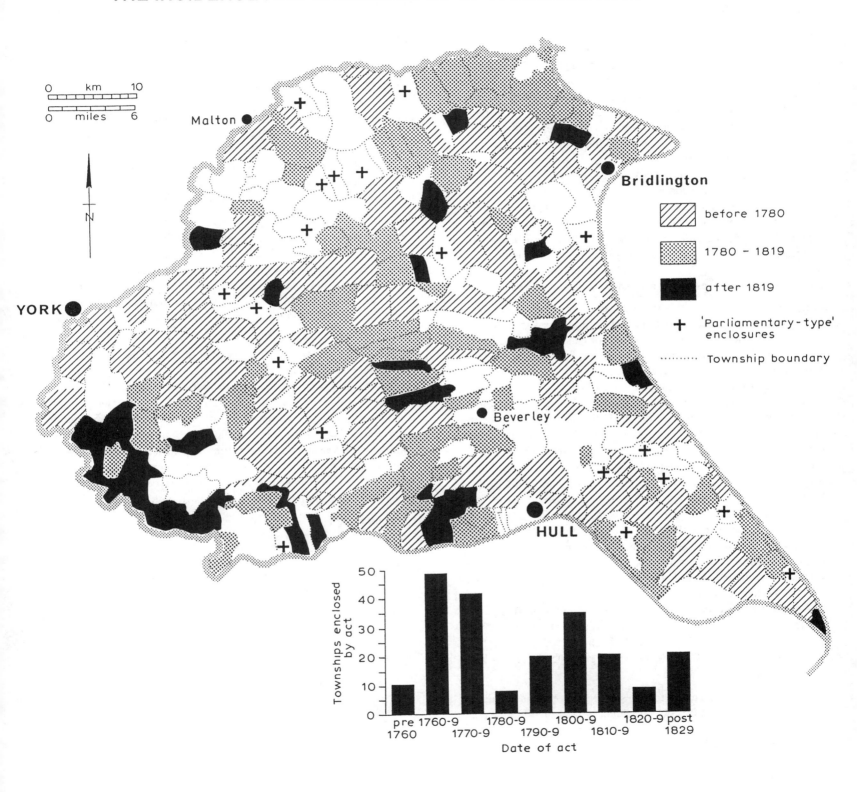

0 km 10

0 miles 6

N

Malton ●

Bridlington ●

YORK ●

Beverley ●

HULL ●

before 1780

1780 – 1819

after 1819

'Parliamentary-type' enclosures

Township boundary

Townships enclosed by act

50
40
30
20
10
0

pre 1760 1760-9 1770-9 1780-9 1790-9 1800-9 1810-9 1820-9 post 1829

Date of act

AGRICULTURAL LAND USE IN 1801

Janice E. Crowther

At the end of the eighteenth century the food resources of the country were in short supply, owing to a series of poor harvests, the diminution of imports during the French wars and the rising population. The government appointed Select Committees to consider the high price of provisions in 1795 and 1799, and in 1801 an inquiry was inaugurated by the Home Office to assess the arable acreage in every parish in England and Wales. Incumbents were required to report the acreage of wheat, barley, oats, rye/maslin, potatoes, turnips/rape, peas, beans and 'other' crops[1] in their parish, adding further information if they wished.[2] W.G. Hoskins was the first historian to highlight the importance of what have come to be known as the '1801 Crop Returns'.[3] In those counties where the coverage was good,[4] crop returns used in conjunction with contemporary accounts[5] provide a means of studying the different patterns of cultivation which prevailed in different districts. In order to show variations in cropping, the East Riding has been divided into eleven districts, based upon topography and soil.[6] The pie charts on the map show percentages for each district.

In England as a whole, wheat was the leading crop, but in the East Riding oats was the most important grain.[7] In the northernmost part of the riding (districts 1 and 2), the acreage for oats almost equalled that for wheat and barley combined. Oats was also the leading crop in the Wold Scarp district, shared equal place with barley in the High Wolds, and took second place to wheat on the Low Wolds, where the clay dip slopes provided a more fertile environment for that grain than did the thin chalky soils of the higher grounds. In the Vale of York oats was also the leading crop. Wheat was the most important crop in Holderness and the Hull Valley (districts 8-11) where heavy clays predominated. In South Holderness 41 per cent of the recorded acreage was devoted to wheat, in Mid Holderness 40 per cent, in the Hull Valley 38 per cent (equal with oats) and in North Holderness 36 per cent. Beans and peas were grown on a large scale in Holderness, which was well-known at that time as 'wheat, oats and bean land'.[8] Wheat only covered thirteen per cent of the recorded acreage of the High Wolds, which was, said Strickland, 'unfavourable' to that grain, whereas 'few districts were better calculated for the growth of barley' than the Yorkshire Wolds.[9] On the High Wolds, barley took up 30 per cent of the recorded acreage, and 20 per cent of both the Wold Scarp and the Low Wolds. Poor people on the Wolds were still eating barley rather than wheaten bread in the late eighteenth century. The only districts where rye was a significant crop were districts 3 and 4 in the Vale of York.[10]

The 'new husbandry', usually four to six-course rotations including turnips and artificial grasses, was particularly well suited to the chalk Wolds, and the returns show that where enclosure had taken place, it was usually well established. Open and enclosed parishes may be compared, and they show much variation. In 1801 a third of the open-field land in Cherry Burton (enclosed 1823-9) lay fallow, and turnips were not an important crop. Similarly, at nearby Etton (enclosed 1818-20) only 100 acres were recorded as turnips or rape. By contrast, at Sledmere (enclosed 1776) 1,000 acres were under turnips, which represented 38 per cent of the cropped area. At North Dalton (enclosed 1778-9) 370 acres were given over to turnips, and the new rotations had been adopted. The incumbent reported that 'there is about the same number of acres in grazing as in tillage, chiefly in sheep walks'. Few reporters were so informative, but from contemporary reports it is clear that much land still lay in sheep walks on the Wolds, and that rabbit warrens, for many years an important part of the economy, still remained, though they were soon to be removed.[11] Few turnips were grown in Holderness; the heavy clay soil was unsuitable. Had returns been provided for Sunk Island, they would have shown potatoes being grown there on a large scale, as they were in the southern part of the Vale of York.

Using the available returns, a conjecture may be made as to the total arable acreage of the East Riding. Turner produced a figure of 29.3 per cent, slightly higher than Churley's 28 per cent.[12] The potential arable acreage in 1801 may well have been over 30 per cent, a regular fallow being still common even in enclosed parishes in many parts of Holderness,[13] whilst in other districts some open-field parishes still had a three- or four-yearly fallow.

Examining the returns parish by parish, especially when the remarks of the incumbents are available, can be productive, providing information on farming practices, the nature of the harvest, and many other matters. The vicar of Sculcoates, with his return, wrote a lengthy essay on the rural economy, the rise of the urban population, the desirability of a General Act of Inclosure, and the need for cultivation of many commons and wastes. The crop returns provide a unique source on arable culture at the opening of the nineteenth century. The picture which they reveal corresponds closely to the accounts of Leatham and Strickland, suggesting that they may be used with some confidence.

Notes on page 145

AGRICULTURAL LAND USE : 1801

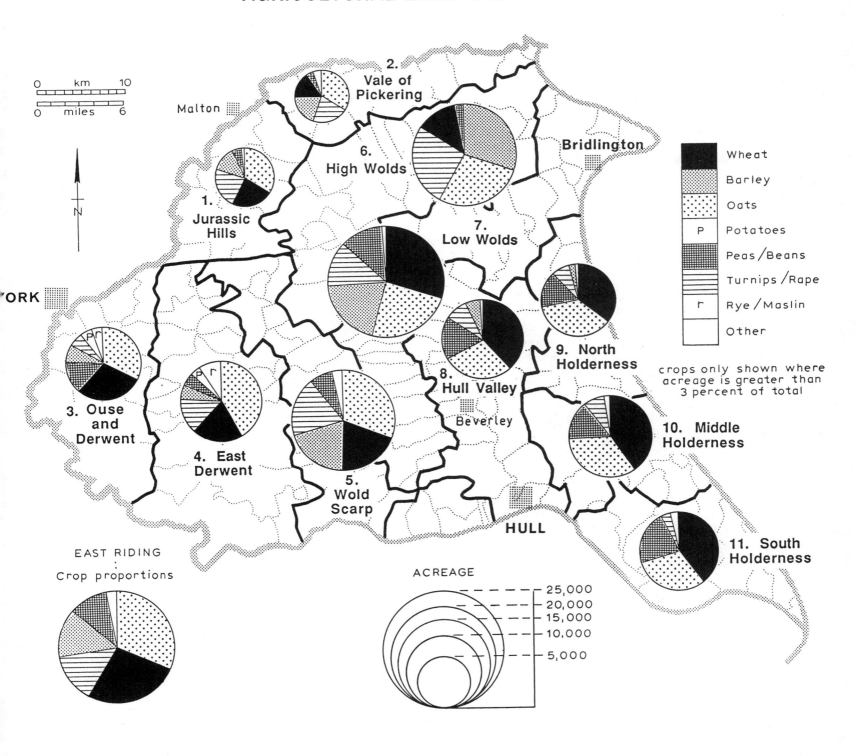

EAST RIDING
Crop proportions

ACREAGE
25,000
20,000
15,000
10,000
5,000

Wheat
Barley
Oats
P Potatoes
Peas/Beans
Turnips/Rape
r Rye/Maslin
Other

crops only shown where
acreage is greater than
3 percent of total

1. Jurassic Hills
2. Vale of Pickering
3. Ouse and Derwent
4. East Derwent
5. Wold Scarp
6. High Wolds
7. Low Wolds
8. Hull Valley
9. North Holderness
10. Middle Holderness
11. South Holderness

Malton
Bridlington
YORK
Beverley
HULL

AGRICULTURAL LAND USE IN THE MID-NINETEENTH CENTURY

Alan Harris and Roger Kain[1]

This cross-section of land use and farming in the East Riding in the mid-nineteenth century is based on land use and cropping data recorded in parish and township tithe files.[2] By c.1840, the East Riding was essentially an arable region. Around 66 per cent (503,821 acres) of the area was devoted to arable crops, grass occupied around 29 per cent (218,765 acres), woodland three per cent (24,810 acres) and common two per cent (7,713 acres). On the higher parts of the Wolds in particular, 'grass was becoming a rarity except on the sides of dry valleys and close to farmsteads, where it was customary to keep a sheltered paddock under grass for the use of dairy cattle and for convenience at lambing time'.[3] The highest proportions of arable were to be found in still unenclosed Wold parishes, while some of the lowest arable to grass proportions were on heavy soils in Holderness, but even here arable exceeded pasture in those tithe districts for which data are available.

Overall, grain and pulse crops occupied some 55 per cent of arable land in the East Riding by comparison with the England and Wales figure of 60 per cent (see table). By 1840, wheat had supplanted oats as the leading grain crop in all the regions shown on the map except the northern Jurassic hills region, but it was only really dominant in Holderness. Elsewhere, the combined acreages of the two spring grains, barley and oats, continued to exceed that of wheat by a considerable margin. Maslin, a rather primitive mixture of wheat and rye, was still sown in some townships where soils were very thin and light.[4] Extensive spreads of oats were sown throughout the riding, but only on the Jurassic hills did the pattern of cropping approach that more usual in England and Wales at this time. Here there was little bare fallowing in winter, with both clover and turnips alternated with grain crops. However, bare fallowing was still widespread in Holderness and the Vale of York. Wheat yields were below the national average in Holderness and on the Jurassic hills, about average overall in the Vale of York, and a little better than this on the Wolds. Some good yields of oats were obtained by Wold and Jurassic hill farmers, but barley and pulse crops (peas and beans) did not do especially well anywhere in the riding at this time. This said, where soils and other physical factors enabled the modern four-course (wheat, turnips, barley, clover) system of cropping or one of its derivatives to be used, as on the chalkland of Millington for example, farming was characterised by an improving air.[5]

East Riding tithe files contain much descriptive comment on farming practices.[6] On light soils, four- and five-course rotations are recorded most often; usually these were: wheat or oats, turnips, barley and then seeds (artificial grasses) for either one or two years to complete the course. On strong soils, rotations were of three- or four-courses as at Menethorpe on the Jurassic hills where 'the usual course of farming is summer fallow, wheat, oats or beans; - clover being sometimes

introduced after the wheat'.[7] 'Low' or under-capitalised and backward farming was noted in several tithe districts, especially where open fields remained or land needed draining.[8] At Waghen (Wawne) in the Hull Valley, it was reported in 1844 that 'the whole of the Arable Land is capable of great improvement which might be effected by underdraining, and improved rotation of cropping to increase the quantity of seeds and green crops, and the consequent increase in the flock of sheep'.[9]

In addition to enclosure and drainage, three other areas of improvement caught the attention of Tithe Commission reporters. On chalk soils, as at Wharram-le-Street, 'the farming is a fair average of the Yorkshire Wolds. It has been much improved within the last 20 years, since the introduction of the Swedish turnip and bones'.[10] On sandy soils, as at Sutton-upon-Derwent in the Vale of York, 'though there is nothing very high in the farming the produce has been much increased within a few years by the cultivation of the heath land which was principally barren or rabbit warren, the principal produce is rye and wheat mixed and oats'.[11] But most spectacular and occasioning much comment was draining and warping (see page 4) in the Humber and Ouse valleys. Characteristic of assistant tithe commissioners' comments are Charles Howard's at Blacktoft in 1837: 'A part of the Land has been rendered highly and permanently valuable by a process known as "warping"... The whole of Blacktoft is capable of this improvement but the expense of it is very considerable, not infrequently exceeding £20 per acre'.[12]

Notes and bibliography on page 146

Arable crops and average yields in the East Riding c.1840

Crop	Mean % of arable	Mean yield per acre*	Estimated acreage in whole county
Wheat	22	19	110,629
Barley	10	28	52,472
Oats	17	33	83,819
Pulses (peas & beans)	6	20	27,696
Turnips	10	3	52,087
Clover & seeds	21	21	106,794
Bare (naked) fallows	14	-	68,259

* Turnips in £s per acre; clover and seeds in hundredweights per acre; all other crops in bushels per acre.

AGRICULTURAL LAND USE IN THE MID-19th CENTURY

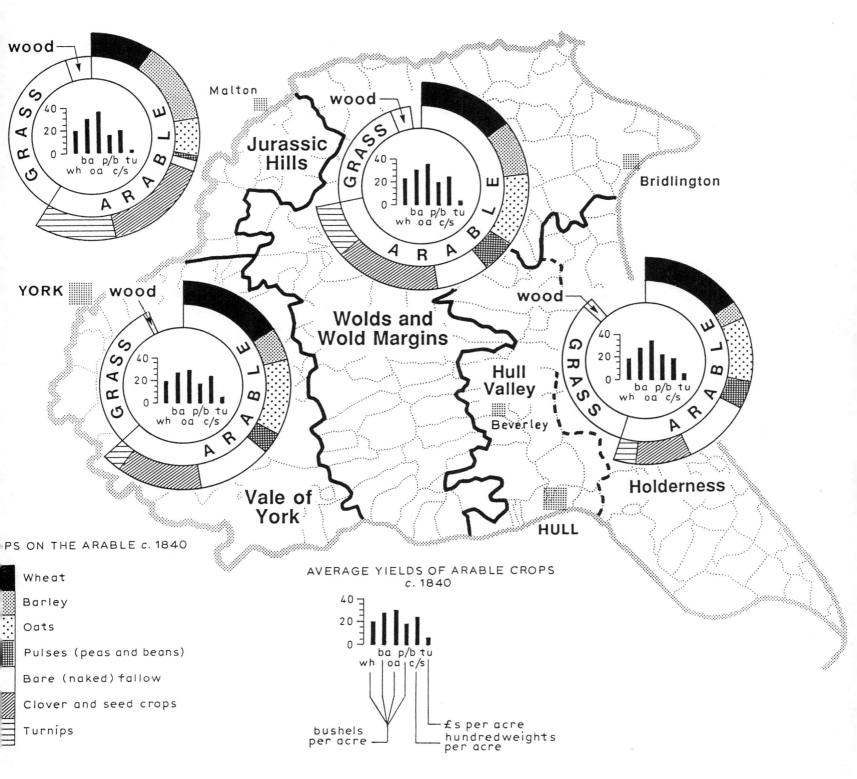

Malton

Jurassic Hills

wood

Bridlington

YORK

wood

Wolds and Wold Margins

Hull Valley

Beverley

Vale of York

Holderness

HULL

PS ON THE ARABLE c. 1840

- Wheat
- Barley
- Oats
- Pulses (peas and beans)
- Bare (naked) fallow
- Clover and seed crops
- Turnips

AVERAGE YIELDS OF ARABLE CROPS
c. 1840

bushels per acre

£s per acre
hundredweights per acre

TRADE AND INDUSTRY

BRANSTON & WRIGHT Sc.

MARKETS AND TOWNS IN THE MIDDLE AGES[1]

D.M. Palliser

After the breakdown of Roman administration in the early fifth century, urban life seems to have died out, even in York. Nevertheless, both natives and invaders in the post-Roman period needed some 'central places' - royal and administrative centres, and holy places - which often became periodic markets as people gathered there for other purposes. It is notable that many East Riding markets and fairs came to be held either at the locations of major churches or at the head manors of the major estates described in Domesday Book; they include Beverley, Bridlington, Driffield, Howden, Market Weighton and Pocklington.[2] Admittedly, most documentary evidence for markets and fairs dates from the period after 1200, but that reflects the limitations of the written sources; many markets and fairs will have originated in gatherings before the Norman Conquest. In one or two cases place-names indicate the early existence of a trading town (*wic* or *port*). York was a *wic* by the ninth century and Howden was probably a *port,* since its dependent settlement of Portington seems to mean 'farm belonging to a town'.[3]

The one clear case of a town east of York developing before 1066 is Beverley, and the evidence there is archaeological, rather than documentary. The only East Riding places credited with 'townspeople' (*burgenses*) in Domesday Book were Bridlington and Pocklington, but it is doubtful whether either was really urban.[4] However, documentary evidence begins to accumulate from the twelfth century of both markets and towns, in some cases apparently providing confirmation of what was already developing, but in others testifying to plantations of new towns. In the 1120s Archbishop Thurstan granted legal and trading privileges to his 'men' or 'burgesses' at Beverley, while later in the century the counts of Aumale founded boroughs at Hedon and Skipsea, and the monks of Meaux created a wool port at Wyke-upon-Hull. In the early thirteenth century Archbishop Gray founded another ecclesiastical borough at Brough, while the fishing port of Ravenser Odd developed on a predecessor of Spurn Point (see pages 8 and 9). Equally important to the region, however, must have been the more numerous smaller settlements with markets but no borough status.

Between about 1200 and 1350 there was a huge increase in the numbers of recorded markets and fairs, as lords hastened to have them licensed by the Crown; almost all those mapped here were first recorded in that century and a half. This was a period of population growth, bringing with it a growing commercialisation of the economy and a demand for increased marketing facilities for agricultural surpluses. However, that growth began well before 1200, and the chronology of recorded markets reflects the growth of a royal monopoly of licensing; many early markets were 'prescriptive', held by customary right rather than royal charter. As grants proliferated, existing holders of markets became worried about competition. In 1279, Edward I granted Meaux abbey a market and fair at Wyke only after a jury had testified that they would not damage neighbouring markets and fairs.[5] It should also be remembered that a market licence secured by a lord, usually as a commercial investment, was not necessarily a success. A revealing royal grant of a market and fair at North Duffield in 1363 explained that they might be held notwithstanding the fact that an earlier grant of 1294 had never been exercised.[6] In many cases no record survives of a market or fair after the initial grant, suggesting that the right was either never exercised or quickly lapsed.

Some places with a weekly market or an annual fair clearly remained agricultural villages. Others became real market towns, as can be seen from both the street pattern (a market place or market street) and repeated references to the continuation of markets. Bridlington, Howden, Kilham, Pocklington, Market Weighton, North Duffield and South Cave all fall into this category. Above them, other places became towns of regional and even national importance, as befitted the one Yorkshire riding which could rank with Lincolnshire and East Anglia in terms of wealth. This was especially true of Beverley, a major cloth making town, and Wyke, which in the customs accounts of 1275-90 usually ranked as the third English port after London and Boston; it was the importance of Wyke that determined Edward I to take it over in 1293 and rename it Kingston-upon-Hull. The importance of the larger towns can be gauged from the lay subsidy of 1334, when in terms of taxable wealth York ranked as the third town in England, Beverley 20th, Hull 33rd and Cottingham - a town if not a borough - 35th. Measured by the 1377 poll tax, they ranked even higher in terms of population - York came second, Beverley eleventh, and Hull 27th.[7]

After the Black Death (1349) and later epidemics, population decreased and agricultural expansion was replaced by contraction. One result was that almost no new markets and fairs were licensed between 1350 and 1500, while many which had been chartered earlier seem to have lapsed. There were also casualties among the larger towns. Hedon declined despite a generous charter of privileges granted in 1348, while its rival, Ravenser Odd, was lost to the Humber in the mid-fourteenth century (see pages 8 and 9). By the fifteenth century Beverley may also have been in decline, though the evidence is ambiguous until the sixteenth century. However, Hull was in contrast one of the great success stories among late medieval English towns, and its royal charters of 1440 and 1447, granting wide privileges including county status, set the seal on its importance.

Notes and bibliography on page 146

MARKETS AND TOWNS IN THE MIDDLE AGES

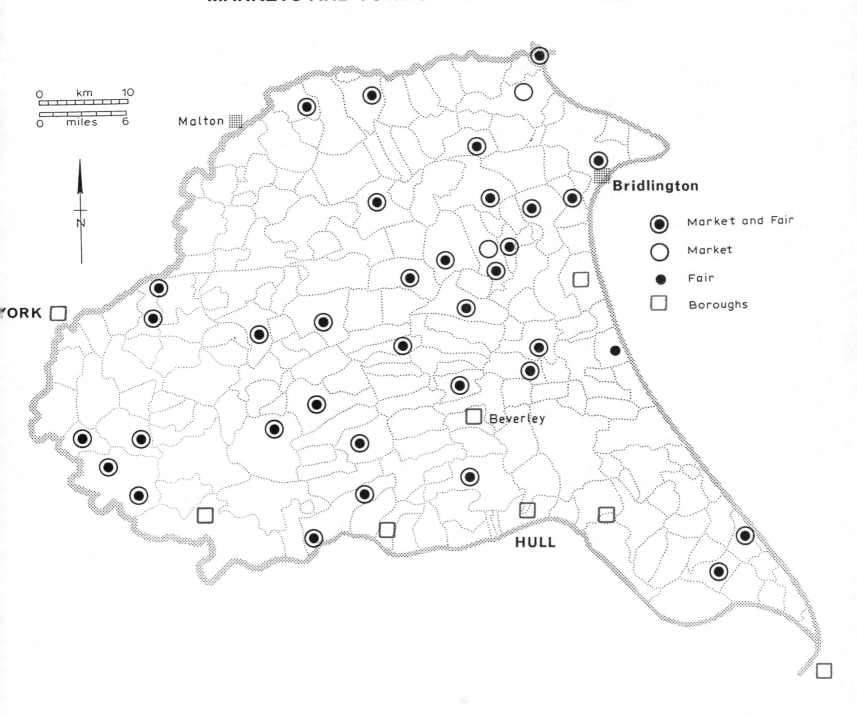

Malton

Bridlington

YORK

Beverley

HULL

● Market and Fair

○ Market

• Fair

□ Boroughs

0 km 10

0 miles 6

N

MARKETS AND FAIRS: 1500-1928
Margaret Noble

At the start of the fifteenth century some 40 communities had been granted the right to hold markets and fairs in the East Riding (see page 75). These were well dispersed throughout the region, but showed a particular cluster on the eastern edge of the Wolds to the southwest of Bridlington. Over the ensuing centuries this number gradually declined, and of the original centres only twelve communities retained their market status at the start of the sixteenth century. The reasons for this reduction include population decline, initial over-provision, and improved transport and communications. Although the fourteenth to sixteenth centuries had already seen a considerable decline in the number of markets serving the region, the thirteen market centres which existed in 1700 were clearly too numerous and the following centuries saw a further reduction in this number. By 1850 the number of market centres was only ten, and by the 1920s just seven centres remained in the East Riding. Throughout the period the markets and fairs in the adjacent settlements of of York, Malton and Selby were of great importance to the residents of the western and northwestern parts of the East Riding.

The granting of a charter to hold a market was usually accompanied by the right to hold a fair. In some small communities, however, fairs existed independently of market towns and several former market centres continued to hold fairs long after weekly markets had disappeared. At the turn of the eighteenth century 20 places held fairs, six of which - Aldbrough, Kirkham, Little Driffield, North Duffield, Brandesburton and Stamford Bridge - held fairs only. Another four fairs were held at Hornsea, Hunmanby, Kilham and North Frodingham where the markets were in serious decline, if not discontinued, by this date. Many places held more than one fair; Beverley, Hedon and Howden each had four and Pocklington six.[1] The fair undoubtedly remained important in the East Riding due to the strength of traditional patterns in a predominantly rural region and the increased volume of produce, particularly livestock, that became available through agricultural improvements in this period. While markets ensured a regular weekly trade their influence tended to be localised, rarely extending beyond a six to eight mile radius, but they could also function as collection and distribution points for the wider market within the region. Fairs complemented the town's role as a market centre by periodically extending trading contact over a wider area.

Some of the region's fairs were notable on an international scale, particularly those that specialised in horses. Howden's October horse fair, which often lasted for up to a fortnight, was attended by agents from France, Spain, Russia, Prussia and Germany well into the nineteenth century.[2] Other fairs traded on a national scale; London merchants regularly attended Beverley's fairs, and Howden's Spring horse fair attracted dealers from the South and Midlands. Regional trade was also important. Market Weighton's September fair, noted for its sale of sheep, attracted farmers from throughout eastern Yorkshire and the West Riding.

Until the eighteenth century most markets and fairs traded in a variety of general produce, but from c.1700 many began to specialise in particular products; such specialisation served to extend the trading area of towns. In the period after 1750 specialisation in market and fair trade became particularly marked and it is clear that those places which relied primarily on general trade had a more uncertain future. The main products traded at markets were corn or livestock, while most fairs specialised in horses, cattle and sheep; fairs at Pocklington and Howden also specialised in cloth. The region's markets handled large quantities of produce which could amount to thousands of quarters of wheat or hundreds of livestock on any given market or fair day. Market Weighton's September fair was said to be 'probably the greatest sheep fair in the kingdom with 70,000 to 80,000 animals annually exposed for sale'.[3]

The most successful market centres were those which were either situated on major thoroughfares or which had access to the region's network of navigable waterways and canals. Indeed, those places without access to good communications often suffered; the corn trade at Bridlington declined following the opening of the Driffield canal and the market at Kilham declined due to the proximity of better served markets at Driffield and Bridlington.[4]

From the middle of the nineteenth century, markets and fairs gradually declined in importance. Population growth, the development of new communication networks by road, water and rail, and changing production encouraged more frequent exchange of goods and an increasing transference of trade to fixed retail outlets. For markets and fairs an increasing amount of trade no longer involved the direct exchange of goods. At fairs livestock were often purchased by intermediaries in advance of the fair days and at markets much trade in grain was by sample. With railway travel, livestock could be transported to more distant markets, resulting in the concentration of trade at three main centres in the East Riding - Hull, Beverley and Driffield - and an increasing transference of livestock to the larger markets of West Yorkshire. By the last quarter of the nineteenth century, Hedon, Patrington and South Cave had lost their trading status and Bridlington, Beverley, Howden, Hull, Market Weighton, Pocklington and Driffield were the only remaining centres which held markets and fairs in the region. By this date only five fairs remained, held at Beverley, Hull and Market Weighton.

Notes and bibliography on page 146

MARKETS AND FAIRS : 1500-1928

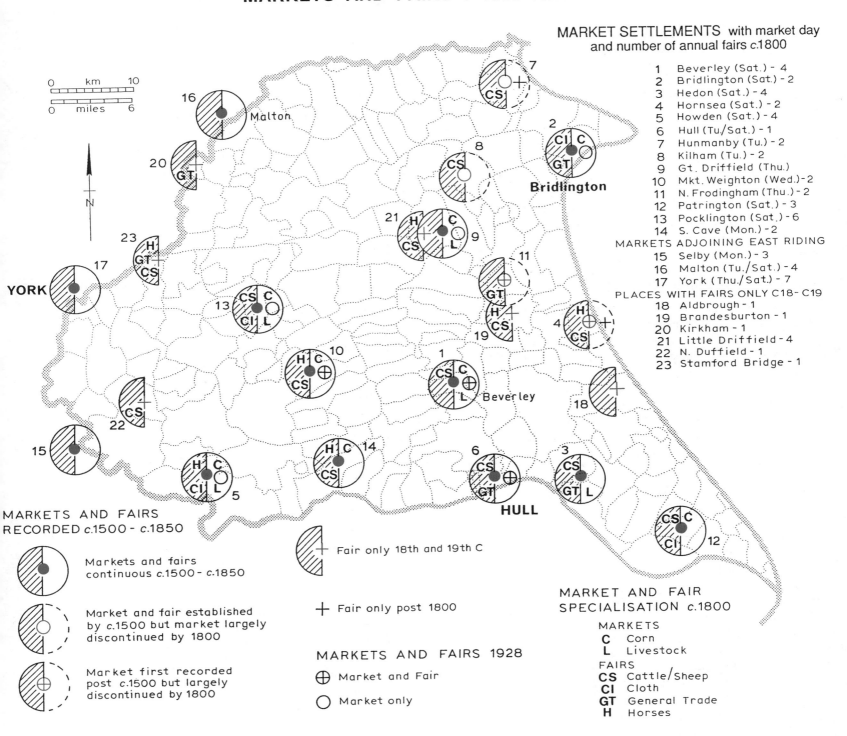

MARKET SETTLEMENTS with market day and number of annual fairs c.1800

1 Beverley (Sat.) – 4
2 Bridlington (Sat.) – 2
3 Hedon (Sat.) – 4
4 Hornsea (Sat.) – 2
5 Howden (Sat.) – 4
6 Hull (Tu./Sat.) – 1
7 Hunmanby (Tu.) – 2
8 Kilham (Tu.) – 2
9 Gt. Driffield (Thu.)
10 Mkt. Weighton (Wed.) – 2
11 N. Frodingham (Thu.) – 2
12 Patrington (Sat.) – 3
13 Pocklington (Sat.) – 6
14 S. Cave (Mon.) – 2

MARKETS ADJOINING EAST RIDING
15 Selby (Mon.) – 3
16 Malton (Tu./Sat.) – 4
17 York (Thu./Sat.) – 7

PLACES WITH FAIRS ONLY C18– C19
18 Aldbrough – 1
19 Brandesburton – 1
20 Kirkham – 1
21 Little Driffield – 4
22 N. Duffield – 1
23 Stamford Bridge – 1

MARKETS AND FAIRS
RECORDED c.1500 – c.1850

Markets and fairs
continuous c.1500 – c.1850

Market and fair established
by c.1500 but market largely
discontinued by 1800

Market first recorded
post c.1500 but largely
discontinued by 1800

Fair only 18th and 19th C

Fair only post 1800

MARKETS AND FAIRS 1928

⊕ Market and Fair

○ Market only

MARKET AND FAIR
SPECIALISATION c.1800

MARKETS
C Corn
L Livestock
FAIRS
CS Cattle/Sheep
Cl Cloth
GT General Trade
H Horses

77

WINDMILLS AND WATERMILLS
Roy Gregory

By the mid-nineteenth century most villages had their own mill producing both flour for human consumption and feed for animals, particularly horses. Waterpower is generally the older and preferred power source, windpower being used when waterpower is not available, a factor well illustrated in East Yorkshire. To the west, the Vale of York had no streams of any consequence, resulting in the windmill reigning supreme, except for three mills on the river Derwent and one on the river Ouse. Moving eastwards, the scarp face of the Wolds produced a number of fast flowing streams where water power predominated, a good example being the Pocklington Beck which powered several mills in succession. The top and dip slope of the Wolds are virtually waterless and such villages as did exist used windpower. Indeed, the now deserted village of Weedley had a windmill as early as 1185, one of the earliest references to a windmill in Western Europe.[1] The Hull valley and the plain of Holderness were also windmill country although a few watermills existed on tributaries to the Hull, and on the Gypsey Race in Bridlington.

Waterpower had many more applications than simply grain milling, being used extensively for industrial purposes. The iron trades in Sheffield, the textile mills in the West Riding and the mining ventures in the North Riding could not have achieved success without waterpower. Such non-milling uses were rare in the East Riding and usually short-lived. In the later eighteenth century textile manufacture was confined to watermills at Boynton, Driffield (Bell Mills) and Wansford. Bell Mills were also used for paper making, as were watermills at Cottingham (Snuff Mill), Goodmanham and North Cave. The Cottingham mill was used for snuff manufacture by the late eighteenth century.[2]

Conversely, although windpower was not used extensively in England for industrial purposes, it made a vital contribution to the industrial activity of East Yorkshire. In Market Weighton and Beverley, windmills were used to grind bark at tanneries and in Beverley and Hessle they were used to crush chalk at whiting works. It was in Hull, however, that the windmill came into its own as the primary source of power, used by the eighteenth-century merchants who needed to process imported materials. Here the first such use was in oil production, having been used for this purpose since the early fourteenth century. By 1800, of the ten largest oil mills in Hull, six were powered by wind and four by steam. Several windmills were used for whiting crushing, a very large windmill was used for timber sawing and another was used to power a paper mill. By the 1850s there were some 26 windmills in Hull.

Windpower was little used in the East Riding for land drainage, but a seventeenth-century example is recorded at Routh. The alluvial clays alongside the Humber and the river Hull have been worked extensively for brick and tile making and a large number of small windpumps were used to drain the workings. These pumps differ from the scoop wheels common in the Fens; in the East Riding the windmill powered a single acting bucket pump, a simple adaptation of the village hand-operated pump. Two of these distinctive structures survive, fully restored, at the former North Howden and Elvington brickworks.[3]

In the East Riding waterpowered cornmills were usually built of local brick, generally two stories high with a loft, thus comprising a three floor module. The loft was used to store grain, the second storey housed the millstones and dressing machinery and the ground floor contained the shutes which delivered the flour into sacks. Most mills were powered by breast shot wheels around 15 ft in diameter (for example the surviving wheel at Beswick), but the wheel at Welton (which also survives) has a diameter of 36 ft 6 ins. At least two mills were converted to turbine.

There were a few larger watermills, for example at Stamford Bridge and Sutton-upon-Derwent, which were fed by impressive weirs across the river Derwent, but perhaps the largest weir was the one which fed Howsham Mill, a small mill of considerable architectural interest, built in the mid eighteenth century in the Gothick style as an eyecatcher from Howsham Hall.

The early windmills were undoubtedly post mills but, by the nineteenth century, the dominant type was the tower mill. Small tower mills started to appear in numbers in the 1770s, in many cases to replace worn out post mills, and stood about 30 ft to the cap. They followed the three-floor module of the existing watermill. An example stands at Bainton, sadly without its sails and working parts. These small free-standing mills offered the miller very little storage space. Thus in the early nineteenth century many had granaries added, as at Skidby, which necessitated raising the height of the tower to enable the sails to turn. Later mills were built to such greater height from the start, for example at Swanland and Walkington.

It was in Hull, however, that windmills achieved a supreme standard, led not by the grain millers but by the oil merchants. Joseph Pease was a prime example; in 1719 he acquired a small tower mill in Church Street which he replaced around 1750 with a much taller mill designed by a Dutch millwright. This design was followed by other oil merchants and eventually taken up by the corn millers. These tall windmills were far in advance of other contemporary mills and applied not only the designs of the Dutch millwrights but also the ideas of the leading Yorkshire engineer John Smeaton. In 1794 an extremely large tower mill was erected for corn milling by the Hull Union Mill Society, standing some 100 ft tall, and thereafter many similar mills were built. In the early nineteenth century, contemporary writers described Hull's mills in glowing terms, one international writer going so far as to say they were the most superb he had seen.[4]

Notes and bibliography on page 147

WINDMILLS AND WATERMILLS

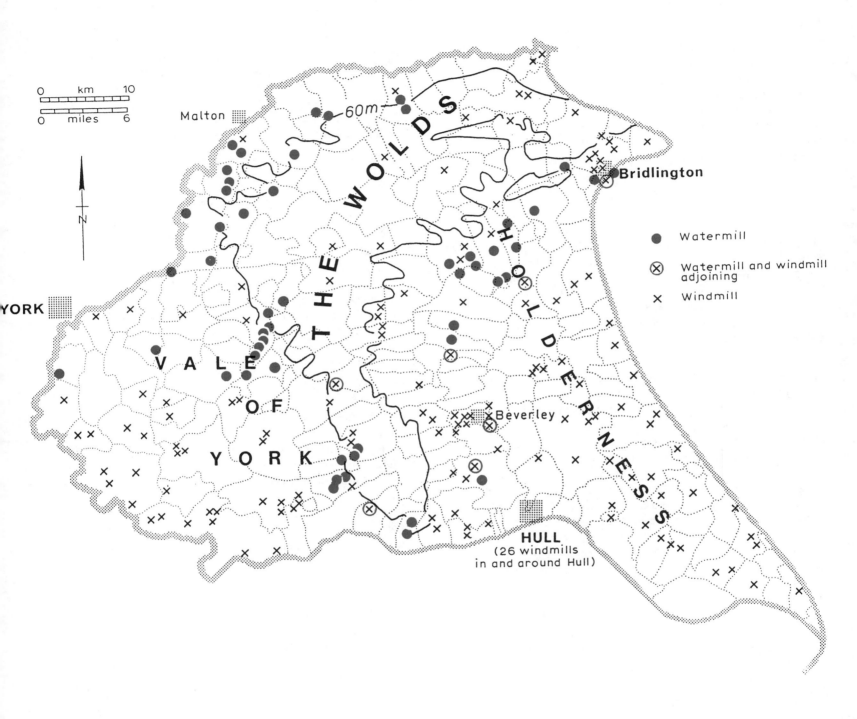

0 km 10

0 miles 6

N

Malton

60m

THE WOLDS

Bridlington

YORK

VALE

OF

YORK

HOLDERNESS

Beverley

HULL
(26 windmills
in and around Hull)

● Watermill

⊗ Watermill and windmill
adjoining

× Windmill

BREWING AND MALTING, ROPEMAKING, TEXTILES AND TANNING

David and Susan Neave

In the nineteenth century the economy of East Yorkshire, outside Hull, was almost entirely dependent on agriculture. It was, as H.E. Strickland noted in 1812, 'as nearly as possible exempt from manufactories'.[1] The riding was not, however, totally devoid of industry, but any development was hampered by the distance from the main markets and the lack of fast-flowing streams, minerals and coal.[2] What industries there were concentrated on the processing of local agricultural produce - milling (see page 78), malting, brewing, ropemaking, textiles and tanning - and the manufacture of agricultural machinery,[3] brickmaking (see page 82) and the quarrying of chalk for whiting.

The accompanying map, based solely on information from trade directories for 1823, 1840 and 1872,[4] shows the extent and distribution of the most widespread of the processing industries - brewing and malting, ropemaking, textiles and tanning - in the nineteenth century.[5] The chief raw materials (barley, hemp, flax, wool, hides and skins) were produced in abundance on the region's farms and it was in the market towns, where these goods were traded, that the processing industries were concentrated.

Brewing and malting

The essential ingredients necessary for brewing and malting were barley (grown on the Wolds) and a good water supply. Until the eighteenth century brewers were less numerous than maltsters, possibly because brewing was still largely done at home or at the alehouse. In the nineteenth century brewers and maltsters are recorded at 42 places; in five cases there is only a maltster recorded and in sixteen cases only a brewer. There were brewers and maltsters in each of the market towns, with the largest numbers at Beverley (six brewers and seven maltsters in 1823) and Bridlington (five brewers and six maltsters in 1823). Most of the larger breweries were in the towns, for example Stephenson's Golden Ball brewery in Walkergate, Beverley rebuilt 1868. Some of the village brewers were innkeepers, as at Burton Pidsea and East Cottingwith in 1840 and Barmston and South Skirlaugh in 1872, who were carrying on the tradition of brewing their own beer. There were larger-scale village breweries at Bubwith, Sherburn and Stamford Bridge, which existed throughout the period 1823-72, and at Foston-on-the-Wolds by 1840. By the later nineteenth century maltings had become major commercial undertakings, exporting malt by rail to Hull and brewery towns in the West Riding. Extensive maltings were built at Nafferton (1840), Great Driffield (1873) and Market Weighton (1875-6).

Ropemaking and textiles

In the middle ages the flourishing Beverley cloth industry was based on locally produced wool, but by the late seventeenth century the principal raw materials for the much reduced textile industry were hemp and flax. Hemp was grown in small hempgarths throughout the Vale of York. When harvested the hemp was rotted in the numerous hemp-pits that surrounded villages such as Holme-upon-Spalding Moor. Almost every East Riding village had one or more weavers to whom home-spun hemp yarn would be taken to be made into the uncomfortable-sounding 'hempen' and 'harden' sheets that are recorded in probate inventories. In 1823 there were only ten village weavers listed in the East Riding, by 1840 only four and in 1872 none. A few larger manufactories were producing sacking, two of which (both at Barmby-on-the-Marsh) also made sailcloth.

Hemp was also the raw material for ropemaking, which occurred at over 20 places in the East Riding in the nineteenth century. There were a number of village ropeworks, for example in the Wolds settlements of Fridaythorpe, Garton, Middleton and Wetwang, all of which specialised in sheep net making, but the greatest concentration was in the principal market towns, each of which had one or more ropewalk. Ropemaking was a speciality of Market Weighton, where an area of the market place was designated the 'hemp market'. There were five ropemakers in the town in 1823 and three in 1872. The elongated crofts running south from the High Street and west from Linegate were ideal locations for the long narrow ropewalks. The port of Hull must have been a ready market for East Riding ropes and nets, particularly after the development of the fishing industry, but the farming community probably remained the principal customer.

Flax growing in the East Riding was limited until the later eighteenth century when it was encouraged by a government subsidy. In the first half of the nineteenth century there were small-scale linen manufactories at a dozen places in the riding, with concentrations at Beverley and in the Howden, Driffield and Bridlington areas. The large flax mill built at Enholmes, Patrington in 1846 by Marshalls of Leeds had nearly 150 employees in 1871, ten years before its closure.[6] In the later eighteenth century woollen and worsted mills, as large as any then existing in the West Riding, had been set up at Boynton (1770), Wansford (1788) and Driffield (1792). These were short-lived ventures, although carpets were made at Wansford until the late 1820s.

Tanning

Hides and skins, oak bark and a plentiful supply of water are the principal requisites for tanning. Oak bark had to be imported into the East Riding but hides were plentiful in the market towns, which abounded in butchers. The selected directories record tanneries at Beverley, Cottingham (Newland), Foston-on-the-Wolds, Great and Little Driffield, Hedon, Howden, Market Weighton and Pocklington. In each of the towns there were also curriers and leather cutters who finished the leather. Beverley was the main centre of tanning in the riding, as it had been since at least the fourteenth century, when there were 30 tanners in the town.

Notes and bibliography on page 147

BREWING AND MALTING, ROPEMAKING, TEXTILES AND TANNING

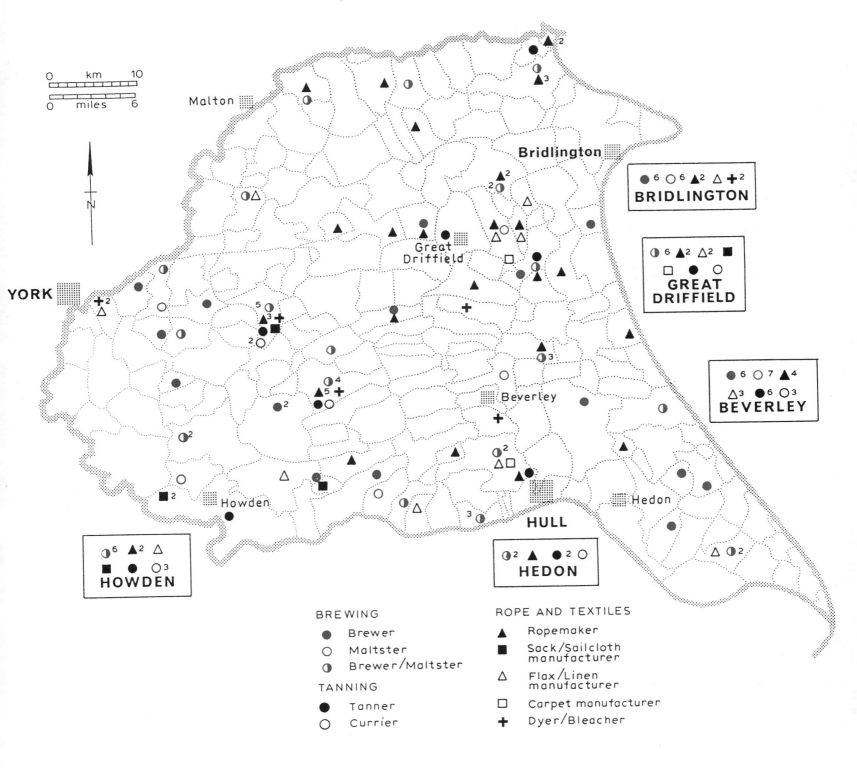

BREWING
- ⬤ (grey) Brewer
- ○ Maltster
- ◐ Brewer/Maltster

TANNING
- ⬤ Tanner
- ○ Currier

ROPE AND TEXTILES
- ▲ Ropemaker
- ■ Sack/Sailcloth manufacturer
- △ Flax/Linen manufacturer
- □ Carpet manufacturer
- ✚ Dyer/Bleacher

BRICK AND TILE MAKING

Peter G. Los and W. Ann Los

The East Riding of Yorkshire has a pre-eminent position in the history of English brickmaking, for the brickworks established at Hull c.1303 and at Beverley by the mid-fourteenth century are amongst the earliest recorded commercial brickyards. At Hull, bricks were used for building the chancel and transepts of Holy Trinity church c.1300-1370 and also the town walls, begun in 1321.[1] Local bricks were used in the building of North Bar, Beverley in 1409-10 and some fifteen years earlier bricks and tiles had been transported from Beverley to Grimsby for building the new town hall.

Although brickmaking at Hull and Beverley may have declined in the later middle ages, there are numerous surviving brick buildings in the East Riding from the late fifteenth century onwards, including the Prior's Lodging at Watton and Paull Holme Tower. Local brickmaking and bricklaying is displayed at its finest in the splendid series of late Elizabethan-Jacobean country houses - Burton Constable, Burton Agnes, Boynton, and Heslington - and in smaller seventeenth century manor houses, particularly Beswick Hall and Knedlington Old Hall. Elaborate brickwork is found on Wilberforce House and Crowle House, two merchant houses in the High Street, Hull built in the 1660s by the bricklayer William Catlyn who had brickworks nearby in Trippet and at Sutton-on-Hull.[2]

From the early seventeenth century there are references to brick making in the rural East Riding. A brick kiln is recorded at Rudston in 1618 and a 'Brick Close' at Deighton near Escrick in 1619. When Henry Best was planning to build himself a new house at Elmswell, near Driffield, in 1635, he contracted John Arlush of Beverley to make 400,000 bricks near the house site.[3] Amongst the first rural brickyards were those linked to landed estates, including those established by Lord Burlington at Thorpe-le-Street by 1679, John Shaw at Bainton by 1727, Sir Marmaduke Constable at Everingham by 1731 and Sir Charles Hotham at Lockington from the early 1730s.[4] When Hotham's father was building his fine town house in Beverley in 1716, he obtained permission from the corporation to dig clay and make bricks on Westwood, the vast common to the west of the town. Here a shed was erected, William Twist built a coal-fired kiln and two brickmakers were 'imported' to make the bricks.[5] There are other references to clay being taken from common land; at Hunmanby in 1713 it was reported that clay had been taken from pits in the outgangs for 30 years.

Although bricks were made almost anywhere there was suitable clay, it was chiefly on the boulder clay of Holderness, the lacustrine clays of the Vale of York and the alluvial clays along the Humber that brickworks were established. There were few brickyards on the Wolds, an exception being the Sledmere estate yard at Garton-on-the-Wolds which was in operation for at least a century up to the First World War. Usually the bricks used in building the many large post-enclosure farmsteads on the Wolds had been carted some distance. In 1805

Eastfield Farm and Kipling House Farm at Middleton-on-the-Wolds were built with bricks from Newport, the brick and tile making settlement established on the Market Weighton Canal in the 1770s. By 1823 there were seven brickworks at Newport producing some 2,000,000 bricks and 1,700,000 tiles annually. Water transport was the cheapest way of carrying bricks. A canal boat could carry up to 25,000 bricks, a railway wagon 20,000, steam traction engines, steam lorries and modern haulage from 1000 to 7000, but a horse and cart only 500.

Brick making was always associated with the manufacture of roofing tiles. The flat or plain tiles made at Beverley and Hull from the early fourteenth century were often called 'thack tiles' to distinguish them from bricks which were termed 'wall tiles'. The distinctive curved pantile was not made in the area until the early eighteenth century although pantiles, imported from Holland, were in use in Hull and the East Riding by the 1660s. By the late eighteenth century pantiles had become the dominant roofing material of the East Riding, and large numbers were exported via Hull to London and many east coast ports from Northumberland to Norfolk. Local pantile manufacture had virtually ceased by the mid-twentieth century but has now been revived with the great expansion of the use of pantiles on housing and commercial buildings.[6]

Many of the tile yards opened in the nineteenth century were for the manufacture of land drain tiles or pipes, not roofing tiles. Agricultural publications in the 1830s and 40s urged farmers to drain their land to improve their crops and advised the establishment of tile yards close to the areas to be drained. Between 1847 and 1861 two-thirds of Yorkshire was drained with two-inch pipes, the cost reducing as more yards were established and more machines developed to mechanise the process.

The early brickyards were very simple with little equipment, and the brick maker may have had a second occupation, most likely that of farmer or builder.[7] The clay was dug out in autumn and left in heaps for the winter weather to break it down as it was turned at periodic intervals. In late spring it was 'trodden' and dug over to obtain the right plasticity, then moulded into bricks which were left to dry for about a month. They were then made into a clamp with turves, wood, refuse or coal and burnt or put into simple kilns with an open top. The brick makers needed only a spade and a mould and within a year the site could be returned to agriculture, leaving a kiln burn mark, a slight hollow and perhaps a pond.

Changes in demand brought about the more mechanised establishments of the later nineteenth century, and the number of yards reduced. In 1850 there had been at least 80 brickyards in the East Riding but only a handful survived after the Second World War with the last closing in the 1970s. Drainage tiles are still produced at the former estate brickworks at Escrick, and pantiles at a large modern works at Broomfleet.

Notes and bibliography on page 147

BRICK AND TILE MAKING

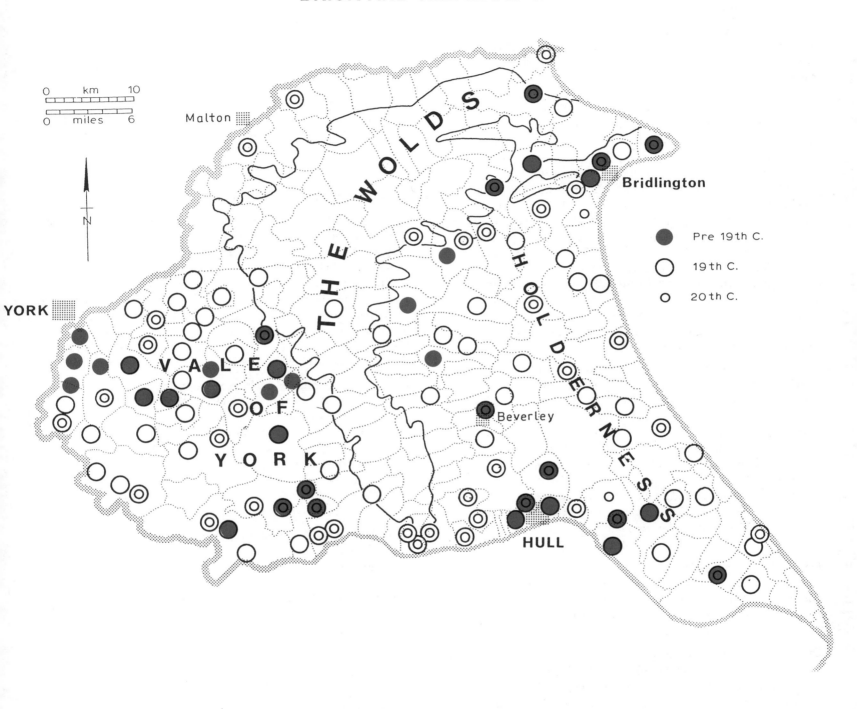

Pre 19th C.

19th C.

20th C.

Malton

YORK

THE WOLDS

Bridlington

HOLDERNESS

VALE

OF

YORK

Beverley

HULL

SHIPBUILDING: 1691-PRESENT

Arthur G. Credland

Hull was one of the three major British shipbuilding centres at the end of the eighteenth century in terms of ship numbers, and ranked fourth or fifth according to tonnage produced. A large proportion of trading vessels were still under 100 tons, so establishing a yard was a simple matter of finding a plot convenient for launching directly into a river at high tide and with easy access by water for timber and other bulky materials. From the late seventeenth century the Humber was supplying the Royal Navy; John Frame at his Hessle Cliff yard, starting in 1691, launched the fireship *Aetna*, two 80 gun vessels and the 60 gun *Kingston* in 1697. Hugh Blaydes (later Blaydes and Co.) launched at Hull no less than fifteen vessels, the largest being the 70 gun *Temple* in 1758. Thomas Hodgson, also in Hull, built another four and John Reed five craft of not more than 24 guns between 1747 and 1757. In 1804-5 Peter Atkinson of Hull launched the sloops *Scout* and *Otter* (382 and 365 tons respectively) and Shepherd of Hull the *Oberon* in 1805. At the Hessle Cliff (also known as North Barton) yard Hawkes constructed the bomb vessels *Hecla* (used by Parry for his arctic expeditions 1819-22) and *Infernal* in 1815, the year of Waterloo. Thomas Steemson (late of Thorne) moved to Paull when he signed a naval contract, and from 1807-12 three ships were built here, the largest being the 74 gun *Anson*.

A noted Hull timber merchant, Alderman William Osbourne, concluding that it was easier to set up a yard adjacent to a convenient source of timber, began, in partnership with Mr Dodsworth, a shipbuilding enterprise at the mouth of the river Spey in northeast Scotland. Timber was floated down from the great pine forests of Glenmore, Rothiemurchus and Abernethy, and between 1786 and 1815 some 50 trading vessels (the largest 613 tons) were produced there, using the skills of many shipwrights who moved north from Hull. The settlement which developed on the site was, in deference to the source of the enterprise, named Kingston-upon-Spey. After closure of the yard many of the craftsmen emigrated to New Brunswick in Canada, where they exercised their skills at Miramichi.

One of Hull's most productive yards was that established in 1805 at Great Union Street, on the east bank of the river Hull, by William Gibson (late of Airmyn). Apart from a brief flirtation with iron shipbuilding at the Groves in the 1840s, the Gibson family confined themselves to wooden shipbuilding and repairs until closure in 1897.

Other than the short-lived experiment by Fourness and Ashton in 1784, steam arrived on the Humber in 1814 with the Clyde-built *Caledonia*, just two years after Henry Bell's *Comet* had proved that a steam-powered vessel was a commercial proposition. The first locally built steamers were constructed on the river Ouse by Richard Pearson of Thorne, and he and a consortium of farmers, brewers and other small capitalists founded the Hull Steam Packet Co. In 1821 the paddle-steamer *Kingston* became the first sea-going vessel registered in the port of Hull. All these early craft were wooden hulled, but in 1831 the first iron steamer, designed for service between Goole and Castleford, was launched from the yard of Aydon and Co. on the Humber bank. Brownlow and Pearson, successors to Richard Pearson of Thorne, built the iron steamer *Jupiter* at Hull in 1841, and two years later T. and W. Pim of Alfred Street launched Hull's first screw-driven steamer, the *Archimedes*, built in sections which had to be carted across English Street for assembly on the Humber bank. In 1853 Hull's greatest single shipbuilding enterprise was founded by Charles and William Joel Earle, though for a number of years they were rivalled by Martin Samuelson who, in February 1857, set up a yard on the site of the old citadel. On one memorable day, 31 October 1863, no less than four ships came off the slips into the Humber, the *Countess of Ripon* and her sister ship *Lightning* both being 1206 tons.

By 1880 iron was the major material for ship construction and in that year half a million (gross) tons of iron (and composite) shipping left British yards, in contrast to only 20,000 tons of wooden vessels; ten years later steel had almost entirely replaced iron. Hull had a long tradition of importing Swedish iron, a cargo which formed the foundation of Thomas Wilson's business before he started in 1831 the development of what became the port's largest steamship company. The waterways flowing into the Ouse and Humber provided a route for bringing iron and steel plates from the foundries of the West Riding, just as they had for native timber.

Earle's was re-formed as a joint stock company in 1871, with Sir Edward James Reed, formerly naval architect and chief constructor to the Admiralty, as chairman and manager. He used his particular expertise to attract orders for naval craft, including the 6,000 ton cruisers *St George* and *Endymion* for the Royal Navy and a variety of war vessels for Turkey, Japan, Germany, Chile and Brazil. In 1873 the steam yacht *Slavyanka* was launched for the Tsarevitch, later Tsar Alexander VI, and nine years later came the launch of the *Zodiac*, the world's first purpose-built steam trawler.

Cook, Welton and Gemmell, which had started on the old Samuelson site, re-established at Beverley in 1901 (although continuing to build at Hull until 1904), taking over the yard vacated by Cochrane's who had moved to a new green-field site on the river Ouse at Selby. For many years these two firms were great rivals in the design and construction of deep-sea trawlers. Both occupied narrow riverside sites and were notable for their spectacular sideways launches. Dunston's, founded at Thorne in 1858, acquired Henry Scarr's shipyard at Hessle Haven in 1932, the same year that Earle's was finally dismantled as a result of the Great Depression. Sadly, Dunston's ceased operation in December 1994, following Cochrane's of Selby in 1992-3 and the Beverley Shipyard in 1975. Currently only two shipyards remain in operation in East Yorkshire - J.R. Hepworth of Paull, founded in 1932-3, and the Yorkshire Dry Dock Co. at Lime Street, Hull.

Bibliography on page 148

SHIPBUILDING : 1691-PRESENT

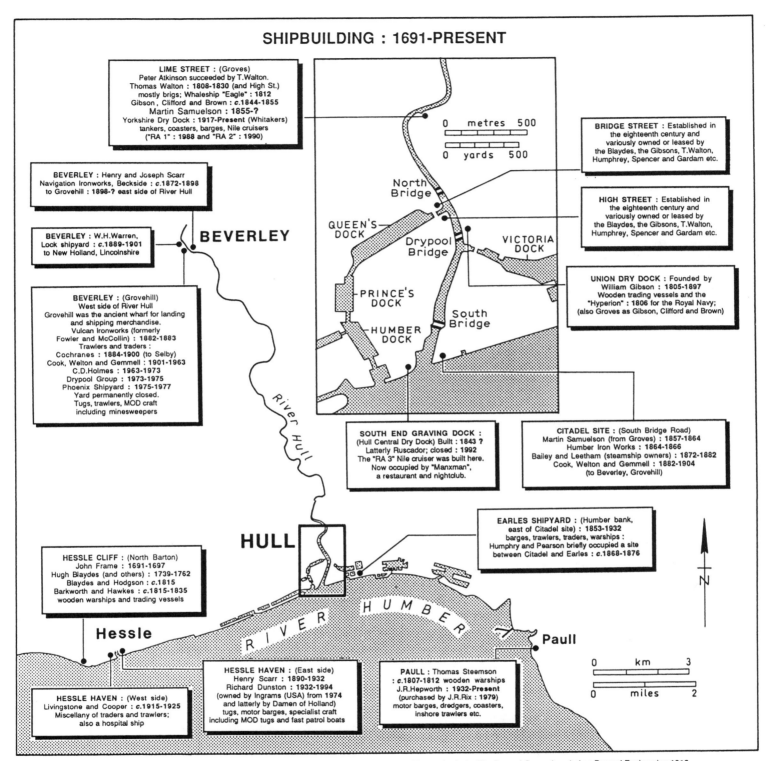

LIME STREET : (Groves)
Peter Atkinson succeeded by T.Walton.
Thomas Walton : 1808-1830 (and High St.)
mostly brigs; Whaleship "Eagle" : 1812
Gibson, Clifford and Brown : *c*.1844-1855
Martin Samuelson : 1855-?
Yorkshire Dry Dock : 1917-Present (Whitakers)
tankers, coasters, barges, Nile cruisers
("RA 1" : 1988 and "RA 2" : 1990)

BEVERLEY : Henry and Joseph Scarr
Navigation Ironworks, Beckside : *c*.1872-1898
to Grovehill : 1898-? east side of River Hull

BEVERLEY : W.H.Warren,
Lock shipyard : *c*.1889-1901
to New Holland, Lincolnshire

BEVERLEY : (Grovehill)
West side of River Hull
Grovehill was the ancient wharf for landing
and shipping merchandise.
Vulcan Ironworks (formerly
Fowler and McCollin) : 1882-1883
Trawlers and traders :
Cochranes : 1884-1900 (to Selby)
Cook, Welton and Gemmell : 1901-1963
C.D.Holmes : 1963-1973
Drypool Group : 1973-1975
Phoenix Shipyard : 1975-1977
Yard permanently closed.
Tugs, trawlers, MOD craft
including minesweepers

BRIDGE STREET : Established in
the eighteenth century and
variously owned or leased by
the Blaydes, the Gibsons, T.Walton,
Humphrey, Spencer and Gardam etc.

HIGH STREET : Established in
the eighteenth century and
variously owned or leased by
the Blaydes, the Gibsons, T.Walton,
Humphrey, Spencer and Gardam etc.

UNION DRY DOCK : Founded by
William Gibson : 1805-1897
Wooden trading vessels and the
"Hyperion" : 1806 for the Royal Navy;
(also Groves as Gibson, Clifford and Brown)

North Bridge

QUEEN'S DOCK

Drypool Bridge

VICTORIA DOCK

PRINCE'S DOCK

South Bridge

HUMBER DOCK

0 metres 500

0 yards 500

SOUTH END GRAVING DOCK :
(Hull Central Dry Dock) Built : 1843 ?
Latterly Ruscador; closed : 1992
The "RA 3" Nile cruiser was built here.
Now occupied by "Manxman",
a restaurant and nightclub.

CITADEL SITE : (South Bridge Road)
Martin Samuelson (from Groves) : 1857-1864
Humber Iron Works : 1864-1866
Bailey and Leetham (steamship owners) : 1872-1882
Cook, Welton and Gemmell : 1882-1904
(to Beverley, Grovehill)

EARLES SHIPYARD : (Humber bank,
east of Citadel site) : 1853-1932
barges, trawlers, traders, warships :
Humphry and Pearson briefly occupied a site
between Citadel and Earles : *c*.1868-1876

HESSLE CLIFF : (North Barton)
John Frame : 1691-1697
Hugh Blaydes (and others) : 1739-1762
Blaydes and Hodgson : *c*.1815
Barkworth and Hawkes : *c*.1815-1835
wooden warships and trading vessels

HULL

BEVERLEY

River Hull

Hessle

RIVER HUMBER

Paull

HESSLE HAVEN : (East side)
Henry Scarr : 1890-1932
Richard Dunston : 1932-1994
(owned by Ingrams (USA) from 1974
and latterly by Damen of Holland)
tugs, motor barges, specialist craft
including MOD tugs and fast patrol boats

HESSLE HAVEN : (West side)
Livingstone and Cooper : *c*.1915-1925
Miscellany of traders and trawlers;
also a hospital ship

PAULL : Thomas Steemson
: *c*.1807-1812 wooden warships
J.R.Hepworth : 1932-Present
(purchased by J.R.Rix : 1979)
motor barges, dredgers, coasters,
inshore trawlers etc.

0 km 3

0 miles 2

N

It may be noted that after the closure of Queen's Dock in 1930 the lock pit was converted into a dry dock. The Drypool Group, founded as Drypool Engineering 1916, by 1966 owned 5 dry docks including Union Dry Dock and Central Dry Dock; acquired Selby shipyard 1969 and Beverley shipyard 1973; went into liquidation 1976. Cochranes which had begun in Beverley resited at Selby in 1900; acquired by Ross Group 1959, Drypool Group 1969 and in 1976 by North British Maritime. The latter was purchased by Howard Smith who closed the yard in 1992. Goole shipyard (W. Yorkshire) founded in 1901 was acquired by Swan Hunter 1968 and closed in 1981. Purchased by Cochranes 1983, finally shut down 1987.

HULL'S ARCTIC WHALING TRADE FROM THE SIXTEENTH TO THE NINETEENTH CENTURY

Arthur G. Credland

Hull vessels were sailing to Vardo at the northern tip of the Scandinavian peninsula in the latter part of the sixteenth century. These were probably trading voyages initially, but reports of cod fish and whale oil brought into Hull from Wardhouse (Vardo) voyages indicate the gradual development of fishing activities. Whaling voyages to the seas around Iceland also took place in the late sixteenth century, certainly in 1598. In 1607 Englishman Henry Hudson re-discovered Spitsbergen, previously sighted by the Dutchman Willem Barents, and the men of Hull were the first to prosecute the whale fishery there, while Jan Mayen is said to have been granted as a fishing station to the Hull Corporation by King James in 1618. Hull whaling continued during the Civil War, but it was the Dutch who came to dominate the whaling trade, largely because the British effort was weakened and fragmented by the monopoly claims of the London-based Muscovy company and their constant disputes with all those they considered 'interlopers' from Hull and the east coast ports. At the close of the seventeenth century, British whaling was moribund, while the huge Dutch fleet, comprising 246 vessels in 1687, was able to supply the whole of Europe with whale oil and baleen.

In the first half of the eighteenth century England was relying on imports of whale products from North America, but when supplies were interrupted by the French, James Hamilton equipped a vessel for the arctic fishery which sailed from Hull in 1754. Added encouragement was provided by a Government bounty of 40 shillings per ship ton, a subsidy of almost £600 per vessel. Subsequently import duty was placed on oil and bone from the colonies, which further encouraged the native enterprise, and in 1766 Samuel Standidge began a substantial investment which laid the foundations of Hull's whaling trade. Wars with England (1780-4) and the blockade of the Netherlands during French domination (1759-1813) effectively killed off Dutch involvement in whaling, and by the end of the eighteenth century Hull's fleet comprised about 40 per cent of the British participants in the trade. The traditional 'bay whaling' method, whereby whales were caught inshore and the carcasses beached for processing on the spot, was abandoned soon after 1670 and new stocks were hunted in the open sea east of Greenland.

As these stocks diminished the whalers pursued new populations on the west side of Greenland in the neighbourhood of Disko. The areas of water clear of ice at the northern end of Baffin Bay were charted by the whalers *Larkins* and *Elizabeth* in 1817. Ships reached here by negotiating the treacherous Melville Bay and sailed into the North Water and then into the West Water adjacent to the Canadian mainland. The existence of the North Water was confirmed by Capt. John Ross in 1818 during his voyage in search of the North West Passage, and the route was firmly established by a contingent of largely Hull vessels in 1820. The voyage was now considerably lengthened, taking vessels far beyond the Arctic Circle, and increasingly at the mercy of the vagaries of the polar climate. Vessels, generally barks or ships of 300-400 tons, left Hull in February or March and instead of returning in summer, would hope to arrive back in October.

During the French wars, when the demand for crews for the Royal Navy made it difficult to reach a full complement, it became usual to pick up fifteen or so men from the Orkney or Shetland Islands, long familiar as the last opportunity to fill up water barrels or take on provisions before heading for the Arctic. The islanders were skilled in handling small craft and were therefore ideal for rowing the whaleboats in which the quarry was pursued with harpoon and lance. From the 1850s vessels would leave home with officers, specialists and a basic sailing crew, and about half of the total complement of some 50 men would be taken aboard at Lerwick or Stromness.

Although the largest fleet (65 vessels) sailed in 1819, the year 1820 proved to be the peak of the Hull whaling trade, when 62 vessels brought back the produce of 688 whales with a value of over £250,000. The following year was disastrous, with the loss of nine vessels, crushed in the ice of Baffin Bay. Many investors withdrew, and the fleet was reduced by a third to only 40 vessels in 1822. In 1830 the whole of the fleet was fishing on the west side of Greenland when disaster befell once more, with six vessels being lost and eight others failing to capture a single whale. Hull, however, remained the chief British whaling port, with 27 ships in 1834; her nearest rival was Peterhead with eleven. Another five Hull vessels were lost in 1835, and in 1836, though all returned, none had more than the produce of two whales. By 1842 there were only two vessels sailing from Hull, but there was a gradual increase during the next decade. In 1857 the installation at Earle's shipyard of a 40 hp engine into the *Diana* made this the world's first steam-powered whaler, enabling it to move through the broken pack ice independently of the wind. Whales were now very scarce and an important part of the catch were large numbers of harp seals, killed on the surface of the ice near Jan Mayen.

By this time the trade was no longer dominated by the great merchant families; investment was provided by a miscellany of small merchants, shopkeepers and artisans. The largest enterprise was the Hull Whale and Seal Fishing Co. which for a time operated the *Diana*, and was managed by Messrs Brown, Atkinson. Two vessels sailed north in 1868, the *Diana* and *Truelove*, the latter a veteran of 72 seasons in the Arctic, then in 1869 the *Diana*, the sole representative of the Hull fleet, was wrecked off Donna Nook on the Lincolnshire coast, homeward bound. It was left to Scottish enterprise to invest in a new generation of specially built auxiliary steamers, which continued to sail in the whale and seal fishery until the outbreak of the Great War.

Bibliography on page 148

HULL'S ARCTIC WHALING FLEET : 16th-19th CENTURIES

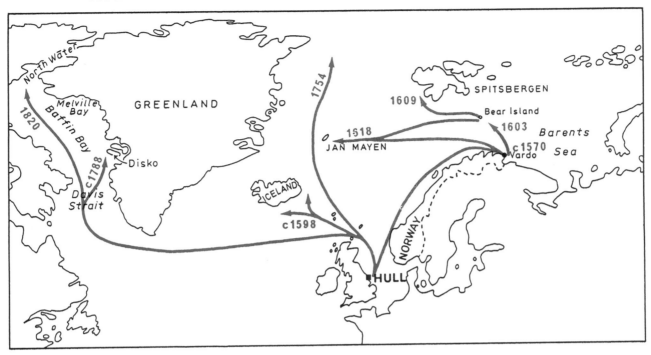

THE HULL WHALING FLEET IN THE ARCTIC : 1810-1842

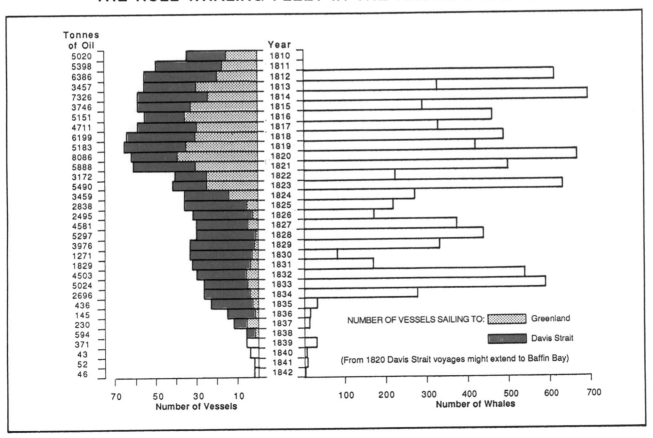

HULL FISHING IN THE NINETEENTH AND TWENTIETH CENTURIES

Arthur G. Credland

The development of fishing as a major industry in Hull began around the middle of the nineteenth century. Before then, fish caught by vessels based in the Humber or brought in by fishermen of other ports was essentially for local consumption. As stocks of fish were depleted in the English Channel and southern North Sea, the Brixham and Ramsgate smacksmen explored further north. Initially on a seasonal basis, they based themselves at Hull, finding a lucrative market in an expanding town, and at Scarborough, where the summer visitors enjoyed the ready supply of fresh fish. Completion of the rail link from Hull to Leeds in 1840 made it possible for fish to be readily transported to the huge population of the industrial North and Midlands. The discovery around the 1840s of the now fabled Silver Pits,[1] a prolific source of sole, further encouraged the southern fishermen to head north and settle on a permanent basis. Consequently, the Hull smack fleet expanded from a modest 21 vessels in 1845 to 313 in 1872.

By the 1870s the small, single-masted fishing craft, the true smack, had been replaced by the 70-80 ton ketch or dandy-rigged smack. Some were built on the south coast, but many others were built in Hull or the Humber region, including Burton Stather on the Trent. Accommodation for the smacks was restricted to the Victoria Pier or a corner of the Humber Dock until the construction of the Albert Dock in 1869. In 1883 St Andrew's Dock was allocated to the fishing fleet when an anticipated growth in coal exports had failed to materialise. To enable fish to be landed in quantity and in a reasonably fresh condition, the box or fleeting system was introduced to Hull by John Sims. The smacks stayed at sea for five or so weeks at a time, off-loading their catch each morning on to a fast cutter in which, packed in ice, it would be rushed to market in Hull or direct to London, vital before the establishment of an efficient rail link with the metropolis; this form of fishing was familiarly known as 'Sims' Railway'. Although well organised and efficient, it placed a heavy burden on the fishermen. The dangers and hardships of the fisherman's life were emphasised in the terrible results of severe weather, as in the great storm of March 1883 in which no less than 47 craft and 260 men were lost from the North Sea fishing fleet. However, closer regulation by the Board of Trade and the work of the Royal National Mission to Deep Sea Fishermen did much to alleviate conditions, and in 1904 when the Hull fleet was fired on by the Russian navy - the infamous 'Russian Outrage' - the Mission steamer was able to provide immediate medical assistance.

Steam arrived first to power the cutters of the box fleet and to drive the trawl winches of the smacks. Then a number of paddle-tugs were converted into trawlers and proved the value of steam in towing a trawl net independently of the vagaries of the wind. In 1882 the first purpose-built steam trawler, the *Zodiac*, entered service following its launch at Earle's, Hull's biggest shipyard. Within the space of 20 years the sailing trawler had vanished, either scrapped or sold to other ports. The higher capital investment required for the new steam trawlers meant that the trade became concentrated in fewer and fewer hands, and the individual owner-skipper became an anachronism. Steam also enabled the efficient use of the Granton trawl, invented in 1895, which replaced the old style beam trawl in which the mouth of the net was kept open by a stout wooden spar. The maximum length of the latter was some 50 feet, but the new trawl with its pair of otter boards or doors attached to the warps, meant that the size of the net was restricted only by the towing power of the trawler's engine and the strength of the winch.

Steam power allowed trawlers to fish further afield, and the exploitation of the Icelandic grounds began in 1891. These vessels fished independently ('single-boaters'), utilising the fish room as a coal bunker on the outward journey, and the catch was packed in crushed ice for the journey home, a round trip of some three weeks. Hull's first ice factory opened in 1891; previously all ice had either been imported from the Norwegian fjords or gathered from local ponds in the winter. By 1898 the Faroes and Iceland were being heavily fished, and from 1905 the grounds around Bear Island and in the Barents Sea ('White Sea') became increasingly important. The demand for fish as a cheap source of protein grew, and the fish and chip shop became an established part of British life. Large imports of herring from Norway, starting in 1884, quickly made Hull the nation's kipper capital, outstripping even Scotland.

Although the emphasis had shifted at the turn of the century to the Sub-Arctic, the box fleet lingered in the North Sea until rising fuel costs and falling fish prices forced it into liquidation in 1936. By the 1930s fishing had reached Spitsbergen and Novaya Zemlya, and there was serious over-production, a problem temporarily solved by the outbreak of war. During two world wars large numbers of trawlers were requisitioned for convoy duties, coastal patrols and minesweeping, and for the remaining fleet large areas of the North Sea were out of bounds owing to the risk of mines and enemy attack. Fleetwood, on the west coast, became the main fishing centre, but soon after hostilities ceased Hull was able to re-assert itself as the major bulk fishing port. By the 1950s the industry was again suffering from over-production and falling prices. Increasingly large and more efficient vessels, many locally built, highlighted the need for conservation of fish stocks.[2] In 1975 Iceland extended its fishing limits to 200 miles and the Hull fishing industry collapsed as other nations followed suit with enlarged limits and restricted quotas. Today only two of the old established companies survive - Boyd's and Marr's - and a large proportion of the fish brought into the port for the city's processing plants now comes overland from elsewhere in Britain or aboard ferries from the continent.

Notes and bibliography on page 148

THE SPREAD OF TRAWLING IN THE NORTH SEA

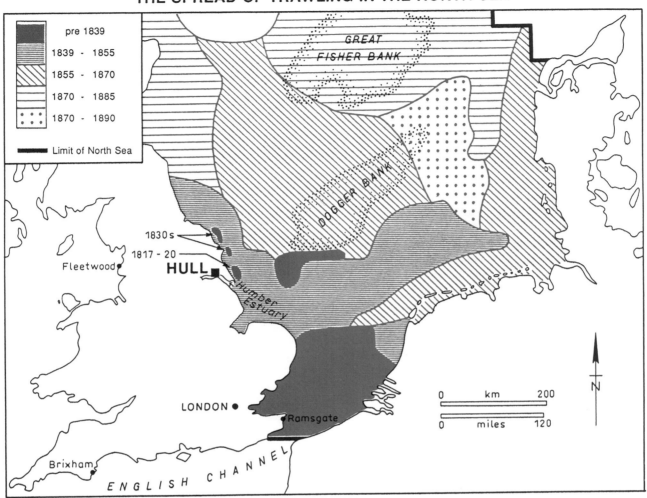

▓	pre 1839
≡	1839 - 1855
⧄	1855 - 1870
═	1870 - 1885
⋯	1870 - 1890
━	Limit of North Sea

GREAT FISHER BANK

DOGGER BANK

1830s
1817 - 20
HULL
Humber Estuary

Fleetwood

LONDON ●
● Ramsgate

Brixham ●

ENGLISH CHANNEL

0 km 200
0 miles 120

THE SPREAD OF HULL DISTANT WATER FISHING

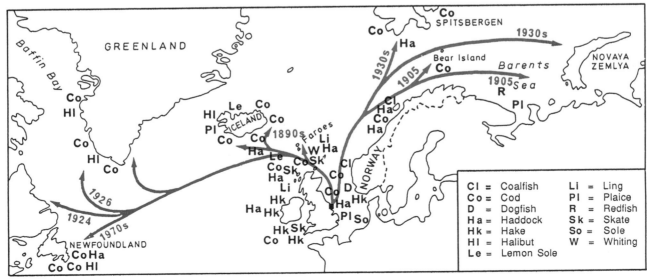

Co SPITSBERGEN
Co
Ha
1930s
1930s
Bear Island
Co
Barents
1905
1905 Sea
R
Pl

GREENLAND

Baffin Bay

NOVAYA ZEMLYA

Co
Hl
Le Co
Hl
Pl ICELAND Co
Co Co
Co 1890s Faroes
Hl Li
Co Ha W Ha
Co Le CoSk Sk
Co Sk Cl
Ha Li Co
Hk D
Ha Co
Ha Hk Ha Hk
1926 Hk Sk Pl So
Co Hk
1924
1970s
NEWFOUNDLAND
CoHa
Co Co Hl

NORWAY

Cl
Co
Ha

Cl =	Coalfish	**Li** =	Ling
Co =	Cod	**Pl** =	Plaice
D =	Dogfish	**R** =	Redfish
Ha =	Haddock	**Sk** =	Skate
Hk =	Hake	**So** =	Sole
Hl =	Halibut	**W** =	Whiting
Le =	Lemon Sole		

THE DOCK SYSTEM OF HULL: EIGHTEENTH TO TWENTIETH CENTURIES

Arthur G. Credland

Throughout most of Hull's history shipping had either berthed in the haven - the lower reaches of the river Hull, usually referred to as the 'Old Harbour' - or anchored in the Hull Roads and transferred its cargo into barges. The principal thoroughfare, High Street, ran along the side of the river Hull, with merchants' houses on either side; those occupying the riverside each had their own private wharf (staith) where the cargoes could be transferred under the watchful eye of the proprietor. However, with the development of trade came congestion of the Old Harbour, leading to increasing demands for improved accommodation for trading vessels, and the Hull Dock Company was established in 1774 to fulfil this aim. The scheme received Government support, but only on condition that the proposed dock should be provided with a 'legal quay' so as to enable the proper collection of customs. Hull, of all the major ports, was unique in having evaded this for so long, and the customs officers had always to scramble along the crowded riverside wharves to assess the dues as best they could, of no doubt with considerable loss to the Crown. In 1778 the whaler *Manchester* was the first vessel to enter the town's first enclosed dock, later known as Queen's Dock. The Humber Dock, with direct access to the Humber, followed in 1809 and the Junction Dock (later known as Prince's Dock) in 1829, so completing a circuit linking the Hull to the Humber and following the line of the medieval wall and defensive ditch which had been destroyed in the process.

Trade was boosted by improvements in the inland navigation system; despite the development of the new town of Goole by the Aire and Calder Navigation Company, Hull was still the best site for the transhipment of goods. The traditional local sailing barge, the Humber keel, with a burden of 80-90 tons, carried every conceivable cargo into and out of Hull, sailing into the heart of the industrial North via the river Ouse and into the Midlands via the river Trent, and there was also a vigorous coasting trade with London and northwards to Newcastle and Scotland. A rail link was established between Hull and Leeds in 1840, the beginning of an elaborate rail network which was to provide an alternative to the movement of goods through the waterways (see pages 98 and 99). It was a more reliable means of transporting perishable goods such as vegetables, fruit and fish as well as coal and other bulk products, which could be loaded by conveyor and hopper and easily discharged into railway wagons. Eventually the North Eastern Railway (NER) so dominated the movement of cargo that in 1893 it purchased the entire dock system from the Hull Dock Company and remained in control until nationalisation of the ports and rail network in 1948.

Steam had arrived on the Humber in 1814, and the first sea-going steamer, the *Kingston*, began trading across the North Sea in 1821. The pioneer steamship company was the Hull Steam Packet Company but this was overtaken by the Wilson Line and Bailey and Leetham in the second half of the century. The Wilson Line absorbed Bailey and Leetham in 1903 to become the largest privately owned steamship company in the world, sending vessels to northern Europe, the Mediterranean, India and North America. Hull also had a larger share of the coasting trade than any other port in the United Kingdom except London.

The old Town Docks system expanded with the completion of the Railway Dock in 1846, and the Albert Dock was constructed parallel to the Humber and opened in 1869. The St Andrew's Dock followed in 1883, and its extension in 1897. As ships became larger, the Town Docks were left to small coasting vessels and short-sea traders and used for fitting out trawlers. The Old Dock or Queen's Dock was filled in during the 1930s and the remaining Town Docks closed down in the 1960s; the Humber and Railway Docks were converted for leisure use as the Hull Marina in the 1980s.

In 1850 the Victoria Dock was completed, the first such facility east of the river Hull. The associated timber ponds and stacks accommodated the large volume of imports from northern Europe. Timber had featured in Hull's continental trade since the middle ages, and in 1897 19,000 loads were cut in the local saw mills. The Alexandra Dock opened in 1885 to the east of Victoria Dock, and a riverside quay was established in 1907 to the south of the Albert Dock to provide a quick turn around for vessels in the provision trade with perishable cargoes. Just before the outbreak of the Great War, King George V opened the dock which was to bear his name. The NER also built the first oil jetty at Salt End in the same year, and this site continues to develop with the expansion of the associated petro-chemical industries. In 1968 the area of tidal mudflats to the east of King George Dock was reclaimed and the Queen Elizabeth Dock was opened in the following year.

The docks, nationalised in 1948, were returned to private hands in 1982 and are now owned and run by Associated British Ports, the body also responsible for controlling navigation on the Humber and maintaining buoys and beacons. Since the Second World War, roads have largely replaced the railways as the national network for movement of goods. The construction of the motorway system, containerisation and the roll-on/roll-off terminals have transformed the throughput of cargo, and the increased mechanisation has resulted in a much reduced labour force but one able to handle a large volume of traffic. A new quay outside King George Dock gives direct access to large roll-on/roll-off vessels in the deepwater channel without the need for them to enter the dock through the narrow lock pit.

Bibliography on page 148

THE DOCK SYSTEM OF HULL : 18th-20th CENTURIES

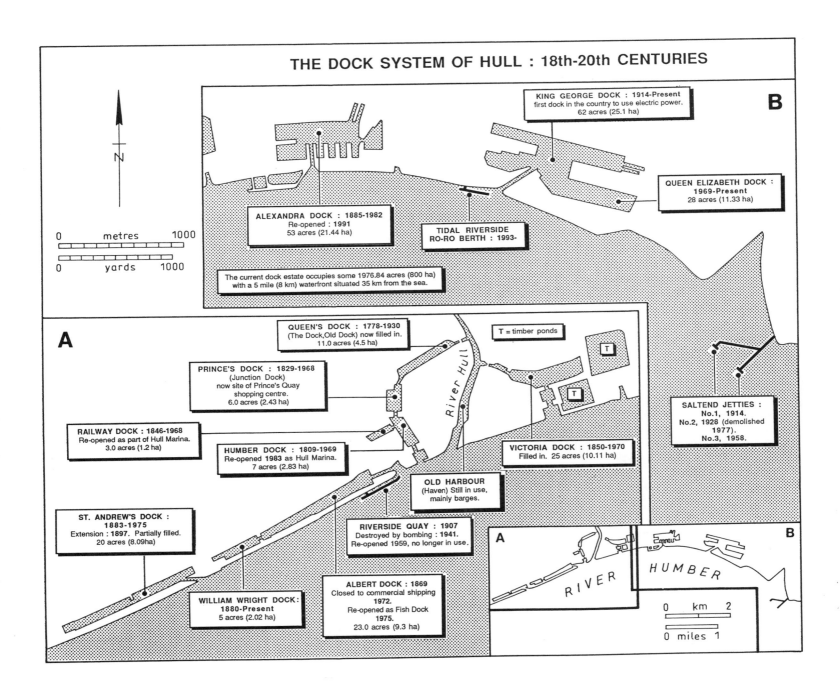

B

KING GEORGE DOCK : 1914-Present
first dock in the country to use electric power.
62 acres (25.1 ha)

QUEEN ELIZABETH DOCK :
1969-Present
28 acres (11.33 ha)

ALEXANDRA DOCK : 1885-1982
Re-opened : 1991
53 acres (21.44 ha)

TIDAL RIVERSIDE
RO-RO BERTH : 1993-

The current dock estate occupies some 1976.84 acres (800 ha)
with a 5 mile (8 km) waterfront situated 35 km from the sea.

0 metres 1000

0 yards 1000

A

QUEEN'S DOCK : 1778-1930
(The Dock, Old Dock) now filled in.
11.0 acres (4.5 ha)

T = timber ponds

PRINCE'S DOCK : 1829-1968
(Junction Dock)
now site of Prince's Quay
shopping centre.
6.0 acres (2.43 ha)

River Hull

SALTEND JETTIES :
No.1, 1914.
No.2, 1928 (demolished
1977).
No.3, 1958.

RAILWAY DOCK : 1846-1968
Re-opened as part of Hull Marina.
3.0 acres (1.2 ha)

HUMBER DOCK : 1809-1969
Re-opened 1983 as Hull Marina.
7 acres (2.83 ha)

VICTORIA DOCK : 1850-1970
Filled in. 25 acres (10.11 ha)

OLD HARBOUR
(Haven) Still in use,
mainly barges.

ST. ANDREW'S DOCK :
1883-1975
Extension : 1897. Partially filled.
20 acres (8.09ha)

RIVERSIDE QUAY : 1907
Destroyed by bombing : 1941.
Re-opened 1959, no longer in use.

WILLIAM WRIGHT DOCK:
1880-Present
5 acres (2.02 ha)

ALBERT DOCK : 1869
Closed to commercial shipping
1972.
Re-opened as Fish Dock
1975.
23.0 acres (9.3 ha)

A

B

RIVER HUMBER

0 km 2

0 miles 1

COMMUNICATIONS

HULL AND SELBY, OR HULL AND LEEDS JUNCTION, RAILWAY.
OPENING OF THE LINE
FOR PASSENGERS AND PARCELS ONLY,
ON THURSDAY, JULY THE 2nd, 1840

THE Public are respectfully informed that this RAILWAY will be OPENED THROUGH-OUT from HULL to the JUNCTION with the LEEDS and SELBY RAILWAY, at Selby, on WEDNESDAY, the First Day of July next, and that PASSENGERS and PARCELS only will be conveyed on THURSDAY, July 2nd; thus presenting a direct Railway Conveyance from Hull to Selby, Leeds, and York without change of Carriage.

TRAINS WITH PASSENGERS WILL START FROM HULL AS UNDER
AT SEVEN O'CLOCK, A.M   AT THREE O'CLOCK, P.M.
AT TEN O'CLOCK, A.M.   AT SIX O'CLOCK, P.M.
ON SUNDAYS, AT SEVEN O'CLOCK, A.M., AND SIX O'CLOCK, P.M.

The Trains from LEEDS and YORK, for HULL, will depart from those Places at the same Hours; and Passengers and Parcels may be Booked through at the Leeds, York, and Hull Stations. Arrangements are also in progress for Booking Passengers to Sheffield, Derby, Birmingham, and London.

THE FARES TO BE CHARGED ARE AS UNDER:

	First Class.	Second Class.	Third Class.
Hull to Selby	4s. 6d	4s. 0d	2s. 6d.
Hull to York	8s. 0d	6s. 6d	4s. 6d.
Hull to Leeds	8s. 0d	6s. 6d	4s. 6d.

No Fees are allowed to be taken by the Guards, Porters, or any other Servants of the Company.

The Trains, both up and down, will call at the Stations on the Line, viz.:—Hessle, Ferriby, Brough, Staddlethorpe, Eastrington, Howden, and Cliff.

Arrangements for carrying Goods, Cattle, Sheep, &c., will be completed in a short time, of which due Notice will be given.

By Order,

GEORGE LOCKING, Secretary.

Railway Office, Hull, June 24th, 1840.

TURNPIKE TRUSTS

Janice E. Crowther

In 1555 an *Act for the Amending of Highways* placed the responsibility for the repair of roads upon the parishes through which those roads went. Each parish elected surveyors to superintend the four days of labour required annually of able-bodied parishioners; the well-to-do provided carts, equipment and additional labour. Parishes which failed in their duties were presented before the Quarter Sessions and fined. 'Statute labour', as it was called, was very unpopular but the system remained in being, with a few modifications, until 1835, when the Highways Act empowered the surveyors to levy a rate for the repair and maintenance of the roads.[1]

The turnpiking system, which came into being in a piecemeal fashion from the early years of the eighteenth century, needs to be considered as an adjunct to the parish system. Under the device of a turnpike trust,[2] established by a private act of parliament, travellers (excluding those on foot) were required to pay tolls towards the repair and improvement of important sections of the public highway which received heavy usage. The Act empowered a body of trustees to 'privatise' an already existing road, locking it at certain points with toll-houses.[3] Turnpike trusts were usually promoted and administered by those such as local landowners, merchants and the corporations of towns, who had an interest in facilitating travel and commerce.[4]

As the map shows, Hull and Beverley became the focal points of several turnpike roads. The earliest turnpike act (1744) in East Yorkshire affected the road from Hull to Beverley. In 1745 the road leading west from Hull to Kirk Ella was turnpiked, as was that from Hull via Preston to Hedon. Then in 1761 the road from Beverley over the river Hull into mid-Holderness, as far as White Cross in the parish of Leven, was turnpiked.

Most early turnpike trust acts remained in force for 21 years. On renewal, further stretches of road were often added. For example in 1764, before the Hull-Beverley Act expired, plans were in hand to include the Beverley-York road, via Market Weighton and Pocklington,[5] and to add a branch to Cottingham. After opposition from the York Corporation, the turnpike ended at Kexby, another trust being established from there to York, with a branch from Grimston to Garrowby Hill.[6]

Turnpiking interest was at its height in the 1760s and several schemes were mooted which came to nothing. An abortive plan in 1767, when the Hull-Beverley Act was to be renewed, suggested turnpiking the road to the river Hull ferry at Wawne, in an endeavour to link southern Holderness with Beverley. Other branches to link the Beverley-White Cross road via Meaux and the Hull-Hedon road via Sutton were also proposed. In the event the only outcome was an act to turnpike the road from White Cross northwards to Bridlington.[7] Before the Hull-Hedon trust expired, an act of 1761 extended the turnpike road as far as Patrington. A minor road to Winestead, for the convenience of Sir

Robert Hildyard, one of the prime movers in the scheme, and a branch to Patrington Haven were also included.[8]

In 1766 the importance of the link between Beverley and Driffield was recognised, with a turnpike trust covering the road as far as Kendale House just to the north of Driffield. The road from Beverley towards Malton as far as Bainton[9] was included in the act, but a proposal to extend the turnpike from the Beverley-Driffield road to Corps Landing on the river Hull was firmly quashed by Beverley Corporation, who feared that such an encouragement to river trade at that point would be detrimental to the town's interests. In 1769 the road from Beverley to Hessle was turnpiked, whilst in 1771 the importance of the Humber ferry at Brough justified the turnpiking of the road from the ferry as far north as South Newbald.[10] An act of 1774 brought the road from Kirk Ella, via Raywell, Riplingham and North Cave, through to Wallingfen under the control of the Beverley-Hessle trust. The turnpiking of that road needs to be seen in the context of the digging of the Market Weighton canal, the enclosure and draining of the extensive commons and carrs, and the subsequent establishment of the brick and tile industry at the new settlement of Newport. The last turnpike act of the eighteenth century was in 1793, when in conjunction with the bridging of the Ouse at Selby and the Derwent at Bubwith, the road from Selby to Market Weighton was placed under a trust. Very few new roads were constructed by turnpike trusts. A notable exception was the road from Hull to Hedon direct, constructed under an act of 1830, and intended to expedite the transport of corn from southern Holderness to Hull.

The coming of the railways naturally had a deleterious effect on the turnpike trusts, especially where there was direct competition. It became progressively more difficult to let the tolls as income dropped, and from *c.*1850 most trusts were wound up. Under the Highways Act of 1862, the obligation for the upkeep of main roads could be transferred back to the parishes, or to a Highways District. This somewhat unsatisfactory system was improved in 1888 when the maintenance of main roads became the responsibility of the newly formed County Councils.

In some counties toll-houses, often of the octagonal style, survive, but none remains in East Yorkshire. Many were quite humble buildings and they were therefore demolished when trusts were wound up. A more lasting memorial of the old turnpike roads is provided by the milestones and mileposts which trustees were under an obligation to erect. The milestones of the East Riding were of two types - the simple 'tomb-stone' design and the mounting-step type - both of which often had inscribed metal plates attached to the stone. Metal mileposts were erected on the short-lived White Cross to Bridlington turnpike and on the Hull to Hedon direct road.

Notes and bibliography on page 148

TURNPIKE TRUSTS

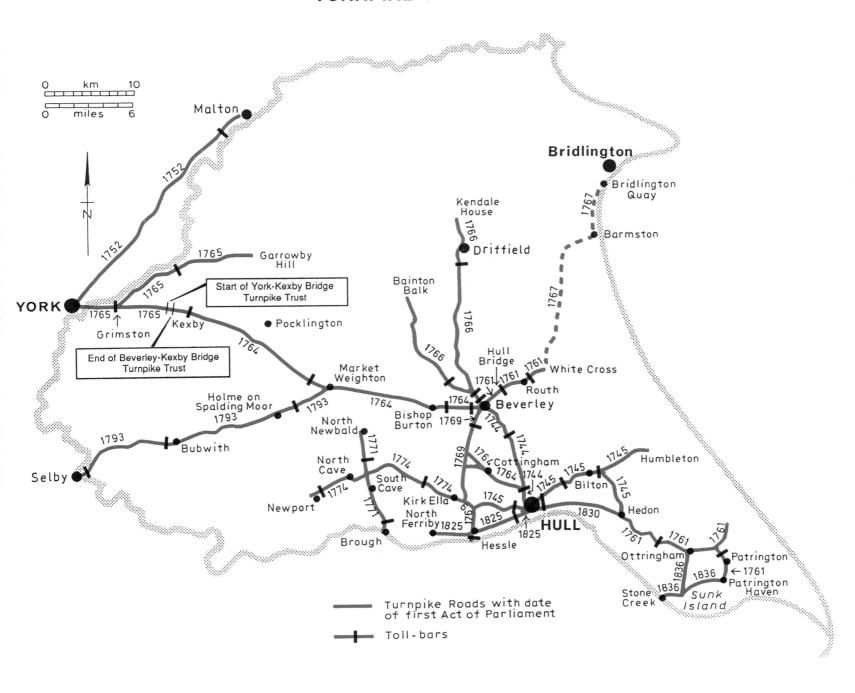

Scale:
0 km 10
0 miles 6

N

Malton — 1752

1752

1765 — Garrowby Hill

YORK

1765
1765
1765
1765

Grimston

Kexby

Start of York-Kexby Bridge Turnpike Trust

End of Beverley-Kexby Bridge Turnpike Trust

1764

Pocklington

Market Weighton

Holme on Spalding Moor
1793

1793

Bubwith

1793

Selby

North Newbald

North Cave

1774

1774

1774

Newport

South Cave

1771

1771

Kirk Ella
North Ferriby

Brough

Hessle

Bainton Balk

Kendale House

1766

1766

Driffield

1766

1766

Bishop Burton

1764

1764

1769

Bridlington

Bridlington Quay

1767

Barmston

1767

White Cross

1761

Hull Bridge

1761 1761

Routh

Beverley

1769

1764

1744

1744

1744

Cottingham

1764

1764

1744

1745

1769

1825

1825

1745

1745

HULL

1825

1745 1745

Bilton

1745

1745

Humbleton

Hedon

1830

1761

1761

1761

← 1761

Patrington

Patrington Haven

Ottringham

1836

1836

1836

Stone Creek

Sunk Island

Turnpike Roads with date of first Act of Parliament

Toll-bars

NAVIGABLE WATERWAYS AND CANALS
Margaret Noble

Like other regions, the East Riding shared in the growth in waterborne transportation systems in the eighteenth and nineteenth centuries. The early success of canals serving towns in the North and Midlands led to their extension into more rural areas where their immediate relevance was less apparent. The development of navigable waterways in the East Riding in the eighteenth century was not, however, a new phenomenon for navigable waterways serving three of the region's towns - Beverley, Hedon and Patrington - date back to the medieval period.

The motives for improving existing, or making new, navigations were essentially local, coming from landlords eager to extend the market for produce from their estates, and from town tradesmen who recognised the boost that such schemes could make to the urban economy through export of goods and import of raw materials. In 1762 William Porter, a cornfactor, landlord of the Blue Bell and one of the chief instigators of the Driffield canal of 1767, wrote, 'if a canal could be made from here to Hull, Driffield would soon emerge as one of the best market towns in the East Riding'. He had good foresight, for between 1750 and 1850 Great Driffield became the most important corn market in the region and was said to be 'frequented by more agriculturists than any other market town in the East Riding'. In the mid-nineteenth century more than 100,000 quarters of corn were exported annually via the town's canal.

In the course of the eighteenth and nineteenth centuries a number of navigation schemes affected the region.[1] These were:

> Derwent Navigation 1702
> Ouse Navigation 1727 and 1732
> Beverley Beck (cleansed and deepened) 1727
> Patrington Haven (improved) 1761
> Driffield Navigation 1767 (further improvements 1797)
> Market Weighton Drainage and Navigation 1772[2]
> Hedon Haven (deepened and improved) 1774
> Leven Canal 1801
> Pocklington Canal 1814

Although the development of the various navigation schemes is well documented, detailed records of the number of ships and tonnages and type of goods using the region's navigable waterways and canals are patchy, and it is the comments of contemporaries that provide the most insight into trading patterns. Following the opening of the Derwent Navigation, Malton was said to have become a 'place of considerable internal commerce due to its facility for the transmission of corn, butter, hams and other articles of provision to Hull, Leeds and various places'.[3] The improvement of Beverley Beck provided 'great facilities for trade by opening up communication with the Humber and coals are brought in large quantities to the staiths for the interior supply of the East Riding.'[4]

Compared to navigational schemes in other parts of the country, those in the East Riding involved low levels of capitalisation; average investment in the region's canals was £20,000, and in river and haven improvement considerably less. The success of navigation schemes was very dependent on the level of financial support and in particular the amount of support which was drawn from beyond the immediate area served by the waterway. For example, the Driffield Canal received a significant amount of external support and by the early 1800s had 27 ships trading regularly with the West Riding via the River Humber; the canal also imported and exported over 40,000 tons of goods per annum. Success was also dependent on the physical location of the waterway and the location of the basin or river wharfage point. On some of the region's waterways these points were at some distance from centres of population, resulting in lower levels of trade; this was the case with both the Pocklington and Market Weighton canals where the basins were some two miles distant from the respective towns. Whereas at Great Driffield the canal head spawned the development of several paper and grain mills, warehouses and a whiting manufactory, only warehouses were built at Pocklington and Market Weighton. On other navigations, problems of silting and dredging served to limit the volume of trade that could be handled. For example, at the small haven at Hedon shipping was badly affected by problems of silting and maintenance, leaving boats little time to unload and often leaving them stranded. Records suggest that as few as ten boats a month may have been using the haven by 1800; this is in sharp contrast to the considerable medieval prosperity enjoyed by the port. Patrington Haven also suffered from problems of silting but did have a regular trade with about 20 boats a month each carrying 70 tons.

The region's navigations dealt primarily in agricultural produce or in industrial products closely associated with agriculture; grain and agricultural products accounted for almost 40 per cent of all trade. Exports of wheat, oats and barley were of particular significance from navigations serving towns with specialised grain markets such as Great Driffield, Market Weighton and Malton.[5] Principal imports to the region were coal, lime, bone dust, gravel, sand, manure and timber, and occasionally products used in local industries. In the 1830s large quantities of bark were imported via the Pocklington canal for use in Pocklington's then flourishing tanning industry. Although the demand for fuel was never cited as a principal rationale for improvement of navigable waterways, imports of coal were significant, accounting for well over 50 per cent of imports.

Navigable waterways in the region enjoyed a century of relative prosperity. From the mid-nineteenth century, however, the importance of the inland waterways of the region, with the exception of the River Humber, began to wane as railways took an ever increasing share of trade. By the early years of the twentieth century, waterborne trade was in decline with most of the navigations functioning at a very low level.

Notes and bibliography on page 149

NAVIGABLE WATERWAYS AND CANALS

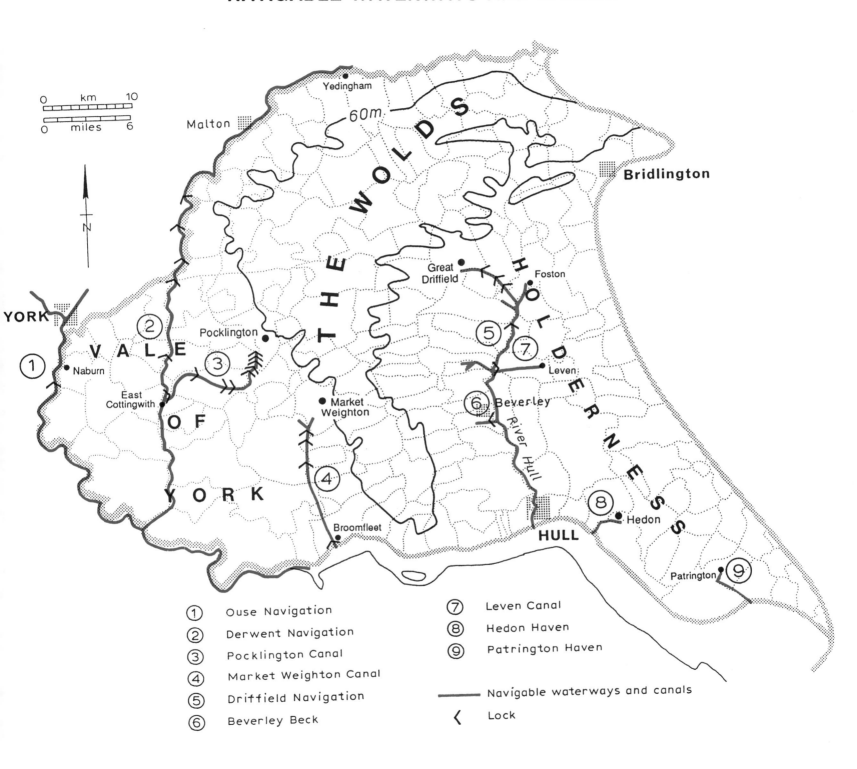

① Ouse Navigation
② Derwent Navigation
③ Pocklington Canal
④ Market Weighton Canal
⑤ Driffield Navigation
⑥ Beverley Beck
⑦ Leven Canal
⑧ Hedon Haven
⑨ Patrington Haven

⎯⎯⎯ Navigable waterways and canals

< Lock

RAILWAYS

J. Allan Patmore

The East Riding provides a classic example of the factors which influenced the evolution of Britain's railway system. At its fullest extent, the county's network reflected the traffic generated by Hull, the coastal resorts and the agricultural hinterland, the inhibiting effect of the relatively moderate relief of the Wolds, and in a modest but striking way, the impact of inter-company competition. The first line to be opened, the Hull & Selby of 1840, was one of the earliest main lines in the country, linking with the even earlier Leeds & Selby of 1834 to give Hull railborne access to the West Riding. The route was near-level and near-straight for much of the way, with the first Hull terminus at Manor House Street adjacent to the original docks. For passengers, this was superseded by Paragon Station in 1848, closer to the town centre. In 1845 the Hull & Selby was leased by George Hudson's York & North Midland Railway, and in the mid-1840s the network expanded dramatically under the aegis of that company. The first routes sought to open up the coast. The York to Scarborough line of 1845 followed easy gradients (maximum 1 in 272), hugging the banks of the river Derwent through the Kirkham Gap. Hull to Bridlington (1846) posed few problems, but between Scarborough and Bridlington (1847) gradients as steep as 1 in 92 were necessary in order to cross the barrier presented by the Wolds.

These four lines mark the essential 'box' of railways in the East Riding, surrounding the Wolds and linking the major settlements. It is no accident that this is essentially the network which still survives today. In the mid-1840s, however, in the feverish years of railway speculation dubbed the Railway Mania, other companies eyed Hull's traffic and not least the route from York to Hull through the gap in the Wolds between Market Weighton and Beverley. George Hudson, the 'Railway King', sought urgently to protect the territorial monopoly of his York & North Midland. He bought the Londesborough estate of 12,000 acres near Market Weighton and rapidly built two lines across the Vale of York to Market Weighton, from York (1847) and Selby (1848), in a classic blocking tactic. Having thus secured the approaches to the Market Weighton gap, the company was in no hurry to exploit it; the line through to Beverley and Hull was not completed until 1865. By then the York & North Midland had become part of the North Eastern Railway, created by amalgamation in 1854.

As the railway became the universal form of transport for all but the most local of traffic in the latter part of the nineteenth century, the gaps in the network to serve rural and commuting needs were filled. An early line through the sparsely settled Wolds was the Malton & Driffield (1853), crossing the watershed north of Burdale in a tunnel almost a mile in length. The nascent resort of Withernsea and the longer established resort of Hornsea were linked to Hull by initially independent railways, but these were soon absorbed into the North Eastern Railway. The last line to be built in the county, the Ministry of Defence Spurn Head Railway excepted, was the purely agricultural Derwent Valley Light Railway of 1913. Other network additions sought to improve existing routes. In 1869 a new outlet from Hull to the south was opened through Goole, shortening the Hull-London distance by nearly 20 miles. The Selby-York link (1871) was a final component of the East Coast main line, until it too was superseded in 1983 by a new line to the west avoiding the subsidence problems of the Selby coalfield. In 1890 a line from Market Weighton to Driffield gave Bridlington a more direct route to the holiday markets of south and west Yorkshire, but at the expense of gradients as steep as 1 in 95 across the Wolds.

Towards the end of the century the North Eastern Railway had a total monopoly of railway provision in the county, and nowhere was that monopoly more keenly felt than in Hull, where the Corporation had strong suspicions that the North Eastern was favouring northeast ports at its expense. With the enthusiastic backing of the Corporation, the Hull, Barnsley & West Riding Junction Railway & Dock Company was promoted, and opened to its new Alexandra Dock in 1885. The new company's route to Hull was a difficult one. West Riding coal had to be brought across the Wolds through the 2,116 yard Drewton tunnel, on gradients of up to 1 in 150, while westbound traffic from the dock faced an even steeper climb at 1 in 100. Rivalry, however, was surprisingly shortlived; by the early twentieth century the Hull & Barnsley and the North Eastern Railways achieved a close understanding, jointly opening the King George V Dock in 1914.

In Hull itself the docks east of the city were reached by two lines circling the built-up area at the time of their construction. The first, to the Victoria Dock in 1853, was built at ground level, necessitating numerous level crossings. The later Hull & Barnsley line of 1885 was built on a high embankment. In the 1960s the network was altered so that this line carried the remaining freight clear of road traffic, and Hull's notorious level crossings declined in number from 22 to four.

Since 1950 the railway network has radically contracted. Early casualties were the rural Malton-Driffield line (1958) and most of the competitive Hull & Barnsley (1959). The Beeching era saw the closure of the routes to the Holderness coast (1964) and of the inland lines crossing at Market Weighton (1965). The independent Derwent Valley Light Railway finally succumbed in 1981. What the maps do not illustrate is the drastic decline of services even on the remaining routes. Many intermediate stations have closed, and the country goods yard is no more. Hull at its zenith had 300 miles of railway sidings; today it has but two regular freight workings a day.

Bibliography on page 149

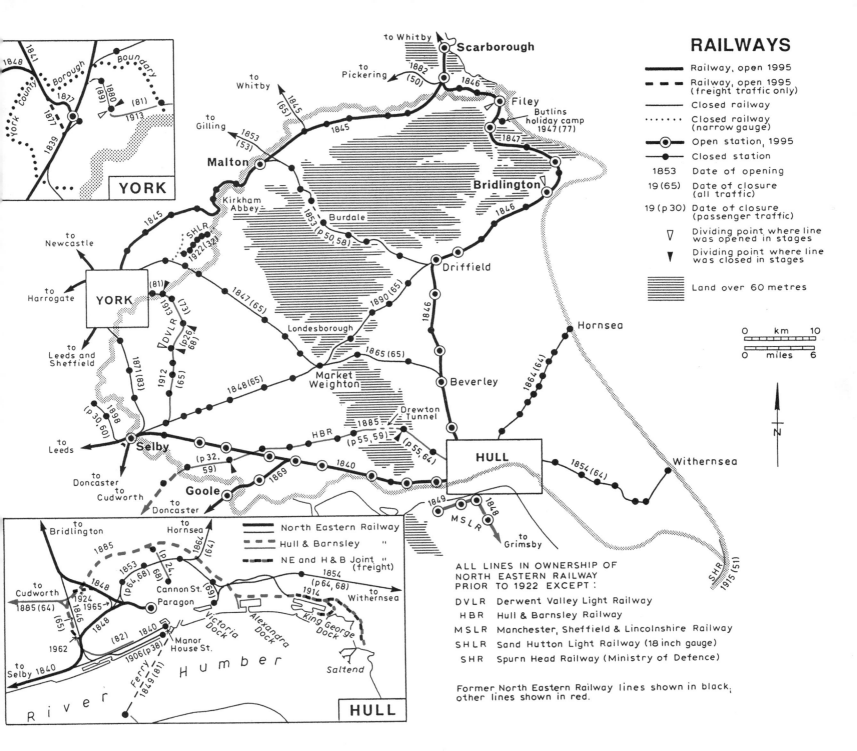

YORK

1848
1848
York County
Borough Boundary
1877
1880
1877
(89)
1839
1913
(81)

RAILWAYS

▬▬▬	Railway, open 1995
▬ ▬ ▬	Railway, open 1995 (freight traffic only)
───	Closed railway
·····	Closed railway (narrow gauge)
⊙	Open station, 1995
●	Closed station
1853	Date of opening
19 (65)	Date of closure (all traffic)
19 (p 30)	Date of closure (passenger traffic)
▽	Dividing point where line was opened in stages
▼	Dividing point where line was closed in stages
▦	Land over 60 metres

to Whitby
Scarborough
to Pickering
1882 (50)
1846
Filey
Butlins holiday camp 1947 (77)
1847
to Whitby
1845 (65)
1845
Bridlington
to Gilling
1853 (53)
1846
Malton
Kirkham Abbey
Burdale
1853 (p 50, 58)
Driffield
to Newcastle
1845
SHLR 1922 (32)
1847 (65)
1890 (65)
1846
Hornsea
to Harrogate
YORK
(81)
1913
DVLR (73)
(p 26, 68)
Londesborough
1864 (64)
to Leeds and Sheffield
1912 (65)
1865 (65)
Beverley
1871 (83)
Market Weighton
1848 (65)
1898 (p 30, 60)
Drewton Tunnel
1885
to Leeds
HBR 1885 (p 55, 59)
(p 55, 64)
HULL
to Doncaster
Selby
1840
1854 (64)
Withernsea
to Cudworth
(p 32, 59)
1869
to Doncaster
Goole
1849
1848
MSLR
to Grimsby
SHR 1915 (51)

0 km 10
0 miles 6

N

ALL LINES IN OWNERSHIP OF NORTH EASTERN RAILWAY PRIOR TO 1922 EXCEPT:

DVLR Derwent Valley Light Railway
HBR   Hull & Barnsley Railway
MSLR Manchester, Sheffield & Lincolnshire Railway
SHLR Sand Hutton Light Railway (18 inch gauge)
SHR   Spurn Head Railway (Ministry of Defence)

Former North Eastern Railway lines shown in black, other lines shown in red.

HULL

to Bridlington
to Hornsea
1885
1864 (64)
1853
(p 24, 68)
1854 (p 64, 68)
Cannon St.
1848 (p 64, 68)
(69)
1914
to Withernsea
to Cudworth
1924
1846
1885 (64)
1965
Paragon
Victoria Dock
Alexandra Dock
King George Dock
(65)
1962
1848
1840 (82)
Manor House St.
1906 (p 38)
Ferry 1849 (81)
to Selby 1840
Saltend
River Humber

▬▬▬	North Eastern Railway
▬ ▬ ▬	Hull & Barnsley "
▬▬▬	NE and H & B Joint " (freight)

RELIGION AND SOCIAL
PROVISION

MEDIEVAL PARISH CHURCHES AND CHAPELS

David Neave

The map opposite shows the distribution of two categories of medieval places of worship - parish churches, and dependent parochial chapels or chapels-of-ease established to serve communities living at a distance from their parish church.[1] Within these categories the survival of any medieval fabric is indicated, whether it is a section of masonry or a complete structure. In some cases the church or chapel has been totally rebuilt on the medieval site, leaving no original feature or, as in the case of the majority of chapels, the site was cleared in the post-Reformation period.[2]

The earliest churches are likely to have been built in the riding in the seventh or eighth century following the re-introduction of Christianity on the conversion of King Edwin by Paulinus in 627. With the exception of the monastery founded by Bishop John of York at Beverley by 700, there is little evidence of ecclesiastical buildings in the East Riding before the early eleventh century.[3] The most substantial Anglo-Saxon architectural remains are the towers of Skipwith and Wharram-le-Street churches, both of the eleventh century, and the contemporary inscription at Aldbrough which records that 'Ulf ordered the church to be built for himself and for Gunwaru's soul'. Fifteen East Riding churches have fragments of Anglo-Saxon sculpture, the largest collection being at Sherburn.[4]

Sherburn is one of the 52 identifiable places in the East Riding with a church, church and priest, or priest recorded in the Domesday Book. In the three cases where a priest alone is mentioned it is likely that there was also a church. It is clear that the Domesday Book does not provide a complete record of the churches in the riding in 1086. For example, there is no mention of a church at Aldbrough or at Wharram-le-Street, nor at Kirby Underdale or Kirby Grindalythe where the place name indicates the presence of a church. The first documentary record of Wharram Percy church is c.1210-20, but excavations on the church site revealed post-holes thought to relate to a timber church of the tenth century. This was replaced by a small stone church, consisting of a rectangular nave and chancel, of the late tenth or early eleventh century. The earliest architectural features in the standing structure are of the early twelfth century.[5] There are 99 East Riding churches and chapels with Norman stone work, ranging from re-used fragments at Hessle and Patrington to the largely Norman churches at Newbald, Garton-on-the-Wolds, Kirkburn, Weaverthorpe and Goodmanham (in descending order of importance). A further seventeen churches have Norman fonts.

The medieval pattern of parishes had been largely established by the thirteenth century. The earliest churches, often built at the principal settlement of a major Anglo-Saxon estate, were 'minsters' or 'mother churches' serving an extensive area which gradually would be divided into smaller sections or parishes. The identification of probable minster churches in the East Riding is based chiefly on the evidence provided by the size and composition of ancient parishes. Pocklington church, built by the eleventh century in the principal settlement of an important royal manor, was clearly a minster church. Here the ancient parish covered 26,360 acres and included eighteen townships until 1252, when it was subdivided on the establishment of the parishes of Barmby Moor with Fangfoss, Great Givendale with Millington, Hayton with Bielby, and Thornton with Allerthorpe. The extensive parish of Howden, covering 18,348 acres and including fifteen townships, remained intact until the mid-nineteenth century.

Few East Riding parishes were as large as these, but over 60 per cent comprised two or more townships and it was here that chapels-of-ease were built in the middle ages. There is evidence for the existence of a medieval chapel in the majority of dependent townships in the East Riding but the list is by no means comprehensive. Information comes from a wide range of sources, for example archbishops' registers, wills, chantry surveys, field names, mid-seventeenth century parliamentary surveys and monastic deeds.[6]

Some chapels were in existence by the twelfth century, but for others the first record is as late as the early sixteenth century. Many may have been short-lived. The chapels of All Saints, Eastburn, St Mary Magdalene, Southburn and St James, Tibthorpe (all in Kirkburn parish) are first mentioned in a will of 1483. There is no further record of the chapel at Eastburn, but weekly services were still being held at Southburn and Tibthorpe chapels when visited by commissioners in 1544. Tibthorpe chapel, deemed 'necessary for slow and impotent persons that cannot go to the parish church to hear mass', had a gilt chalice, vestments, albs, an altar cloth and two small bells. Southburn was amongst the numerous chapels that passed into the hands of John Bellew, the notorious surveyor of Crown lands in the East Riding. By 1556 Bellew had demolished at least eleven chapels for their lead and building materials.[7]

Many parochial chapels were demolished in the mid-sixteenth century, but some survived, often in a neglected state, into the seventeenth century and beyond. Bewholme chapel was said to be in decay in 1615, as was Out Newton chapel in 1650. Ruins of the latter still stood near the cliffs in south Holderness in 1911. A number continued in use, for example at Skidby where the chapel became a parish church in its own right in 1859.

Notes and bibliography on page 149

MEDIEVAL PARISH CHURCHES AND CHAPELS

MEDIEVAL PARISH CHURCHES

⊙   Church with some medieval fabric

●   Post-1700 church on site of medieval parish church

⊕   Site of medieval parish church

MEDIEVAL CHAPELS

⊙   Chapel or former chapel, with some medieval fabric

●   Post-1700 church or chapel on site of medieval chapel

⊕   Site of medieval chapel

CHURCHES IN DOMESDAY BOOK : 1086

CP   Church and priest

C   Church only

P   Priest only

MEDIEVAL RELIGIOUS HOUSES
Susan Neave

Two monastic houses are recorded in the East Riding in the Saxon period - a nunnery at Watton, mentioned by Bede, and the monastery of *Inderauuda* ('in the wood of Deira'), the site of which is usually identified with Beverley. A monastic revival in this part of Yorkshire began in the early twelfth century with the founding of a house of Augustinian canons by Walter de Gant at Bridlington around 1113.[1] Augustinian priories were subsequently established at Kirkham (*c.*1122), Warter (1132) and North Ferriby (?*c.*1140).[2] Almost two centuries later, in 1320, Thomas Wake was licensed to found another house of Augustinian canons, at Cottingham near Hull. Building work had already commenced when the priory was moved to a new site further south in 1326, where it became known as Haltemprice priory.

The Benedictine presence in the East Riding was confined to an alien cell and a handful of nunneries. Burstall priory at Skeffling, close to the Humber estuary, was an alien cell of Benedictine monks from Aumale abbey, founded *c.*1115. In 1396 it was sold to Kirkstall abbey in the West Riding; there is no record of its existence after this date. The houses of Benedictine nuns were at Nunburnholme (*c.*1150), Nunkeeling (*c.*1152), Wilberfoss (by 1153) and Thicket (by 1180). A Benedictine nunnery was also founded at Yedingham, sometime before 1158. Although the village of Yedingham lies within the East Riding, the priory site was on the other side of the river Derwent, in the North Riding.

The Cistercians, a reform movement of the Benedictines, entered the East Riding *c.*1150, when William le Gros founded Meaux abbey. The Cistercian nunnery at Swine also dates from the mid-twelfth century.[3]

A new monastic order was founded in England by Gilbert of Sempringham (Lincolnshire) in the early twelfth century. Some Gilbertine priories were double houses, accepting both canons and nuns, for example Watton, established *c.*1150. The canons followed the rule of St Augustine, and the nuns the rule of St Benedict. The East Riding's other Gilbertine house, Ellerton priory, established by 1207, was for canons only.

A Carthusian priory was founded at Hull in 1378 by Michael de la Pole. Attached to the priory was a hospital or maison dieu for thirteen poor women and thirteen poor men. The present almshouse known as the Charterhouse has its origins in the medieval hospital.

The principal mendicant orders were to be found at Hull and Beverley. A Carmelite friary was established in Hull *c.*1290. It moved to a new site in 1307; the street called Whitefriargate takes its name from the friary. The Augustinian friars held land in Hull from 1303, and were granted a messuage and plot of land on which to build in 1317 (see page 35). At Beverley a house of Franciscan or Grey friars was established sometime before 1267. It moved to a new site outside Keldgate Bar in 1297. The Dominican friary was founded by 1240, on a site close to the Minster (see page 41).

The military order known as the Knights Templars was introduced to England in 1128. Its purpose was to protect pilgrims making journeys to Jerusalem and to defend the Holy City during the time of the Crusades. When the order was abolished in 1312 many of its possessions passed to the Knights Hospitallers, another military order which had been established to care for poor and sick travellers and crusaders. A preceptory of the Knights Templars was founded at Faxfleet in Howdenshire, probably before 1220. At its dissolution it was the wealthiest preceptory in Yorkshire. The Knights Hospitallers had a preceptory at Beverley, founded *c.*1201. This was dissolved in 1540. The site has recently been excavated.

Colleges of secular canons were established at Beverley, Howden, Lowthorpe, Sutton-on-Hull and Hemingbrough. Throughout the East Riding there were many small hospitals (not mapped) for the poor or infirm, including leper houses. A number of these hospitals were directly associated with monastic houses, for example the hospital of St Giles at Beverley, which was annexed to Warter priory.

Most of the East Riding's religious houses were dissolved between 1536 and 1539, followed by the colleges of secular canons a decade later. Although the majority of monastic buildings were partially destroyed at the Reformation, and their ruins systematically plundered in the following centuries, remnants survive. The most impressive monastic remains in the East Riding are those of Kirkham priory, on the banks of the river Derwent. These include the late thirteenth-century gatehouse with elaborate heraldry. The gatehouse or Bayle also survives at Bridlington, together with the aisled nave of the monastic church. At Swine part of the late twelfth century nuns' church survives. The Gilbertine priory at Watton is represented by the prior's lodging, a brick and stone building dating largely from the late fourteenth and fifteenth centuries. It is now a private house. An excavation of the priory site was carried out in the late nineteenth century.

Monastic stone is evident in many post-Reformation buildings, for example Howsham Hall near Kirkham, built *c.*1610, Manor House (Coatgares) Farm at Warter, which dates from the early eighteenth century, and in the foundations of houses in the High Street, Bridlington. Haltemprice Priory Farm incorporates stonework from the priory site, as does Manor House Farm at Nunkeeling. Thirteenth-century floor tiles are amongst the artefacts found on the Meaux abbey site.

Remains of friary buildings are confined to the remnant of the Dominican friary at Beverley, which may represent the fifteenth-century dormitory and library, rebuilt after a fire in 1449. It is now a Youth Hostel. The site of the Augustinian friary in Hull has recently been excavated prior to redevelopment.

Notes and bibliography on page 149

MEDIEVAL RELIGIOUS HOUSES

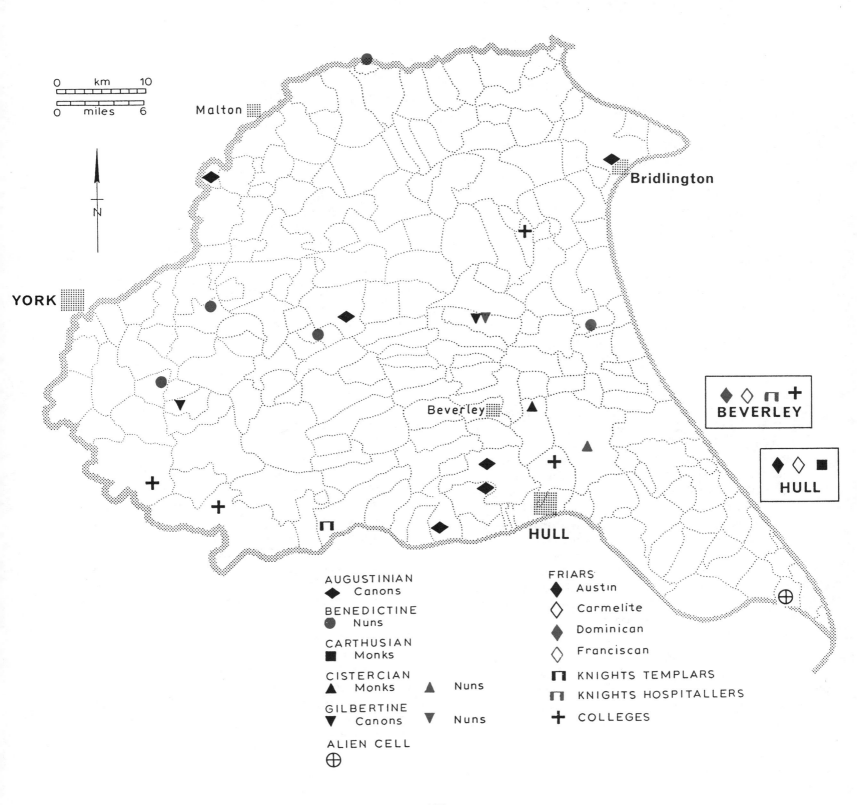

0 km 10

0 miles 6

N

Malton

YORK

Bridlington

Beverley

HULL

AUGUSTINIAN
Canons

BENEDICTINE
Nuns

CARTHUSIAN
Monks

CISTERCIAN
Monks   Nuns

GILBERTINE
Canons   Nuns

ALIEN CELL

FRIARS
Austin
Carmelite
Dominican
Franciscan

KNIGHTS TEMPLARS
KNIGHTS HOSPITALLERS
COLLEGES

BEVERLEY

HULL

PROTESTANT NONCONFORMITY AND ROMAN CATHOLICISM IN THE SEVENTEENTH AND EIGHTEENTH CENTURIES

Rodney W. Ambler

The seventeenth and eighteenth centuries were a period of considerable change for the Protestant dissenting churches, both in terms of the legal framework within which they worked and of their spiritual development. The relaxation of prohibitions on the activity of Protestant nonconformists with the Toleration Act of 1689, meant that they were free to build chapels and meeting houses, a particularly important development for the study of the geography of religious practice, since fixed and purposely provided centres of worship can be identified and mapped.

Until permanent meeting places were provided worship took place in rooms in private houses or even outbuildings. This might be only for relatively short periods of time since owners or occupiers could move, alter their opinions or be forced to cease allowing their premises to be used in this way. This meant that the location of Protestant nonconformist worship could change relatively frequently. However, such changes usually took place within areas where a particular denomination had enough adherents for them to gather a reasonably stable congregation, so that the provision of a chapel or meeting house usually represented a period of consolidation in the history of a local church.

Independent and Presbyterian meeting houses were built in Hull and the markets towns of the area from the 1690s. Those in Hull, Beverley and Bridlington were reported as having congregations of between 300 and 500 in the period 1715-29, and there were also large churches in the neighbourhood of Hull in Cottingham, Swanland and South Cave. Independents and Presbyterians also met in Howden. The location of these meetings was related to the composition of their congregations. There were a few East Riding gentlemen and women who favoured dissenting preachers, but their main support was in urban churches. Here the artisans, merchants and tradesmen of the towns and neighbouring villages gathered to worship. In the 30 years after 1662, clergymen who had lost their Church of England livings as a result of the Restoration settlement sometimes ministered where they resided, although it needed favourable milieux, both in terms of potential congregations and freedom from persecution, for permanent churches to develop from their work.

The establishment of an hierarchical structure of meetings by the Society of Friends or Quakers in the 1660s systematised their organisation. They had been active in the East Riding since the 1650s and the distribution of their meeting houses reflects their strength among farmers and rural craftsmen and tradesmen in the seventeenth century. This was particularly marked in Holderness, where a few leading families were influential in sustaining a Quaker presence, although numbers began to decline from the early eighteenth century.

Movement into the towns and the development of a middle class less closely tied to the land meant that meetings with an urban base became relatively more important in Quaker life.

The most significant changes in the geographical distribution of Protestant nonconformity in the East Riding during the seventeenth and eighteenth centuries were the result of the evangelical revival, and particularly the development of Methodism in the later eighteenth century. The effect of the revival on the older dissenting churches was more limited. It was not until the late 1790s that Fish Street Chapel in Hull began to establish churches in Holderness, while the small number of Baptist churches in East Yorkshire did not begin to expand until after the end of the eighteenth century.

The gains of the evangelical revival in the East Riding were consolidated primarily through the institutions of the Methodist connexion. There were Methodists in Hull from the 1740s, but York was a more important centre and Methodism spread from the city into the market towns and villages of the Vales of York and Pickering in the eighteenth century. The distribution of chapels and meetings shows the extent to which its organisation, with its city-based circuits, provided the institutional framework through which local societies were sustained in the places where Methodists were able to meet and build chapels.

The distribution of centres of Catholicism in the East Riding in the eighteenth century reflects older patterns of worship and allegiance rather than the changes which began to affect the English Catholic community in that period. Catholicism had depended for its survival on the patronage and protection of local Catholic gentry. Services were held in their houses and attended by people from the area, many of whom were their tenants and servants. From the early eighteenth century, rooms began to be set aside as chapels in these houses. This pattern of provision was, however, changing and the first separately built Catholic chapel in the East Riding, at Marton in Holderness, is indicative, but not a measure, of this process. Although a local gentleman, William Constable, paid for it, the chapel, which was built in 1789, was representative of new developments within the English Catholic community. Dependence on the gentry lessened as a Catholic middle class of tradesmen and farmers became more prominent, while migration led to the growth of an urban Catholic community who provided and exercised a greater degree of control over their own places of worship.

The growth of Methodism increased the number of places in the East Riding in which there were Protestant nonconformist chapels and meetings by nearly a third, although the situation in the Roman Catholic church was more static. Yet, despite the considerable growth in Protestant nonconformity, there were still at the end of the eighteenth century only 64 out of the 184 parishes in the area which had places of worship not belonging to the Church of England.

Bibliography on page 150

PROTESTANT NONCONFORMITY AND ROMAN CATHOLICISM :
17th-18th CENTURIES

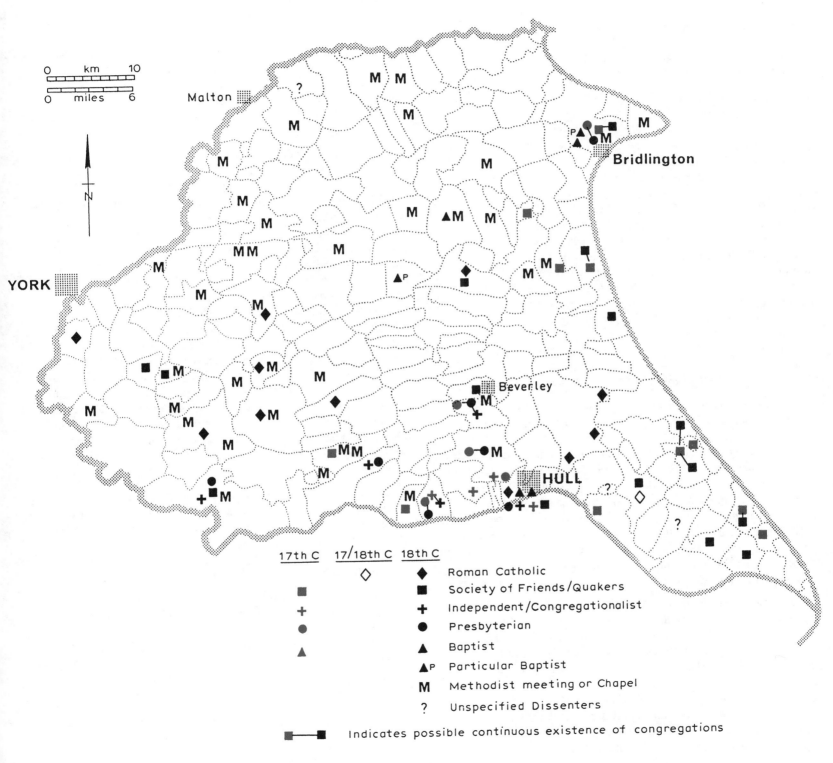

17th C	17/18th C	18th C	
	◇	◆	Roman Catholic
■		■	Society of Friends/Quakers
+		+	Independent/Congregationalist
●		●	Presbyterian
▲		▲	Baptist
		▲P	Particular Baptist
		M	Methodist meeting or Chapel
		?	Unspecified Dissenters

■——■ Indicates possible continuous existence of congregations

PROTESTANT NONCONFORMIST CHAPELS AND MEETING HOUSES

David and Susan Neave

The map shows the location of all Protestant nonconformist chapels and meeting houses recorded in the East Riding (excluding Hull[1]) between the late seventeenth century and the outbreak of the First World War.

The earliest dissenting groups - Baptists, Independents, Presbyterians and Quakers - all built meeting houses in the riding in the late seventeenth and early eighteenth centuries. The first three groups were largely confined to the towns or nearby villages. Presbyterian meeting houses were built at Beverley (by 1694), Cottingham (by 1697) and Bridlington (1698); Independent meeting houses at Swanland (1693), South Cave (1718) and Howden (1722); and a sole Baptist meeting house at Bridlington (1699, rebuilt 1713). The latter sect was said to have been introduced into Bridlington by a Scotsman seeking shelter at the port on his way home from London, where he had been converted. Bridlington also had one of the earliest recorded Quaker meeting houses (1678), but generally the Society of Friends had its main following in villages throughout Holderness, the Vale of York and the Wolds. Quaker meeting houses were built at Skipsea, Elloughton, Owstwick (c.1670), North Cave (1687), Beverley (1702), Hutton Cranswick and Barmby Moor (1707), Hornsea (1711) and Welwick (1718). Quaker membership in the East Riding declined sharply after 1720 but isolated groups built meeting houses at East Cottingwith (1788), Knapton (by 1815) and Bubwith (1879).

In the wake of the late eighteenth century religious revival the Baptists and Independents grew in strength, and many new chapels were built in the East Riding, sometimes as a direct result of missionary work by established congregations. Baptists from Bridlington opened chapels at Driffield, Hunmanby and Kilham, and members of Fish Street chapel, Hull, were responsible for the building of eight Congregational chapels in Holderness in the years 1801-20. In some cases it was the wealth and influence of a single person that led to a chapel being built, as at Thorngumbald where the Hull whaling ship owner, Sir Samuel Standidge, built an Independent chapel in 1800. Despite the increase in Congregational and Baptist chapels, by the mid-nineteenth century they were still insignificant in number compared to Methodist chapels.

Methodism, which had reached York by 1743 and Hull by 1746, spread rapidly into the East Riding but it was not until the 1770s that purpose-built meeting houses were opened. The earliest were in the market towns and larger villages - Bridlington (1775), Great Driffield (1777), Beverley (1782), Market Weighton (1786), Holme-upon-Spalding Moor (1787), Garton-on-the-Wolds (1788), Howden (1788), Kilham and Newport (1789) and Acklam (1790). Newport, a newly established industrial settlement, and Acklam, a quarrying village, were typical of the places where Methodism found its earliest followers, but support was as strong in purely agricultural communities. Over 100 Methodist chapels had been built in the riding by the beginning of 1819, when the dominance of Wesleyan Methodism was challenged by the arrival of Primitive Methodism, which had spread steadily up the Trent valley since its establishment in 1811. The 'missionary' work of William Clowes and 'Praying Johnny' Oxtoby met with immediate success, and within a surprisingly short time Primitive Methodist chapels had been built in every part of the East Riding. The first to be opened was at North Cave in 1819, followed by chapels at Pocklington (1820), Acklam, Flamborough, Flixton, Great Driffield, Leavening, Melbourne, Middleton, North Duffield, Seaton Ross and Skirlaugh (all 1821).

By the later nineteenth century there were few settlements without a Methodist chapel. Many of the places without a chapel were estate villages with a resident landowner, for example Birdsall, Boynton, Brantingham, Escrick, Everingham, Londesborough, Rise, Scampston and Winestead. At Warter in the 1860s Lord Muncaster actively prevented the Primitive Methodists from meeting in any building in the village or acquiring land on which to build a chapel. Other landowners, such as Sir Tatton Sykes II at Sledmere, accepted the fact that most tenants were likely to be Methodist, and gave or leased land for both Primitive and Wesleyan chapels. Of the 241 East Riding settlements with chapels, 115 had both Wesleyan and Primitive Methodist chapels, 91 only Wesleyan and 31 only Primitive. Neither group dominated any area of the riding except perhaps in the western part of the Vale of York, where Wesleyan Methodist chapels were more numerous. The many other Methodist splinter groups had little following in the East Riding. There were Methodist New Connexion chapels at Dunswell and Meaux, and both Independent Methodist and Wesleyan Methodist Association chapels at Heslington. The Church Methodists built chapels in 1825 at Beverley, Cherry Burton and Woodmansey, and the Wesleyan Reformers had chapels at Ellerker, Bridlington and Beverley.

Outside Hull there were few buildings belonging to the category 'other denominations'. There were Salvation Army citadels at Beverley, Bridlington, Cottingham, Great Driffield and Norton. The presence of an Inghamite chapel at Howden can be explained by the town's proximity to the West Riding where this sect, followers of the eighteenth century evangelist Benjamin Ingham, was at its strongest.

The two peak periods of rural chapel building, 1820-45 and 1860-70, coincided with periods of religious revival and a relatively buoyant economy. Agricultural depression and a great decrease in rural population led to a decline in chapel building from the late 1870s. The earliest chapels are simple rectangular buildings of brick with hipped or gabled roofs, but from the mid-nineteenth century they become much more elaborate, adopting a Classical Italianate or Gothic style. The average cost of an East Riding village chapel rose from £111 in 1820-39 to £731 in 1880-1909.

Note and bibliography on page 150

PROTESTANT NONCONFORMIST CHAPELS AND MEETING HOUSES

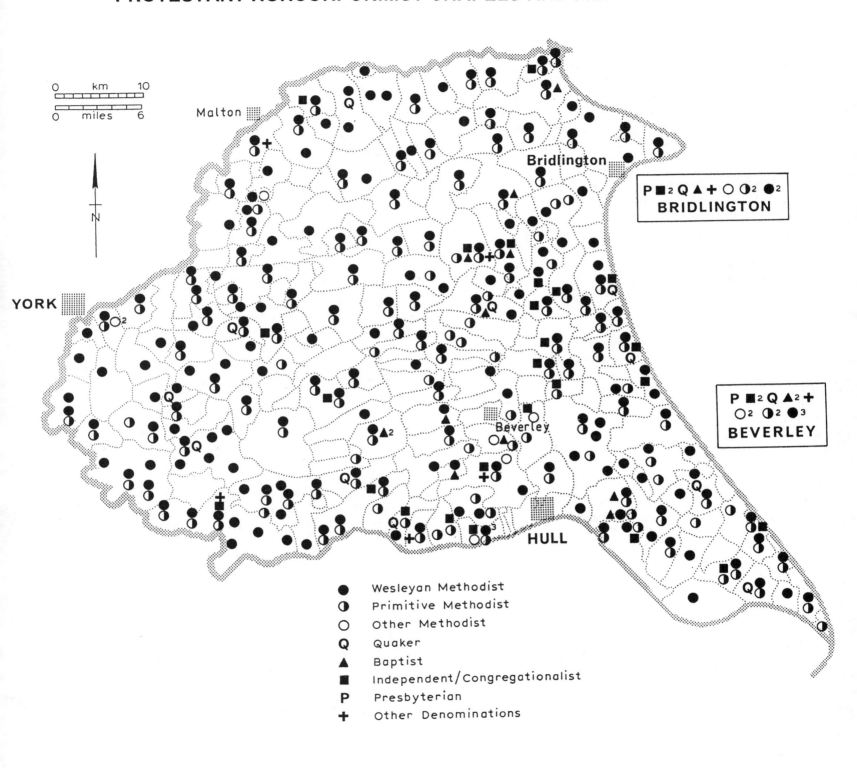

P ■₂ Q ▲ + ○ ◑₂ ●₂
BRIDLINGTON

P ■₂ Q ▲₂ +
○₂ ◑₂ ●₃
BEVERLEY

● Wesleyan Methodist
◑ Primitive Methodist
○ Other Methodist
Q Quaker
▲ Baptist
■ Independent/Congregationalist
P Presbyterian
+ Other Denominations

ANGLICAN CHURCH BUILDING: 1701-1900

David Neave

Between the Reformation and the early eighteenth century there was a hiatus in church building in the East Riding.[1] Although churchwardens' accounts record regular expenditure on the maintenance and furnishings of churches in this period, there was neglect, particularly by the recipients of the great tithes who often failed in their duty to repair the chancel. At Eastrington, an inscription records that the chancel was rebuilt after it 'fel' in 1632, but when the roof and upper walls of the choir of Howden collapsed in 1696 it was left a ruin.[2]

With the exception of the restoration of Beverley Minster, 1717-31, no major church works were carried out in the East Riding throughout the Georgian period. Churches were crammed with galleries, box pews and three-decker pulpits, stonework was patched with brick, and domestic sash windows were introduced, but rarely was a church wholly rebuilt or a new one provided for an expanding community. Some 20 churches were built in the East Riding in the eighteenth century, of which all but one - St John the Evangelist, Hull, 1791-2 - were in rural areas. Half of these are close together in the Vale of York. The earliest and best of this group of modest brick churches is at Thorganby, with a nave of 1710 and chancel of 1719. Here the medieval tower was retained, as at Everingham, c.1763 and Wheldrake, 1778-9, which are larger buildings with apsidal chancels and some architectural pretension. The churches at Yapham, 1777-8; Barlby 1779-80; East Cottingwith, 1780; and Seaton Ross, 1788, differ little from contemporary nonconformist chapels except for the presence of a tower or cupola. Costs were met by subscriptions or gifts from the patron or landowner. At Wressle the absentee landlord, the earl of Egremont, supplied bricks and salvaged material for the new church, built in 1799 to replace the chapel destroyed in a fire at the castle.[3] It is a mean building compared to the charming Gothick church at Boynton, built in 1768 by Sir George Strickland.

In the first four decades of the nineteenth century only eighteen churches were built or rebuilt in the East Riding. Around 1840 the pace of church building suddenly accelerated and, under the influence of the Oxford Movement and the Ecclesiological Society, the quality of the church architecture improved dramatically. In the years 1841-1900 some 152 Anglican churches were built, rebuilt or extensively restored in Hull and the East Riding, the numbers rising each decade - 23 in 1841-50, 27 in 1851-60, 33 in 1861-70 and 44 in 1871-80 - before dropping to only twelve in the 1880s and thirteen in the 1890s. Fifteen of the new churches were in Hull, two each in Beverley and Bridlington and one in Great Driffield; the rest were built in villages.

Victorian church building in the countryside owed much to the patronage of wealthy landowners. In the western part of the riding the Lords Wenlock and family spent £26,000 on rebuilding the church in their estate village of Escrick in 1856-7, paid for a new church at Kexby in 1852 and met half the cost of the restoration of Riccall church in 1864-5. Similarly, the church at South Dalton was built at a cost of £25,000 by the third Lord Hotham in 1858-61, following the lead of his land agent, James Hall, who spent £5,000 rebuilding the smaller church at Scorborough in 1857-9. Such expenditure and building activity is modest in comparison to the achievements of Sir Tatton Sykes II, fifth baronet of Sledmere who, between 1863 and 1913, built seven new churches on his estate and restored another eight. His father, Sir Tatton I, had already restored three churches on the Wolds and built one at Hilston on the Holderness coast. Sir Tatton II spent an average of £10,000 on each of the churches, employing the leading ecclesiastical craftsmen and artists and the foremost architects - J.L. Pearson,[4] G.E. Street[5] and Temple Moore. Street designed seven new churches for Sir Tatton II - Wansford, Thixendale, Fimber, Helperthorpe, West Lutton, East Heslerton and Duggleby (the last was never built) - and restored or refurnished a further five, including Garton-on-the-Wolds.[6] The agricultural depression of the 1880s curtailed Sir Tatton's church building activities, but in 1893-8 he spent over £60,000 on rebuilding the church at Sledmere.

It is significant that two of the areas with noticeably few Victorian Anglican churches - the southern Vale of York and southern Holderness - are the locations of the estates of the major Roman Catholic landowners: the Constables of Burton Constable, Lord Herries of Everingham, the Langdales of Houghton, and the Stourtons of Holme-upon-Spalding Moor. The southern part of the Vale of York provides a particular contrast to the northern Wolds in quality and quantity of Victorian churches. It is an area of large ecclesiastical parishes - five of them (Howden, Hemingbrough, Eastrington, Holme and Bubwith) covered 55,000 acres and included 32 townships, many a considerable distance from the parish church. In 1851 this vast area was served by only five medieval parish churches and three chapels-of-ease. In the second half of the century there was a limited increase in provision. Three new parishes were carved out - Laxton (1858), with a new church built 1875-6, Barmby-on-the-Marsh (1864), where the former chapel-of-ease was restored in 1870, and Newport (1895). It had taken the Anglican church a long time to provide a place of worship in the last settlement, which had grown up at the edge of three parishes in the late eighteenth century. The new church of 1897-9, an ambitious urban-style building, cost £7,000 in contrast to the £350 spent by T. Sotheron Estcourt, a former Home Secretary, on the nearby chapel-of-ease at Bursea (Holme-upon-Spalding Moor), designed by William Butterfield (1870-2).[7]

A number of nineteenth century churches have been demolished, two in the rural areas at Acklam and Leppington, and fifteen in Hull, where only three Victorian Anglican churches remain - St Matthew, Boulevard, 1870; St John the Baptist, St George's Road, 1878; and St Giles, Marfleet, 1884.[8]

Notes on page 150

ANGLICAN CHURCH BUILDING : 1701-1900

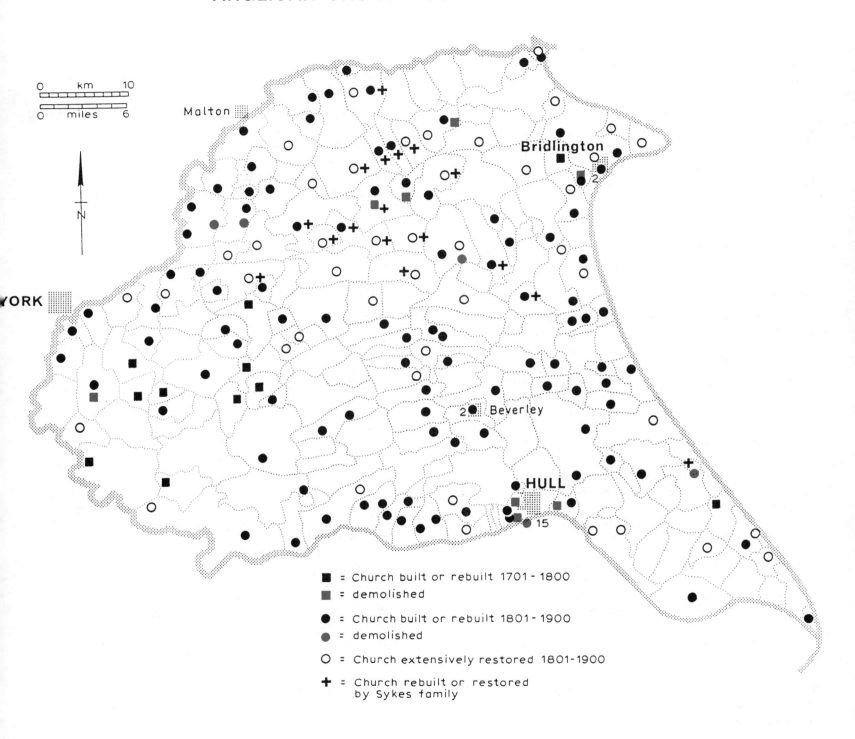

= Church built or rebuilt 1701 - 1800

= demolished

= Church built or rebuilt 1801 - 1900

= demolished

○ = Church extensively restored 1801-1900

✝ = Church rebuilt or restored by Sykes family

ATTENDANCE AT RELIGIOUS WORSHIP, 1851

Rodney W. Ambler

The 1851 Census of Religious Worship was a unique event in British religious history. For the first and last time the government obtained information on attendance at religious worship throughout England and Wales. On Census Sunday - 30 March, the same day as the decennial census of population - material was gathered on the numbers who attended services, the amount of accommodation available for worship and, for some Anglican churches, on endowments.

The original returns for individual places of worship are preserved in the Public Record Office, London, and are the ultimate source for any investigation into religious practice at a local level. An analysis of them was published as a Parliamentary Paper and the registration districts used in it provide the basis of this map of attendance at religious worship in the East Riding in 1851. It includes the municipal borough of Hull as well as material for the whole Riding. Where the boundaries of registration districts overlap those of the county the figures have been recalculated to include only places in it, indicated on the map by the word 'Parts'.[1]

Attendance at religious worship in each registration district has been mapped in two ways - to show the proportion of the total population present at worship in the morning, afternoon and evening of Sunday 30 March (an index of attendance) and the percentage share of these worshippers who attended three main denominations or groups of denominations. These were the Church of England, the various branches of Methodism and a third, more heterogeneous group in which the Independent churches had the largest attendances over the whole county. This group also included Roman Catholics with the next largest attendances, followed by the Baptists, smaller groups of Quakers and Unitarians, three congregations belonging to the Mormons, and single congregations of Scottish Presbyterians, Brethren and Jews. There were also four isolated congregations who do not appear to have had any wider allegiance.

The largest proportion of the population of the East Riding as a whole worshipped on the morning of Sunday 30 March, when the index of attendance was 23 per cent. This was also the time when the third group of churches had their highest attendances. In the evening the full strength of Methodism in the East Riding became apparent. The overall index of attendance then was slightly lower than in the morning, but attendance at the various branches of Methodism constituted just over 65 per cent of total worshippers. These would include people who had fulfilled their obligations to the established church by attending its morning or afternoon services, although the 10,592 Primitive Methodists in 134 chapels and meetings were less likely to have this dual loyalty.

The composition and times of the largest indices of attendance varied from district to district. In Beverley, an index of attendance of 29 per cent in the morning, of whom just over 60 per cent attended the Church of England, showed the Anglican church at its most successful in fulfilling its mission as the national church. There were parts of the East Riding where the Church of England attained an even higher percentage share of worshippers, particularly in the part of the York registration district which was in the East Riding, and also in the Patrington, Skirlaugh and Scarborough districts, but these were based on lower indices of attendance than in Beverley.

Although there was some variation across the East Riding, attendances at the Church of England were generally higher in the morning and afternoon, while those of the Methodists were greater in the evening. The level of attendance at the other churches was more varied, although when their attendances are added to those of the Methodists the number of worshippers exceeded those at the Church of England in the East Riding as a whole at all times of the day.

Just over 77 per cent of all worshippers in Bridlington district in the evening when the index of attendance, at 34 per cent, was the highest in the East Riding, were Methodists. In Driffield, Howden, Pocklington, Selby and Skirlaugh districts, Methodist, and particularly Wesleyan Methodist, attendances outnumbered those of the Church of England at both afternoon and evening services. There were, however, almost as many Primitive Methodist worshippers (1660) at evening services in Driffield registration district as there were Wesleyans. The differences in the relative success of the various branches of Methodism reflects the strength of Wesleyan institutions in some areas from the eighteenth century (see page 106). In the first half of the nineteenth century the Primitive Methodists reached out to social groups less influenced by the Wesleyans and this was seen in their greater comparative success in the Driffield area.

The lowest index of attendance in the East Riding was three per cent at afternoon services in Hull municipal borough. Hull was exceptional because there were no Methodist services in the afternoon, whilst the distribution of the percentage share of worshippers at all services in the city showed the greater strength in the city of the third group of churches. Nonetheless, the indices of the overall levels of attendance at morning and evening services were comparable with those for the rest of the East Riding.

The general level of religious observance of the people of Hull reflected that in the countryside from which many of them had migrated, although the city offered more varied opportunities for religious practice. The lower level of accommodation in the churches and chapels of Hull in proportion to its population, compared with that in the rural East Riding, was indicative of the problems faced by the churches as they sought to maintain allegiances developed in a rural context. When the results of the 1851 Census of Religious Worship are mapped, the distribution of these allegiances becomes apparent.

Note on page 150

ATTENDANCE AT RELIGIOUS WORSHIP : 1851

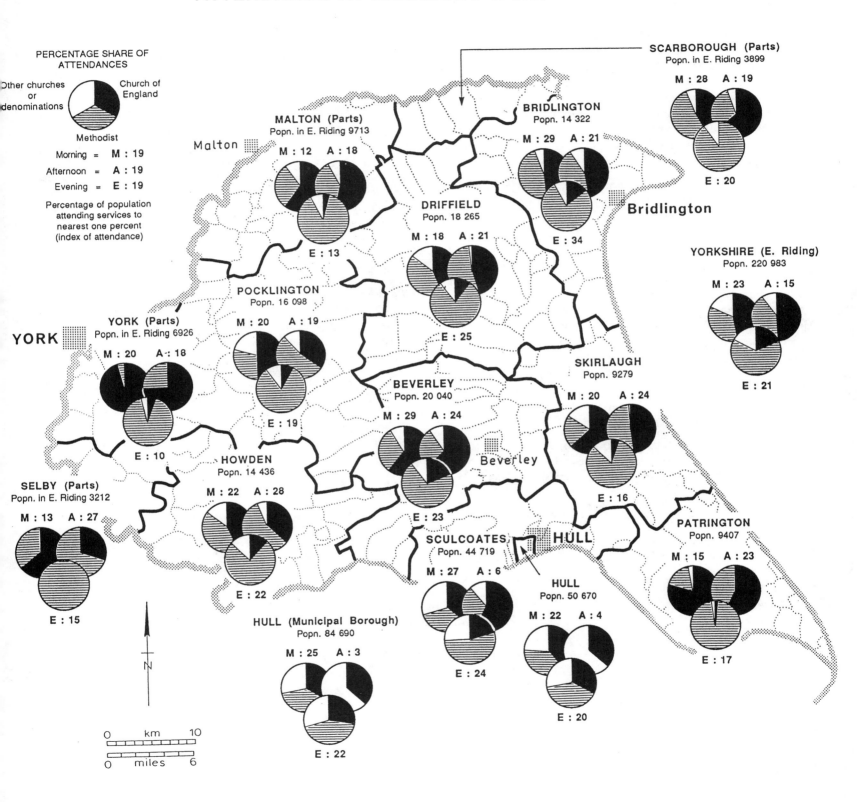

PERCENTAGE SHARE OF ATTENDANCES

Other churches or denominations — Church of England

Methodist

Morning = M : 19
Afternoon = A : 19
Evening = E : 19

Percentage of population attending services to nearest one percent (index of attendance)

Malton

SCARBOROUGH (Parts)
Popn. in E. Riding 3899
M : 28   A : 19
E : 20

MALTON (Parts)
Popn. in E. Riding 9713
M : 12   A : 18
E : 13

BRIDLINGTON
Popn. 14 322
M : 29   A : 21
E : 34

Bridlington

DRIFFIELD
Popn. 18 265
M : 18   A : 21
E : 25

YORKSHIRE (E. Riding)
Popn. 220 983
M : 23   A : 15
E : 21

YORK

POCKLINGTON
Popn. 16 098
M : 20   A : 19
E : 19

YORK (Parts)
Popn. in E. Riding 6926
M : 20   A : 18
E : 10

SKIRLAUGH
Popn. 9279
M : 20   A : 24
E : 16

BEVERLEY
Popn. 20 040
M : 29   A : 24
E : 23

Beverley

HOWDEN
Popn. 14 436
M : 22   A : 28
E : 22

SELBY (Parts)
Popn. in E. Riding 3212
M : 13   A : 27
E : 15

N

SCULCOATES
Popn. 44 719
M : 27   A : 6
E : 24

HULL
Popn. 50 670
M : 22   A : 4
E : 20

HULL
Popn. 84 690

PATRINGTON
Popn. 9407
M : 15   A : 23
E : 17

HULL (Municipal Borough)
Popn. 84 690
M : 25   A : 3
E : 22

0   km   10
0   miles   6

113

ELEMENTARY EDUCATION: 1850-1902
David Neave

The map plots the distribution of public elementary schools which existed in the East Riding between 1850 and 1902.[1] During this period there were many other schools privately run for profit. In 1851, of the 650 schools recorded in the East Riding outside Hull, 433 were private ventures.[2] Individual references to schools and/or schoolteachers are recorded for most East Riding settlements well before 1850 but purpose-built schools and continuous educational provision were not common before the early nineteenth century, except in the case of charity schools.[3]

The Church of England led the way for more structured provision with the founding, in 1812, of the National Society for Promoting the Education of the Poor in the Principles of the Established Church. The society raised funds, chiefly by voluntary subscription, to support schools. The first National school in the East Riding was opened in Minster Moorgate, Beverley before the end of 1812. Many more followed in the next half-century, particularly after the introduction of school building grants by the government in 1833. The new breed of resident Anglican clergy, imbued with the ideals of the Oxford Movement, were active in school building, men such as Archdeacon Robert Wilberforce at Burton Agnes and Revd Francis Orpen Morris at Nafferton. By 1870 the great majority of primary schools in the East Riding were formally linked with the Anglican church and most were National schools. The Methodist church, despite its strength in the East Riding, provided few schools; only eighteen were built, all Wesleyan, and of these half had closed by 1902.

Landed gentry and their families played a major part in the provision of schools. In 1902 sixty elementary schools in the East Riding were owned by landed families. Lord Middleton, Lord Wenlock and Colonel Harrison-Broadley each owned three but the great church-builder Sir Tatton Sykes led the way with nine village schools, all of which he had built or enlarged.[4] Not all the gentry-schools were Anglican; Roman Catholic squires built schools for their own denomination at Everingham, Holme-upon-Spalding Moor and Marton in Holderness.

Under the 1870 Elementary Education Act where school accommodation was insufficient school boards were established, voluntarily or compulsorily, to levy an education rate. Forty-three school boards were formed in the East Riding, chiefly in the towns and open parishes where church and gentry provision was limited or non-existent. All but five of the boards built new schools, superior in scale and design to most of the National schools. This is particularly so of the schools designed for Hull school board by John Bilson. School boards were abolished by the Education Act of 1902 when four education authorities were recognised for the area - the East Riding County Council, the county borough of Hull and the boroughs of Beverley and Bridlington.

Beverley schools
In 1902 there were ten elementary schools - eight National schools (boys, girls and infants) associated with the Minster and St Mary's parish, a Wesleyan and a Roman Catholic school. Two charity schools had closed since 1850.[5]

Hull schools
In 1902 there some 71 elementary schools. The majority, 42, were board schools, all built since 1874. There were fifteen Church of England schools, six Roman Catholic schools, and one Wesleyan school. Three Anglican and three Wesleyan schools had closed since 1850.[6]

Notes on page 151

East Riding and Hull School Boards and their date of formation[7]

1. Atwick 1876
2. Barmby-on-the-Marsh and Asselby 1874/1893
3. Blacktoft with Yokefleet 1892
4. Bridlington 1879
5. Broomfleet 1880
6. Bubwith 1875
7. Burstwick-cum-Skeckling 1872
8. Burton Fleming 1873
9. Cottingham Without 1877 (part taken into Hull 1883)
10. East Cottingwith 1876
11. Eastrington 1876
12. Faxfleet 1880
13. Fridaythorpe 1880
14. Great Driffield 1871

15. Hedon 1872
16. Hemingbrough 1875
17. Holme-upon-Spalding Moor 1874
18. Holmpton 1876
19. Hornsea with Burton 1884
20. Hutton Cranswick 1872/1895
21. Keyingham 1873
22. Kingston-upon-Hull 1871 (area enlarged 1883 and 1897)
23. Langtoft 1896
24. Langton 1897
25. Melbourne 1875
26. Newington 1879 (dissolved and taken into Hull 1883)
27. Newport Wallingfen 1877
28. Owthorne 1875

29. Preston 1875
30. Reighton 1875
31. Rillington 1874
32. Scalby 1894
33. Skerne 1876
34. South Duffield 1886
35. Spaldington 1875
36. Sutton and Stoneferry 1875 (part taken into Hull 1883, dissolved 1896)
37. Thorngumbald 1875
38. Thwing 1881
39. Walkington 1873
40. Willerby 1875
41. Withernwick 1892
42. Wold Newton 1879
43. Yedingham 1892

ELEMENTARY EDUCATION : 1850-1902

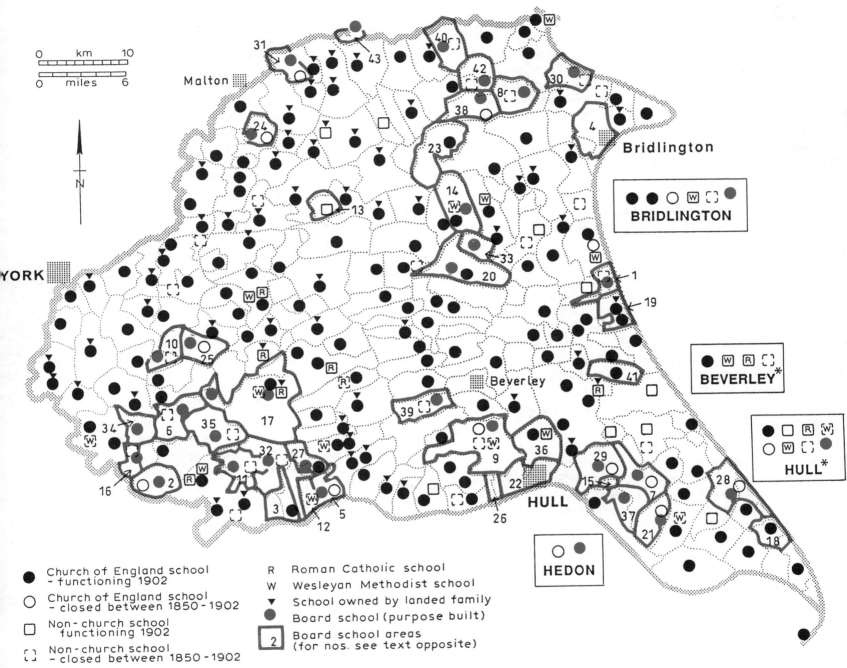

O ———— km ———— 10
O ———— miles ———— 6

Malton

YORK

Bridlington

BRIDLINGTON

BEVERLEY *

HULL *

Beverley

HULL

HEDON

• Church of England school
  - functioning 1902

○ Church of England school
  - closed between 1850-1902

□ Non-church school
  functioning 1902

[] Non-church school
  - closed between 1850-1902

R Roman Catholic school

W Wesleyan Methodist school

▼ School owned by landed family

● Board school (purpose built)

2 Board school areas
   (for nos. see text opposite)

* For fuller details on Beverley and Hull schools see text

FRIENDLY SOCIETIES: 1800-1914
David Neave

During the nineteenth century over 350 friendly societies were established in the East Riding (excluding Hull), all of which had as their primary purpose the provision of a substantial sickness benefit and a decent funeral for members and their wives in return for subscriptions regularly paid into the club 'box'.[1] Friendly societies are of two main types - local societies (autonomous village or town benefit clubs), and branches of the national affiliated order friendly societies. The main affiliated orders with branches (variously known as 'lodges', 'courts' and 'tents') in the East Riding were: the Independent Order of Oddfellows Manchester Unity (IOOF MU), the Grand United Order of Oddfellows (GUOOF), the Ancient Order of Foresters (Foresters), Loyal Order of Ancient Shepherds (Shepherds), United Ancient Order of Druids (Druids), National United Order of Free Gardeners (Gardeners), Independent Order of Rechabites (Rechabites) and the Order of the Sons of Temperance. Most societies, until the twentieth century, restricted their membership to adult males, but there were a few female societies.

The earliest recorded local society was established at Howden in 1751, and by 1830 at least 44 societies had been opened in 27 towns and villages in the riding. Half were based in market towns, with few in purely agricultural settlements. An exception was the Etton Amicable and Friendly Society, founded in 1789. At its peak in 1827 it had 764 members, living in 61 different towns and villages. Many local societies had already closed or were in decline when the affiliated orders arrived in the 1830s. In the years 1830-1912 244 branches of the orders were established in the East Riding, of which 143 were opened in 1836-43.

The affiliated orders combined the functions of the local friendly society with an elaborate ritual, regalia and secrecy more commonly associated with the freemasons. The majority of the orders had their origins in the expanding industrial towns of Lancashire and the West Riding, and it was from the west that they entered the East Riding. The first order to appear was the Independent Order of Oddfellows Manchester Unity, which opened lodges at Howden (1831), Beverley (1832), Market Weighton and Great Driffield (1833), Pocklington (1834) and Bridlington (1836). From these centres the order missioned the surrounding area, so that by 1843 there were 55 Oddfellows lodges in the riding, 39 of them in villages. The development of the second major order, the Ancient Order of Foresters, was similar. The first branch or court was opened at Howden in 1836 by a court from Goole, which in turn had been opened by a Doncaster court the year before. By the end of 1844 48 courts had been opened in the East Riding.

The Shepherds, Gardeners and Druids had their greatest following in the north and west of the riding. In 1837-8 the Leeds district of the Loyal Order of Ancient Shepherds opened lodges at Malton, Beverley and Hull, and these three lodges were directly responsible for opening

a further 27 lodges in the area in 1838-46. Thirteen were opened from Malton. Three of the four lodges of the Ancient Free Gardeners opened 1838-9 were also founded from Malton. The initiative for opening seven 'gorsedds' of the Loyal Order of Druids in the northeast of the riding in 1839-43 came from Scarborough. In the same period the temperance Independent Order of Rechabites opened eight 'tents' which, with the exception of Skipsea and North Cave, were in towns.

In 1848-52, owing to the depressed state of agriculture and internal disputes, many branches closed, but in the years 1856-70 friendly societies experienced another boom period. Branches were opened in the East Riding by the Grand United Order of Oddfellows, the Independent Order of Oddfellows Kingston Unity, the National United Order of Free Gardeners and the United Ancient Order of Druids. The Druids, with a strong following in Holderness, continued to expand locally, particularly after the order's national headquarters were moved to Hull in 1875. The final order to be established in the riding was the Order of the Sons of Temperance, which had close links with nonconformist chapels. Fifteen branches, or sub-divisions, were opened between 1893 and 1915 by which time the heyday of friendly societies was over. Many factors, including the implementation of National Insurance in 1912-13, and the First World War, hastened the decline.

Friendly societies were most likely to be established in market towns or large, open villages. A high proportion of East Riding members were agricultural workers, but it was the village craftsmen - shoemakers, tailors, blacksmiths and wheelwrights - who played the major role in the establishment and management of the affiliated order branches. A society's anniversary meeting or club feast day became for many village communities their chief annual celebration, with processions led by a brass band, feasting, sideshows, sports and a great gathering of friends and relatives. Although many societies were short-lived, others lasted for a century or more. Court Friendship of the Ancient Order of Foresters at Keyingham, founded in 1839, is one of a handful of East Riding societies that still exist in 1996.

Hull Friendly Societies
Seventy-four local societies were founded in Hull in 1727-1820.[2] The first affiliated order branch (IOOF MU) was opened in Hull in 1827. No systematic research has been carried out on Hull affiliated order friendly societies, and the following statistics of numbers of branches may therefore not be complete: Independent Order of Oddfellows, Manchester Unity - 20, Grand United Order of Oddfellows - 24, Independent Order of Oddfellows, Kingston Unity - 8, National Independent Order of Oddfellows - 21, Loyal United Order of Oddfellows - 16, Ancient Order of Foresters - 22, Loyal Order of Ancient Shepherds - 33, United Ancient Order of Druids - 35, Order of Druids - 22, National United Order of Free Gardeners - 27, Sons of Temperance - 15, Independent Order of Rechabites - 13. Total: 256.

Notes and bibliography on page 151

FRIENDLY SOCIETIES : 1800-1914

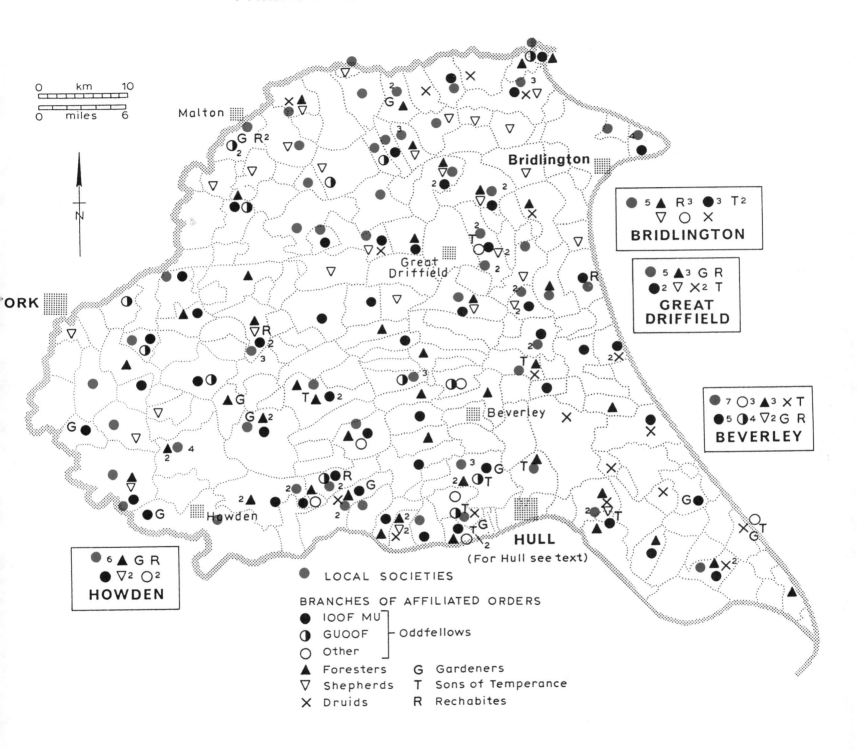

0 km 10
0 miles 6

Malton

York

Bridlington

Great Driffield

Beverley

Howden

HULL
(For Hull see text)

BRIDLINGTON
● 5 ▲ R 3 ◐ 3 T 2
▽ ○ ✕

GREAT DRIFFIELD
● 5 ▲ 3 G R
◐ 2 ▽ ✕ 2 T

BEVERLEY
● 7 ○ 3 ▲ 3 ✕ T
◐ 5 ◑ 4 ▽ 2 G R

HOWDEN
● 6 ▲ G R
◐ ▽ 2 ○ 2

● LOCAL SOCIETIES

BRANCHES OF AFFILIATED ORDERS
● IOOF MU ⎤
◐ GUOOF ⎬ Oddfellows
○ Other ⎦
▲ Foresters   G Gardeners
▽ Shepherds   T Sons of Temperance
✕ Druids   R Rechabites

117

RIOT AND REBELLION

TERRIBLE AND TRVE

NEVVES FROM

BEVERLEY

AND THE

CITY OF

YORKE

Wherein is a true Relation
of the beseiging of the Town of *Hull*,
by the Kings Majesty, with six thousand Horse
and foot, on Thursday, *Iuly* 7. 1642.

ALSO

Of Sir *John Hothams* drowning the
Country within foure miles of *Hull*, and what
hath happened since, and his Maiesties Resolution
concerning it.

WITH

The Lord *Digbies* entertainment at
the Court, and divers remarkeable passages at
Yorke; from the third of *Iuly* to the ninth of the
same, sent in a letter from *Yorke* to a freind in
London. *Iuly* the twelfth. 1642.

London printed fot *M. T.* 1642.

THE PILGRIMAGE OF GRACE: 1536-37

David Neave

In October 1536 the East Riding was the scene of a popular and, initially, highly successful rising against the government of Henry VIII. This revolt, termed by its participants 'the Pilgrimage of Grace', although partly a response to the suppression of the lesser monasteries and other measures taken in the early stages of the English Reformation, had no single cause. A long list of grievances - religious, economic, constitutional and legal - united the commons, gentry and clergy in opposition to the king's ministers.[1]

The revolt had its immediate origins in the short-lived Lincolnshire rising which began at Louth on 2 October. News of this rising rapidly reached the already disaffected East Riding, partly through the activities of Robert Aske of Aughton who was recruited as one of the 'captains' of the Lincolnshire host by rebels at Caistor on 4 October. Aske, the prime mover of the rising in the East Riding and eventual 'grand captain' of the Pilgrimage of Grace, was on his way from Aughton to London, where he practised as a lawyer, when he fell in with the Lincolnshire rebels.

Aske was soon spreading the word north of the Humber. A letter he sent to one of the governors of Beverley giving instructions on how to organise a rising was said to have been a key factor in the agitation that took place in the town on Sunday 8 October which signalled the beginning of the Pilgrimage of Grace. That afternoon and on the three subsequent days 'the town' met fully armed on the great common of Westwood.

Over the next few days the rest of the riding rose in response to the ringing of bells and firing of beacons. Musters were called and an oath of allegiance sworn in each wapentake in turn.

Firstly, on Wednesday 11 October the men of the Ouse and Derwent wapentake gathered on Skipwith Moor and those of Howdenshire at Ringstanhirst near Howden. A mob appeared at the gate of Wressle Castle and shouted 'Thousands for a Percy'. On Thursday 12 October some 3,000 men from Watton, Cottingham, Hessle and other parishes in the Bainton beacon and Hunsley beacon divisions of Harthill wapentake and Hullshire met at Hunsley beacon.[2] The same day Holderness was also reported to be 'up to the sea side' with a general muster at Nuttles in Burstwick parish and another at Sutton Ings on 13 October. The two northern wapentakes of Buckrose and Dickering do not appear to have fully risen until 17 October when 3,000-4,000 mustered on the wold above Staxton and three days later when an estimated 10,000 from both the East and North Ridings met at Malton under the leadership of Sir Thomas Percy of Seamer, brother of the earl of Northumberland.

By the date of the Malton muster much had already been achieved by the rebel forces. On 13 October Robert Aske led the men of Howdenshire and the Marshland to Weighton Hill where they met up with the combined force of those who had earlier mustered at Beverley and Hunsley beacon. Here on 14 October it was decided that the Howdenshire force should march on to take York whilst the rest turned their attention to Hull. Aske quickly secured the bridges over the river Derwent at Kexby and Sutton and, after a muster outside the walls of York, entered the city without opposition on Monday 16 October.[3]

Hull was not so easily secured. On the morning of 15 October a muster was held at Wyndeoak, near Cottingham from which the rebel force was dispersed to besiege Hull. Some 200 horsemen and all the foot soldiers from Holderness were stationed on the east side of the river Hull, the Beverley host was encamped at Sculcoates to the north with a company from Cottingham adjoining them on the west, and at the Hermitage to the west of Hull were 100 horsemen from Holderness and all the force from Hullshire. On the afternoon of 19 October reinforcements arrived from York, whereupon Hull was yielded to the 'pilgrims' who entered the town early the next day.

The besiegers were then summoned to rejoin the main body of 'pilgrims' at Pontefract. They arrived there on 22 October, the day after the castle had been surrendered to Aske. The greatly increased 'pilgrim' army, now consisting of over 30,000 well-armed men, moved on to Doncaster, where on 26 October they confronted a royal army of some 11,000 under the Duke of Norfolk. On the following day a truce was agreed and the rebel army dispersed awaiting the king's response to their request for a general pardon and a parliament in the north to consider their grievances. After lengthy delay and much discussion these terms were finally confirmed on 8 December.

However, discontent remained in the East Riding and, at the beginning of 1537, Sir Francis Bigod of Settrington and John Hallam, a farmer from Watton, who had been active in the original rising, drew up an ill-conceived plan to capture Hull and Scarborough.[4] They called a muster for the Buckrose and Dickering wapentakes at 'Borough' (now represented by Burrow Nook on the High Street northeast of Cowlam) on Tuesday 16 January 1537. From here George Lumley of Thwing was despatched with a force to take Scarborough Castle and on the same day Hallam with a small group went from Watton to take Hull. Neither was successful and Hallam was seized. Bigod then set out for Hull, mustering troops at his manor at Bainton before occupying Beverley on 18 January. Here early the next day the rebel force was routed by Sir Ralph Ellerker, and Bigod fled to Cumberland where he was finally captured on 10 February.

The failure of the second rising provided the king with the excuse to take revenge on Aske and the other leaders of the Pilgrimage of Grace. Many from the East Riding were executed including Hallam, Bigod and Lumley, the prior of Bridlington, the sub-prior of Watton, two canons of Warter, Sir Thomas Percy and Sir Robert Constable. Finally, on 12 July 1537, Robert Aske was hung, drawn and quartered at Clifford's Tower, York.

Notes and bibliography on page 151

THE PILGRIMAGE OF GRACE : 1536-37

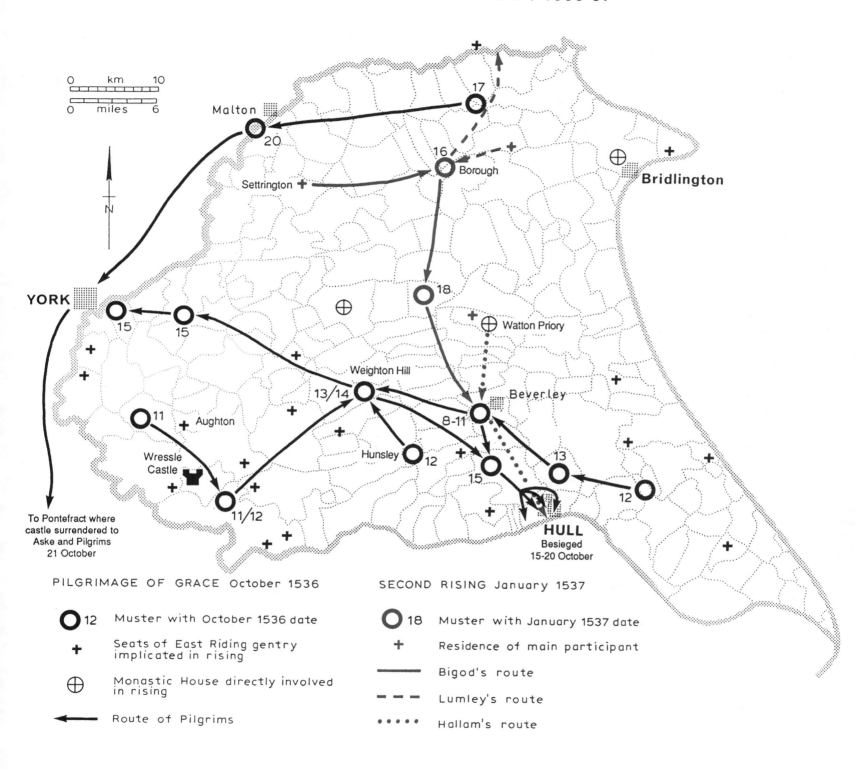

0 km 10
0 miles 6

N

Malton 20

Settrington +

Borough 16
17

Bridlington ⊕ +

YORK

15 15

+ +

Weighton Hill

11 Aughton +

Wressle Castle

+

Hunsley 12

13/14

Watton Priory ⊕

Beverley

8-11

+

15 13 12

To Pontefract where castle surrendered to Aske and Pilgrims 21 October

11/12

+ +

HULL
Besieged
15-20 October

18

PILGRIMAGE OF GRACE October 1536

◯12 Muster with October 1536 date

+ Seats of East Riding gentry implicated in rising

⊕ Monastic House directly involved in rising

← Route of Pilgrims

SECOND RISING January 1537

◯18 Muster with January 1537 date

+ Residence of main participant

—— Bigod's route

- - - Lumley's route

• • • • Hallam's route

THE CIVIL WAR IN THE EAST RIDING: 1642-45

David Neave

Although the East Riding was not the location of any of the great battles of the English Civil War, the strategic importance of Hull, York and Scarborough ensured that the area experienced considerable military activity. The king's attempt to take control of the arsenal at Hull on 23 April 1642, when he was refused entry by the governor Sir John Hotham, was one of the most significant events leading to the outbreak of war.[1] A second attempt in early July led to the first siege of Hull, which lasted until 27 July when the royalist troops withdrew. Less than a month later the king raised his standard at Nottingham and the Civil War began.

By the end of 1642 the East Riding was largely controlled by the parliamentarians. York, however, was firmly in royalist hands and was the initial objective of Queen Henrietta Maria when she landed at Bridlington Quay on 22 February 1643 with a vast quantity of arms and ammunition from Holland. The queen spent almost two weeks at Bridlington, while transport was arranged and a safe passage made through to York. By early March the north part of the riding had been cleared of parliamentary forces and the queen set out with a convoy of 500 waggons travelling via Burton Fleming and Malton to York, which she reached on 8 March.

During the summer of 1643 the royalists took control of the whole of the East Riding with the exception of Hull and Wressle castle. In June and July sorties were made as far as Market Weighton and Beverley by Sir Hugh Cholmley, the governor of Scarborough castle, who in March had declared for the king. The changing fortunes of the parliamentarians at Beverley were noted by the sympathetic parish clerk of St Mary's. On 30 June he wrote 'A great scrimmage in Beverley yesterday, and God gave us victory at that time... War in our gates.'[2] By late summer Hull became once again the chief objective of the royalists. The earl of Newcastle with some 16,000 men reached Beverley on 28 August and Sir Thomas Fairfax, the parliamentarian commander with far inferior forces, was forced to retreat to Hull. Beverley was sacked by the royalists, who on 2 September began their second siege of Hull. The siege lasted for five and a half weeks with the besieging forces constantly harried by parliamentarians. On 9 September an attack on the royalist headquarters at Anlaby was only repulsed with considerable loss, and later in the month the royalist magazine at Cottingham was blown up. Early in October the royalist forts at Paull and Barton-on-Humber were destroyed, and finally on 11 October Lord Fairfax rode out of Hull and soundly beat the royalists who abandoned the siege, pillaging Beverley once again on their way back to York.

In early 1644 there was much military activity in the East Riding as John, Lord Belasyse tried vainly to retain royalist control of the territory between York and Scarborough in the face of raids made by Sir William Constable from Hull.[3] Constable, from an encampment on the Wolds, attacked royalist positions as far away as Pickering. Royalist troops sent from York to confront Constable set up camp at Cowlam (not Kilham as is sometimes stated).[4] There at night they were surprised by Constable who took 160 prisoners. The Cowlam fight probably took place on 10 February; soon after Constable captured Bridlington and was involved in skirmishes with royalists at Driffield and Helperthorpe.[5]

The parliamentarians gained their greatest success at Selby on 11 April when the royalists were decisively defeated. The fighting spread into the East Riding, with a force of 120 royalist cavalry being captured at Hemingbrough and lodged in the church overnight. The parliamentarians then mopped up the remaining royalist outposts on the borders of the East Riding. Stamford Bridge was taken on 24 April, Buttercrambe castle on 16 May, Cawood castle on 19 May and finally the fort at Airemouth, Airmyn on 22 May. York, which had effectively been under siege from 23 April, was temporarily relieved by Prince Rupert on 30 June but was again besieged after the great royalist defeat at Marston Moor on 2 July. The city was finally taken on 16 July, leaving Scarborough as the only place in East Yorkshire still in royalist hands. Scarborough castle was at once besieged but was not surrendered until 22 July 1645.

During the Civil War the gentry of the East Riding were fairly evenly divided between the two parties. J.T. Cliffe has calculated that of 142 gentry families in the riding, 44 could be classed as royalist, 37 as parliamentarian, 19 as divided in their loyalties, and 42 as neutral.[6] Mapping the seats of the active gentry does not show any particular pattern, although there are clusters of royalist gentry in the Vale of York and Holderness. Here were the seats of the leading Catholic families, all royalists - the Constables of Everingham, the Constables of Burton Constable and the Langdales. Sir Marmaduke Langdale was one of the most skilled of the royalist cavalry commanders. In 1634 he purchased the Holme-upon-Spalding Moor estate from Sir William Constable. Constable, a Puritan, was the riding's most active parliamentarian leader, and, along with Colonel John Alured of Hull, was amongst the signatories of the king's death warrant. Sir Matthew Boynton of Barmston, another Puritan, was the parliamentarian governor of Scarborough castle from 1645 until his death two years later when he was succeeded by his second son Matthew, who soon afterwards changed sides and held the castle for the king. It was Matthew Boynton who captured Sir John Hotham in Beverley in June 1643 after the correspondence of Hotham and his eldest son with the royalists had become known to parliament. For their 'treason' the Hothams were executed on consecutive days at the beginning of January 1645.

Notes and bibliography on page 151

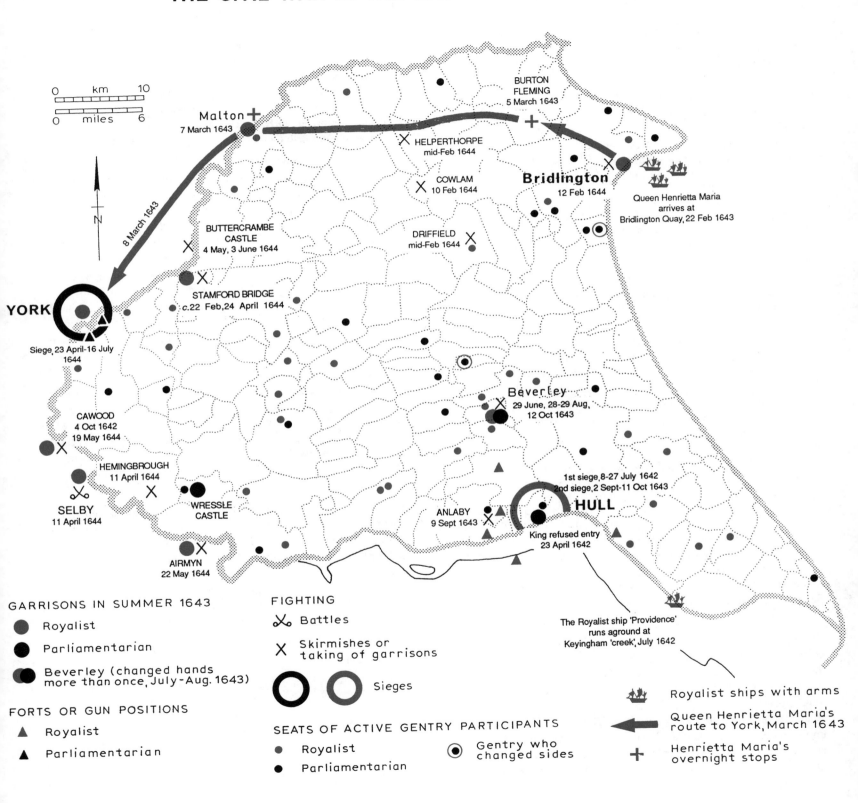

THE CIVIL WAR IN THE EAST RIDING : 1642-45

0 km 10

0 miles 6

Malton
7 March 1643

BURTON
FLEMING
5 March 1643

× HELPERTHORPE
mid-Feb 1644

× COWLAM
10 Feb 1644

Bridlington
12 Feb 1644

8 March 1643

N

Queen Henrietta Maria
arrives at
Bridlington Quay, 22 Feb 1643

BUTTERCRAMBE
CASTLE
4 May, 3 June 1644

DRIFFIELD
mid-Feb 1644 ×

STAMFORD BRIDGE
c.22 Feb, 24 April 1644

YORK

Siege, 23 April-16 July
1644

Beverley
29 June, 28-29 Aug,
12 Oct 1643

CAWOOD
4 Oct 1642
19 May 1644

HEMINGBROUGH
11 April 1644

1st siege, 8-27 July 1642
2nd siege, 2 Sept-11 Oct 1643

SELBY
11 April 1644

WRESSLE
CASTLE

ANLABY
9 Sept 1643

HULL

King refused entry
23 April 1642

AIRMYN
22 May 1644

The Royalist ship 'Providence'
runs aground at
Keyingham 'creek', July 1642

GARRISONS IN SUMMER 1643

● Royalist

● Parliamentarian

● Beverley (changed hands
more than once, July-Aug. 1643)

FORTS OR GUN POSITIONS

▲ Royalist

▲ Parliamentarian

FIGHTING

✂ Battles

× Skirmishes or
taking of garrisons

◯ ◯ Sieges

SEATS OF ACTIVE GENTRY PARTICIPANTS

● Royalist

● Parliamentarian

◉ Gentry who
changed sides

Royalist ships with arms

Queen Henrietta Maria's
route to York, March 1643

Henrietta Maria's
overnight stops

123

ANTI-MILITIA RIOTS: 1757

David Neave

In September 1757 the East Riding community experienced what was probably its most serious period of unrest since the Pilgrimage of Grace.[1] Day after day hundreds of men, women and children, armed with guns, swords, pitchforks and scythes, gathered at the houses of gentry, clergy and law officers, threatening to pull the buildings down unless a stop was put to implementing the new Militia Act. Money, food and drink were extorted, windows were broken and roofs untiled. There was a complete breakdown of law and order, for as the High Sheriff of Yorkshire, Henry Willoughby of Birdsall, lamented 'When the whole populace rise in arms against the magistrates where is then the authority of civil power?'.[2]

The 'Act for the better ordering of the Militia Forces', passed on 28 June 1757, was needed to provide a militia to keep peace at home and thus release the regular troops for service in one of the numerous theatres of the Seven Years War. The act radically changed the method of obtaining men for the militia, laying the responsibility on all adult males instead of just on the propertied classes. Previously, any person with an annual income from land of £50 per annum or an estate valued at £500 had been charged with providing and equipping an infantry man. Under the new act, the militia was to be chosen by ballot from all men between eighteen and 50 years of age in England, except peers, officers of the militia and regular forces, clergy, dissenting ministers, peace and parish officers, articled clerks, apprentices and seamen. If chosen, a man could serve himself or provide a substitute. For the poorer classes it meant that some would have to serve and leave their work, homes and families for up to three years, unless they were able to contribute to a parish fund for the payment of a substitute.[3] It is no wonder that much of the population felt aggrieved, not least because this new imposition came at a time of severe hardship when the price of corn was at its highest for 30 years.

The riots coincided with the collecting in of the lists of men liable to serve in the militia from each parish or township by the chief constables of the wapentakes or divisions. The chief constables had been summoned to take the lists to a meeting of the justices and deputy lieutenants of the East Riding at Beverley fixed for Saturday 17 September. Action was therefore taken to destroy the lists before they reached Beverley.

Rioting began on Thursday 8 September at North Frodingham in the north division of Holderness. The following day the unrest spread to the middle and south divisions, where 400 people threatened to pull down the house of Sir Robert Hildyard at Winestead. On Saturday 10 September, 500 rioters forced money from the attorney Henry Waterland at Hedon and tore up the lists. The same day there was unrest in the Hunsley Beacon division at Cottingham. Disturbances continued on the Sunday. People from the Wilton Beacon division gathered in Pocklington and spent all night drinking in the town's 30 alehouses. The next day, Monday 12 September, they went to Kilnwick Percy Hall where, after laying siege all morning, 'the main mob got into the house, which was brimful of men, women and children, and they broke into the larder, filled the kitchen, took roast beef, spitt and all and fell a fighting, took the calves head and a great family pudden'.[4] The rioters, on being given money, finally dispersed and Sir Edmund Anderson counted 1,500. The same day rioters in Bainton Beacon division broke the windows of Lund vicarage and demanded liquor, and at Beverley rioters threatened to burn the town and began to demolish the house of a magistrate, Christopher Goulton.

On Tuesday 13 September it was the turn of the wapentakes of Buckrose, Howdenshire, and Ouse and Derwent to rise. At Birdsall the High Sheriff was visited by an armed mob from 40 townships numbering, he claimed, 3,000. Six hundred rioters surrounded the hall at Howsham, some of whom went on to visit the rectors of Settrington and Scrayingham, saying 'It is a pity some example is not made of them'.[5] The rising in Dickering wapentake, for which there had been much active recruiting the previous Sunday, took place on Wednesday 14 September when about 1,000 gathered at Hunmanby Hall where they broke all the windows before going on to Buckton Hall. The chief constable, injured in the attack on his house, was forced to call at Burton Agnes, Boynton and Thorpe Hall, Rudston, to give a warning and collect money.

The last recorded riots occurred on Thursday 15 September at Bubwith, Laytham and Foggathorpe in Holme Beacon division.[6] On this day the Lord Lieutenant, Lord Irwin, with the backing of the High Sheriff and other East Riding gentry who had fled to Temple Newsam, issued a notice calling off the proposed militia meeting at Beverley on 17 September and the further collection of lists.[7] This notice, much criticised in London and the West Riding, effectively brought a halt to the rioting.

Much to the disgust of the government, no action was taken by an apprehensive magistracy until December, when the first rioters were arrested. At the York Assizes in March 1758 over 100 people were tried for their part in the anti-militia riots, some 80 coming from the East Riding. Of these, 40 were imprisoned for short terms and four were found guilty of high treason and ordered to be hung, drawn and quartered. Only the unfortunate Robert Cole of Bridlington was actually hung, despite a request for his reprieve from East Riding gentry.[8]

Notes on page 152

ANTI-MILITIA RIOTS : 1757

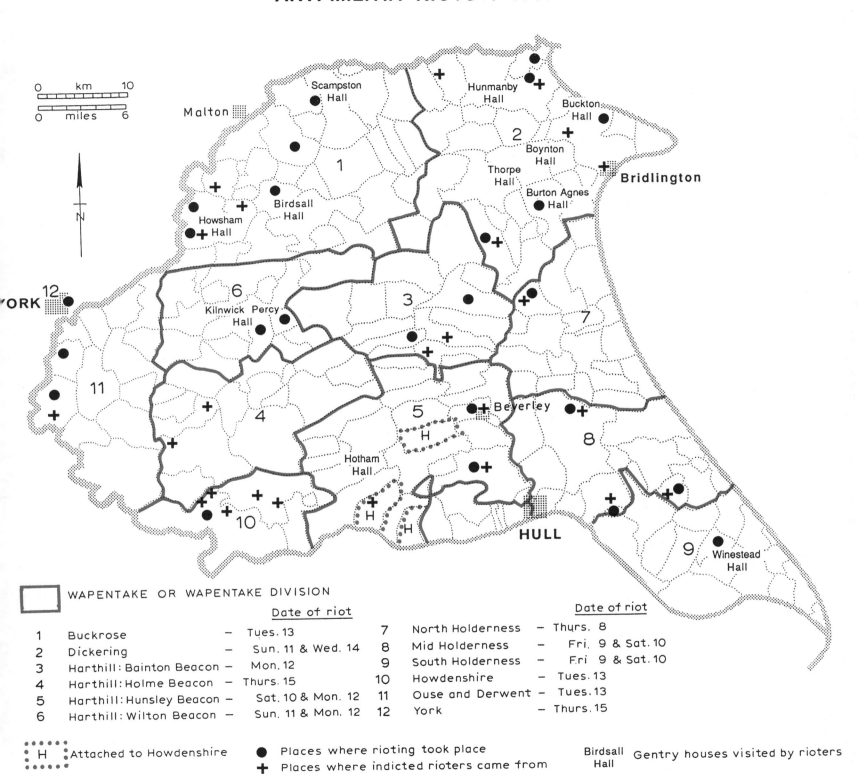

0 km 10
0 miles 6

Malton

Scampston Hall

Hunmanby Hall

Buckton Hall

1

2

Boynton Hall

Thorpe Hall

Bridlington

Burton Agnes Hall

Birdsall Hall

Howsham Hall

YORK
12

6

Kilnwick Percy Hall

3

7

11

Beverley

5
H

8

Hotham Hall

H

H

4

10

HULL

9

Winestead Hall

WAPENTAKE OR WAPENTAKE DIVISION

		Date of riot			Date of riot
1	Buckrose	— Tues. 13	7	North Holderness	— Thurs. 8
2	Dickering	— Sun. 11 & Wed. 14	8	Mid Holderness	— Fri. 9 & Sat. 10
3	Harthill: Bainton Beacon	— Mon. 12	9	South Holderness	— Fri 9 & Sat. 10
4	Harthill: Holme Beacon	— Thurs. 15	10	Howdenshire	— Tues. 13
5	Harthill: Hunsley Beacon	— Sat. 10 & Mon. 12	11	Ouse and Derwent	— Tues. 13
6	Harthill: Wilton Beacon	— Sun. 11 & Mon. 12	12	York	— Thurs. 15

H ⋯ Attached to Howdenshire

● Places where rioting took place

✚ Places where indicted rioters came from

Birdsall Hall Gentry houses visited by rioters

125

ADMINISTRATIVE UNITS

ADMINISTRATIVE UNITS

Mike Rogers

Ecclesiastical boundaries: deaneries and peculiars

After the Reformation the ecclesiastical parish became the basic administrative unit for both secular and religious matters.[1] For the purposes of diocesan administration, parishes were grouped in deaneries and the deaneries in archdeaconries. Certain parishes or groups of parishes, termed peculiars, were, until 1846, exempt from the jurisdiction of the archbishop or archdeacon, and were administered by a range of ecclesiastical officials, chiefly dignitaries and prebendaries of York Minster. The most extensive peculiars in the East Riding were those of the dean of York and the dean and chapter of Durham.[2]

Deanery boundaries and the location of peculiars are of particular relevance to family historians. Before 1858 probate of wills was granted by ecclesiastical courts and in the Borthwick Institute of Historical Research, University of York, the original wills and associated documents (including administration bonds, inventories and tuition bonds) for the diocese of York are arranged chronologically by month in deanery and Prerogative court bundles or in the many boxes relating to the ecclesiastical peculiars.

The map shows boundaries *c*.1840. In 1896 the deanery of Bulmer was transferred from the archdeaconry of Cleveland to the archdeaconry of the East Riding which then covered all but a small portion of the administrative county of the East Riding. This changed in 1936 when the western part of the area comprising the then rural deaneries of Buckrose, Pocklington, Weighton and Escrick was transferred to the archdeaconry of York.

Wapentakes and divisions

Wapentakes emerged in the twelfth century and replaced the eighteen 'hundreds' found in Domesday Book.[3] The four divisions of Harthill wapentake appeared in Elizabeth I's reign, possibly connected with assessments for the maintenance of beacons. Holderness wapentake was also sub-divided into three divisions.

The borough of Kingston-upon-Hull was created in 1299 from Harthill wapentake and became a county in its own right in 1440 with the addition of Myton. Additional townships in the west were added in 1447 to create Hullshire, which continued until 1835. Beverley and its liberties were sometimes treated separately, with varying boundaries. Howdenshire, regarded as a wapentake from the mid-fourteenth century, included the detached townships of Ellerker, Melton and Welton, and large parts of Brantingham and Walkington.

With minor variations of boundaries, these units were used for the assessment of taxes such as hearth tax, window tax and land tax, and for militia assessments. The county Quarter Sessions used the divisions (excluding boroughs) for jury lists, licensing of alehouses and bastardy returns.

At the beginning of the nineteenth century, local administration lay in the hands of oligarchic municipalities, Improvement Commissioners appointed under local acts, justices of the peace, vestries and manors. The wide-ranging reforms of the nineteenth century resulted in the formation of elected bodies with specific duties and powers. The extension of the franchise by successive Acts of Parliament increased the representative nature of these bodies and their accountability. The Municipal Reform Act of 1835 altered the manner in which boroughs were governed, and other acts had effects on the administration of justice, the treatment of the poor, public health, education and highway maintenance, laying the foundations of modern local government.

Petty Sessional divisions

Courts of Quarter Sessions, held four times a year, originated in an Act of 1362 and continued until abolished as courts of law from 1 January 1972. Locally they were held for the East Riding (at Beverley), and for the boroughs of Beverley (until 1836), Hedon (until 1860) and Hull. In addition to the administration of justice at a lesser level than the Assizes, the Quarter Sessions had many administrative functions prior to the creation of County Councils and County Boroughs in 1889 - bridges, weights and measures, licensing, asylums, prisons (until 1877), police, and the registration of gamekeepers, dissenters, Roman Catholics and friendly societies. The clerks of the peace were responsible for deposited plans and inclosure awards.

From at least the sixteenth century, justices of the peace could exercise summary jurisdiction in lesser cases. Courts of Petty Sessions, held by local justices of the peace, developed in the course of the eighteenth century to deal with these cases and certain licensing functions. Specific Petty Sessional divisions were created after 1828.[4] In the East Riding these were largely based on wapentakes and divisions, but with the splitting of Hunsley Beacon into North and South divisions, and a compact Howdenshire division. Beverley and Hull retained their own magistrates.[5] The boundaries of the divisions were slightly adjusted in 1935 in conjunction with a review of local government districts (see below). Little Kelk had been transferred to Bainton Beacon from its anomalous position in Dickering in 1902.[6] The Petty Sessions evolved into the modern magistrates courts.

Poor Law Unions

From 1601 until the 1830s the Poor Law was administered at the level of townships and parishes. Locally chosen overseers were responsible for the collection of poor rates and the payment of relief. Settlement examinations and removal orders were made by JPs at the petition of overseers. Parish poor houses were sometimes provided under Gilbert's Act, 1782, and it was possible for groups of parishes to combine to fund a workhouse, as at North Dalton.[7]

The Poor Law Amendment Act, 1834, led to the union of parishes as Poor Law Unions, mostly centred on market towns.[8] The Unions were administered by elected Boards of Guardians who met regularly and were overseen by the Poor Law Commissioners in London (the Poor

Law Board from 1847, and the Local Government Board from 1871 - the precursor of the Ministry of Health). The Unions did not correspond to the boundaries of the East Riding or to existing internal administrative boundaries. Thus it was that certain parishes were assigned to Unions based in Malton, Scarborough, Selby and York. In the East Riding the Guardians first met in late 1836 and early 1837. The existing Hull Incorporation for the Poor was not brought fully within the national system until about 1850.[9] Guardians and their paid staff were responsible for duties ranging from the administration of indoor and outdoor relief, to school attendance (from 1877) and vaccinations. Unions were also used as units for civil registration of births, marriages and deaths from July 1837. Large workhouses were built to house the poor and act as offices, and increasingly to function as infirmaries. After 1894 district councillors acted as Guardians for their respective parishes, rather than being directly elected. Overseers of the Poor continued to collect parish poor rates until 1925.

The formation of an Ouse and Derwent Union was recommended in 1888 by Parliamentary Commissioners, and in 1889 the Boundaries Committee of the newly formed East Riding County Council made a number of proposals to rearrange Unions within the county boundary, including the creation of new Unions for Cottingham, Norton, and Ouse and Derwent. These proposals were not adopted but in 1894 the Escrick and Norton Out Relief Unions were created to carry out all functions except indoor relief in the workhouses, which remained the responsibility of York and Malton Unions respectively.[10]

The Boards of Guardians were superseded in 1930 by local Guardians Committees. Outside Hull these were under the auspices of the County Council, namely for Beverley (Beverley and Haltemprice from 1935), Bridlington, Derwent (from 1935), Driffield, Howden, Norton (from 1935), Patrington (Holderness from 1935) and Sculcoates (until 1935).[11] The Committees were made up of County and District councillors and other appointed persons. In 1948 the functions of the Guardians Committees were divided between the County Council and the new National Health Service. Some workhouses became hospitals (Beverley, Hull, Sculcoates), homes for the elderly (Bridlington), or local government offices (Skirlaugh).

Local Authority areas
Under the Public Health Act, 1848, elected Local Boards of Health were created for Beverley (1851), Bridlington (1863), Cottingham (1864), Great Driffield (1874), Filey (1868), Hedon (1860), Hornsea (1865), Hull (1851), Malton (1854, to include Norton until 1890[12]), Newington (1872-82), Norton (1890), Pocklington (1893) and Wallingfen (1871, extended 1877-9 and renamed South Cave and Wallingfen). The boards dealt with matters such as sanitation, street cleaning, drainage, nuisances, slaughter houses and lodging houses, and might appoint paid staff such as a clerk, treasurer, medical officer of health, inspector of nuisances and surveyor. Beverley and Hull corporations took over the functions of their Local Boards in 1872 and 1876 respectively. From 1872 the Local Boards were also known as

Urban Sanitary Authorities and the system was extended to areas not already covered.[13] Accordingly, Boards of Guardians set up special committees to act as Rural Sanitary Authorities.

In 1889 the County Council of the East Riding of Yorkshire was elected to cover the whole administrative county outside Hull.[14] Hull became a county borough and in 1897 it was given the status of a city. The East Riding County Council was based in Beverley and inherited the administrative functions of the East Riding Quarter Sessions. The East Riding Constabulary was subsequently administered by a Standing Joint Committee of the County Council and the Quarter Sessions. Highways were taken over in the 1890s from Highway Boards and Districts (created after 1862), and rural roads in 1929, although trunk roads passed to the Ministry of Transport in 1937. The County Council was initially responsible for technical instruction only, but in 1903 it took over primary education from elected local School Boards (established after 1870), the National Society, and the British and Foreign Schools Society. However, the boroughs of Beverley and Bridlington exercised separate education functions until 1945. Smallholdings were created after 1892 and motor vehicle licensing was run by the county from 1903 until the 1970s. The Fire service was added to the county's responsibilities in 1948.

In 1894 the county outside the boroughs was divided into Urban and Rural Districts (U.D.s and R.D.s) with elected councils (U.D.C.s and R.D.C.s), which superseded the Urban and Rural Sanitary Authorities, but were to be wholly within the county boundary.[15] Urban Districts were initially created for Bridlington (made a Municipal Borough in 1899), Cottingham, Great Driffield, Filey, Hornsea, Pocklington and Norton. Hessle (from Sculcoates R.D.) and Withernsea (from Patrington R.D.) both became Urban Districts in 1898.[16] Rural Districts were created for Beverley, Bridlington, Driffield, Escrick, Howden, Norton, Patrington, Pocklington, Riccall, Sculcoates, Sherburn and Skirlaugh. South Cave and Wallingfen Local Board was split between Howden and Beverley R.D.s. The district councils were given powers over planning, housing, refuse collection, water supply and sewerage, cemeteries and, in Urban Districts, minor roads.

Also in 1894 civil parishes were created in the Rural Districts, based primarily on township boundaries.[17] Those parishes with electorates greater than 300 (or 200 if the parishioners so chose) were to have an elected parish council. Parishes with smaller electorates were to hold a parish meeting at least once a year, and could choose to have parish councils with the agreement of the County Council. Parish councils took over the civil functions of vestries and were made responsible for allotments, street lighting, village greens, shelters and village halls, and could provide burial grounds. After 1974 urban areas could be parished and adopt the title of Town Council.

The first substantial alteration of this system of local councils took place in 1935.[18] The boundaries of Filey U.D. and the boroughs of Bridlington and Hedon were extended, while the boundaries of

Driffield U.D. were reduced and Pocklington was integrated into the surrounding Rural District. Patrington R.D. and Skirlaugh R.D. were combined to form the new Holderness R.D. In the area surrounding Hull, extensions to the city boundary in 1929 and 1935 made the existing authorities unviable. As a result the civil parishes of Melton, North Ferriby, Sutton, Wauldby, Welton and much of Swanland were transferred from Sculcoates R.D. to Beverley R.D., and a new Haltemprice U.D. was formed by the amalgamation of Cottingham U.D., Hessle U.D. and the remaining parts of Sculcoates R.D. west of the River Hull. In the north of the county, the small Sherburn R.D. was divided between Bridlington R.D. (Folkton and Muston civil parishes) and Norton R.D. (Ganton, Sherburn and Willerby civil parishes). The civil parishes of Butterwick, Foxholes with Boythorpe, Helperthorpe, Luttons Ambo and Weaverthorpe (from Driffield R.D.), and Scrayingham, Thixendale and part of Kirby Underdale (from Pocklington R.D.) were transferred to Norton R.D., while Fridaythorpe (from Pocklington R.D.) was transferred to Driffield R.D. Finally, Escrick R.D. and Riccall R.D. merged with the townships of Hemingbrough and Brackenholme with Woodhall (both from Howden R.D.) to form Derwent R.D. There were also a number of smaller adjustments involving parts of parishes.

At the same time, significant changes were made to the pattern of civil parishes. Many small parishes were amalgamated with their neighbours, reducing the overall number, and some others were renamed. Anlaby, Haltemprice, Kirk Ella, West Ella and Willerby were abolished because they now lay in an Urban District.

The boundaries of Hull were extended in 1882, 1897, 1929, 1935, 1955 and 1968, and there were extensions to Bridlington Municipal Borough in 1923 and 1935, Hedon borough in 1935 and 1964, and Withernsea U.D. in 1911.[19] The boundaries of York were extended into East Riding parishes in 1832, 1884 and 1967.

The council areas described above remained in place until 1 April 1974 when the Urban Districts, Rural Districts and Boroughs were replaced by new larger Districts, and the East Riding County Council was abolished. The Districts of Beverley (later East Yorkshire Borough of Beverley), North Wolds (later East Yorkshire), Holderness and part of Boothferry, which were all later designated as Boroughs, and the city of Hull, were included in the new county of Humberside. The remaining areas of the East Riding were transferred to the county of North Yorkshire and formed parts of the Districts of Selby, Ryedale and Scarborough. A further re-organisation of local government on 1 April 1996 created Unitary Authorities for Hull and for the East Riding of Yorkshire (to include the area around Goole which had been in the West Riding until 1974, but not those East Riding areas which had been transferred to North Yorkshire). The area of the City of York was extended to include, amongst others, the parishes of Deighton, Dunnington, Elvington, Fulford, Heslington, Kexby, Naburn and Wheldrake which until 1974 had been in the East Riding. The 1996 boundaries are shown on the key map at the end of the atlas.

Parliamentary boundaries

Before 1832, with the exception of the franchised boroughs, the whole of Yorkshire was represented by just two members of parliament (increased to four in 1826). In addition, the medieval boroughs of Kingston-upon-Hull, Beverley and Hedon each elected two representatives. Under the 1832 Act the East Riding became an electoral division returning two MPs, Hedon was disfranchised and Norton was included in the North Riding borough of Malton.[20] Malton's two representatives were reduced to one from 1868,[21] and it ceased to be a parliamentary borough in 1885. Beverley, with extended boundaries, retained two representatives until 1870, when it was disfranchised following an enquiry into electoral malpractices (in the 1868 election), and incorporated into the East Riding constituency. Hull's parliamentary boundary was extended beyond the municipal boundary in 1868, and subsequent extensions to the municipal boundaries resulted in further adjustments to electoral boundaries.

In 1885 the East Riding was arranged into three divisions - Buckrose, Holderness and Howdenshire - each with one representative.[22] These divisions, with minor adjustments, were retained until 1948. The largest revision came in 1918 when Fridaythorpe and Scrayingham were transferred from Buckrose to Howdenshire; Lund and Kilnwick from Buckrose to Holderness; Skipsea from Holderness to Buckrose; and Cottingham, Rowley, Skidby and South Dalton from Howdenshire to Holderness. Ulrome had been transferred from Holderness to Buckrose in the course of 1891. Also in 1885 the number of members for an enlarged Hull was increased from two to three, and specific constituencies created - Central, East and West. The Hull constituencies were increased to four in 1918 as Central, East, North West and South West.

From 1948 the Hull constituencies were re-arranged as East, Central, North and Haltemprice (the latter comprising Haltemprice U.D. and the two Hull wards of Pickering and St Andrew's).[23] The remainder of the East Riding was divided into the two county constituencies of Beverley and Bridlington, based on district boundaries.

In 1955 the Haltemprice constituency was altered to include the areas of Beverley Borough, Beverley R.D. and Haltemprice U.D., while Driffield U.D and R.D. were transferred from the Bridlington constituency to join the rest of the county as the new Howden constituency. At the same time the Hull constituencies were again re-arranged as East, North and West (to include Pickering and St Andrew's wards).[24] The Bransholme area was added to Hull East in 1968.[25] A further alteration in 1970 created Central, East and West constituencies for Hull.[26] New constituencies of Beverley, Boothferry and Bridlington, created in 1983, reflected the post-1974 county boundaries.

Notes and bibliography on page 152

ECCLESIASTICAL BOUNDARIES : DEANERIES AND PECULIARS

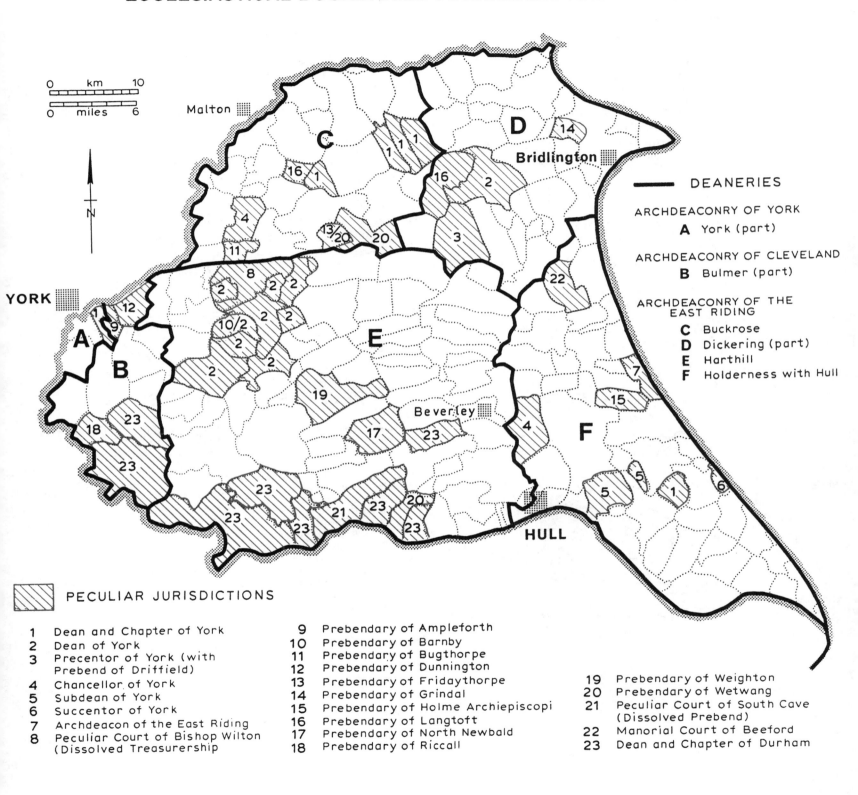

0 km 10

0 miles 6

Malton

YORK

Bridlington

Beverley

HULL

A

B

C

D

E

F

—— DEANERIES

ARCHDEACONRY OF YORK
A York (part)

ARCHDEACONRY OF CLEVELAND
B Bulmer (part)

ARCHDEACONRY OF THE
EAST RIDING
C Buckrose
D Dickering (part)
E Harthill
F Holderness with Hull

PECULIAR JURISDICTIONS

1 Dean and Chapter of York
2 Dean of York
3 Precentor of York (with Prebend of Driffield)
4 Chancellor of York
5 Subdean of York
6 Succentor of York
7 Archdeacon of the East Riding
8 Peculiar Court of Bishop Wilton (Dissolved Treasurership
9 Prebendary of Ampleforth
10 Prebendary of Barnby
11 Prebendary of Bugthorpe
12 Prebendary of Dunnington
13 Prebendary of Fridaythorpe
14 Prebendary of Grindal
15 Prebendary of Holme Archiepiscopi
16 Prebendary of Langtoft
17 Prebendary of North Newbald
18 Prebendary of Riccall
19 Prebendary of Weighton
20 Prebendary of Wetwang
21 Peculiar Court of South Cave (Dissolved Prebend)
22 Manorial Court of Beeford
23 Dean and Chapter of Durham

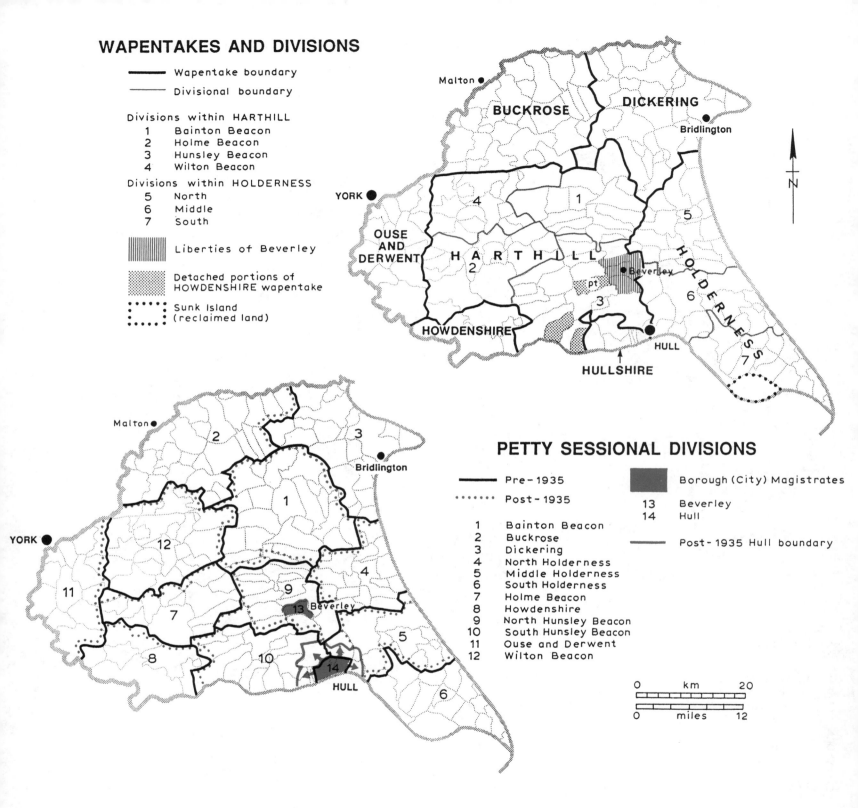

WAPENTAKES AND DIVISIONS

——— Wapentake boundary

——— Divisional boundary

Divisions within HARTHILL
1   Bainton Beacon
2   Holme Beacon
3   Hunsley Beacon
4   Wilton Beacon

Divisions within HOLDERNESS
5   North
6   Middle
7   South

▦   Liberties of Beverley

▦   Detached portions of HOWDENSHIRE wapentake

⋯   Sunk Island (reclaimed land)

BUCKROSE

DICKERING

Malton

Bridlington

YORK

OUSE AND DERWENT

4

1

5

HARTHILL

2

Beverley

Pt

HOLDERNESS

3

6

HOWDENSHIRE

HULL

7

HULLSHIRE

N

PETTY SESSIONAL DIVISIONS

——— Pre-1935

⋯⋯ Post-1935

1   Bainton Beacon
2   Buckrose
3   Dickering
4   North Holderness
5   Middle Holderness
6   South Holderness
7   Holme Beacon
8   Howdenshire
9   North Hunsley Beacon
10   South Hunsley Beacon
11   Ouse and Derwent
12   Wilton Beacon

■   Borough (City) Magistrates

13   Beverley
14   Hull

——— Post-1935 Hull boundary

Malton

2

3

Bridlington

1

YORK

12

11

7

9

13 Beverley

4

8

10

5

14

HULL

6

0   km   20

0   miles   12

132

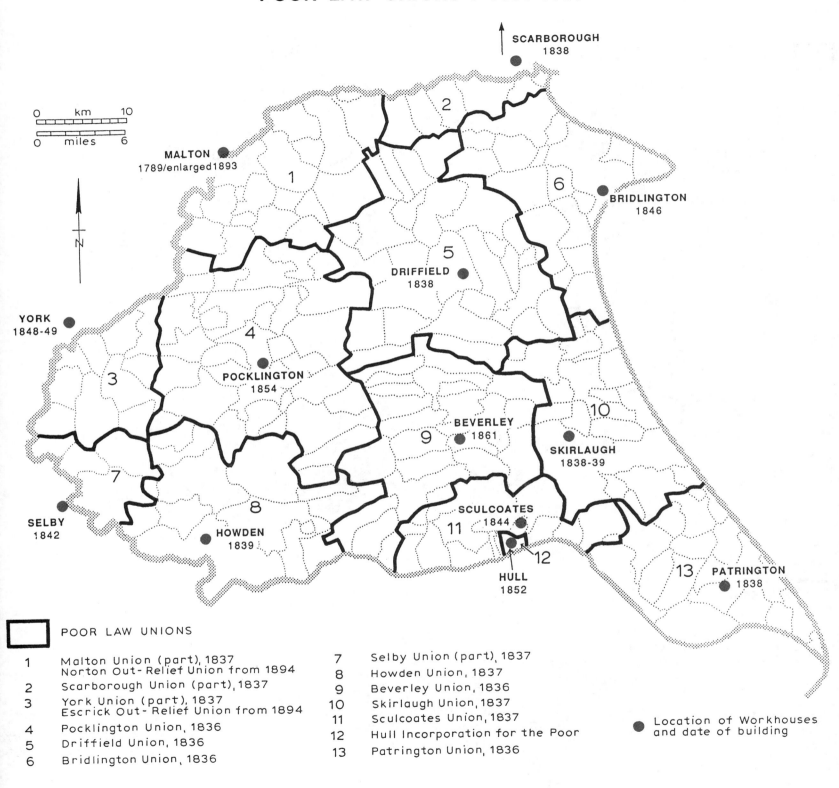

POOR LAW UNIONS : 1836-1930

SCARBOROUGH
1838

MALTON
1789/enlarged 1893

BRIDLINGTON
1846

6

2

1

5

DRIFFIELD
1838

YORK
1848-49

4

POCKLINGTON
1854

3

BEVERLEY
1861

10

9

SKIRLAUGH
1838-39

7

8

11

SCULCOATES
1844

SELBY
1842

HOWDEN
1839

HULL
1852

12

13

PATRINGTON
1838

0   km   10

0   miles   6

N

POOR LAW UNIONS

1   Malton Union (part), 1837
    Norton Out-Relief Union from 1894
2   Scarborough Union (part), 1837
3   York Union (part), 1837
    Escrick Out-Relief Union from 1894
4   Pocklington Union, 1836
5   Driffield Union, 1836
6   Bridlington Union, 1836

7   Selby Union (part), 1837
8   Howden Union, 1837
9   Beverley Union, 1836
10 Skirlaugh Union, 1837
11 Sculcoates Union, 1837
12 Hull Incorporation for the Poor
13 Patrington Union, 1836

•   Location of Workhouses
    and date of building

LOCAL AUTHORITY AREAS : PRE-1894

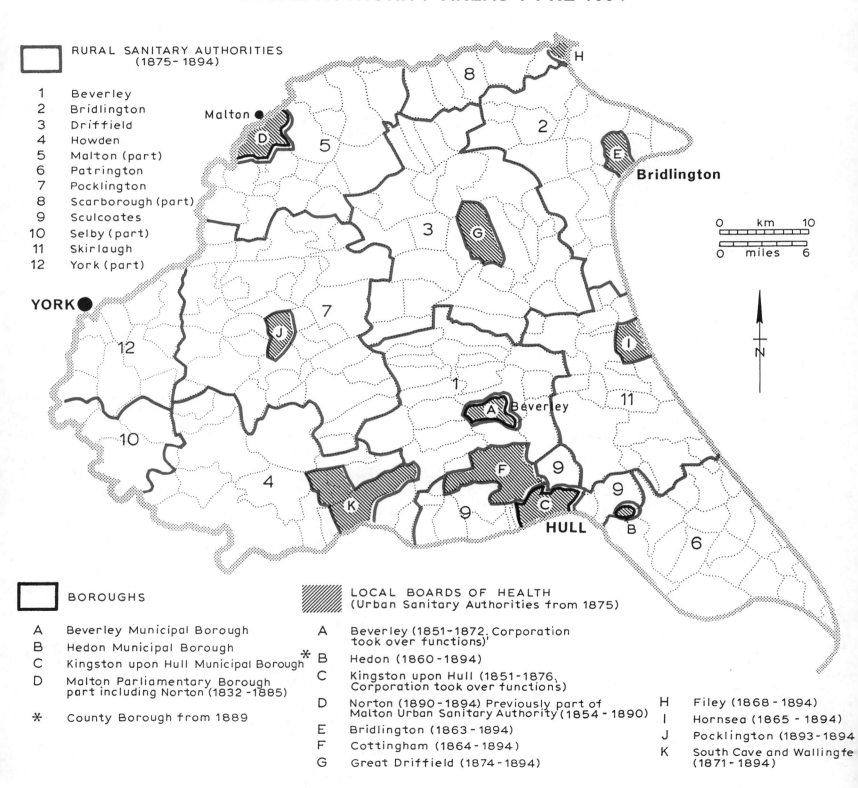

RURAL SANITARY AUTHORITIES
(1875-1894)

1 Beverley
2 Bridlington
3 Driffield
4 Howden
5 Malton (part)
6 Patrington
7 Pocklington
8 Scarborough (part)
9 Sculcoates
10 Selby (part)
11 Skirlaugh
12 York (part)

BOROUGHS

A Beverley Municipal Borough
B Hedon Municipal Borough
C Kingston upon Hull Municipal Borough *
D Malton Parliamentary Borough
   part including Norton (1832-1885)

* County Borough from 1889

LOCAL BOARDS OF HEALTH
(Urban Sanitary Authorities from 1875)

A Beverley (1851-1872, Corporation
   took over functions)'
B Hedon (1860-1894)
C Kingston upon Hull (1851-1876,
   Corporation took over functions)
D Norton (1890-1894) Previously part of
   Malton Urban Sanitary Authority (1854-1890)
E Bridlington (1863-1894)
F Cottingham (1864-1894)
G Great Driffield (1874-1894)

H Filey (1868-1894)
I Hornsea (1865-1894)
J Pocklington (1893-1894)
K South Cave and Wallingfe
   (1871-1894)

LOCAL AUTHORITY AREAS : 1894-1935

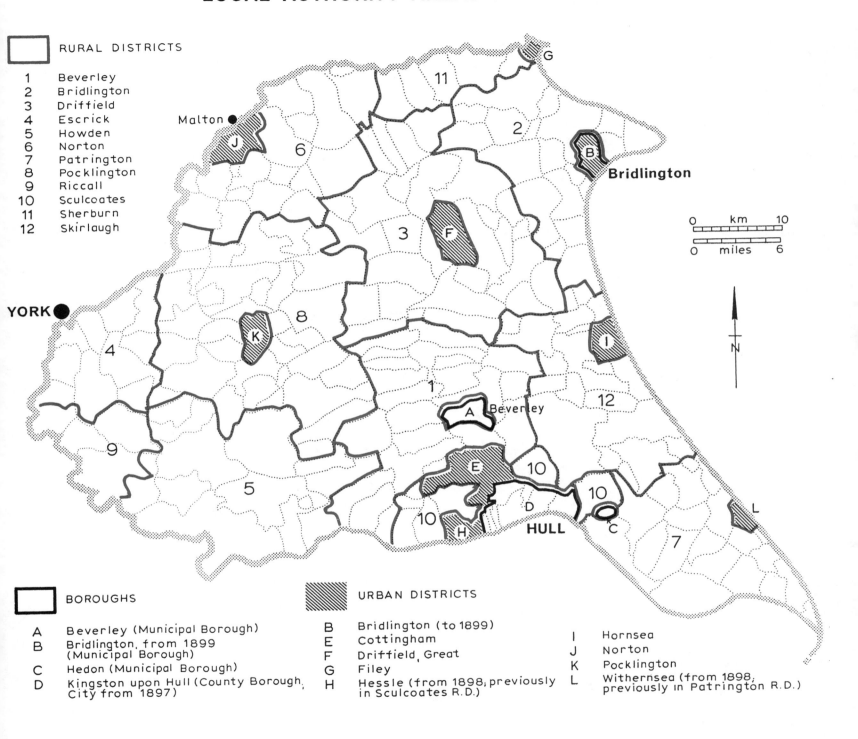

RURAL DISTRICTS

1   Beverley
2   Bridlington
3   Driffield
4   Escrick
5   Howden
6   Norton
7   Patrington
8   Pocklington
9   Riccall
10   Sculcoates
11   Sherburn
12   Skirlaugh

BOROUGHS

A   Beverley (Municipal Borough)
B   Bridlington, from 1899 (Municipal Borough)
C   Hedon (Municipal Borough)
D   Kingston upon Hull (County Borough, City from 1897)

URBAN DISTRICTS

B   Bridlington (to 1899)
E   Cottingham
F   Driffield, Great
G   Filey
H   Hessle (from 1898; previously in Sculcoates R.D.)

I   Hornsea
J   Norton
K   Pocklington
L   Withernsea (from 1898; previously in Patrington R.D.)

LOCAL AUTHORITY AREAS : 1935-1974 and 1974-1996

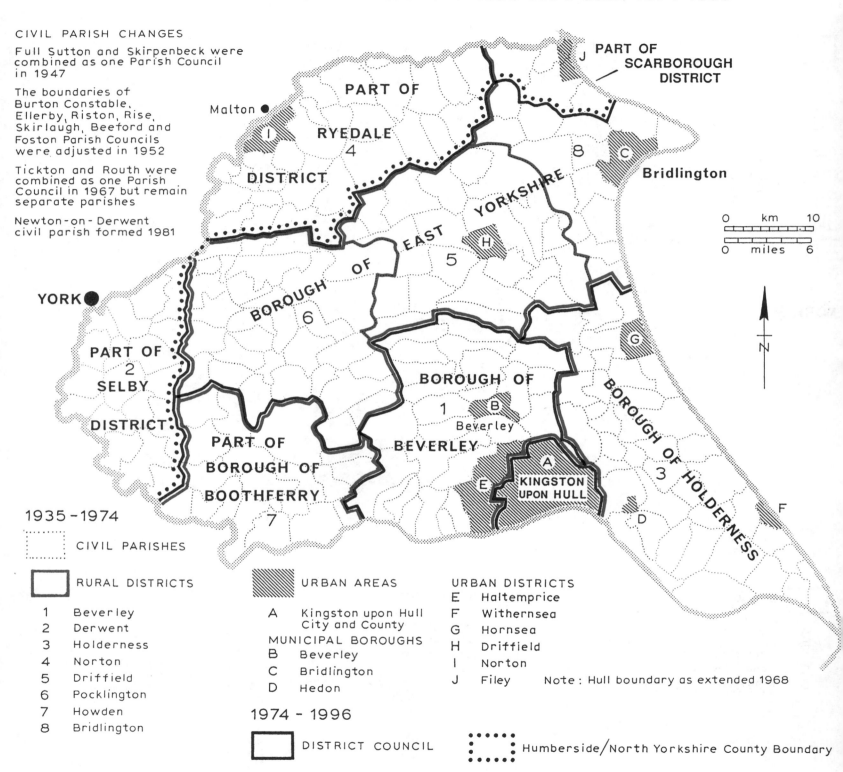

CIVIL PARISH CHANGES

Full Sutton and Skirpenbeck were combined as one Parish Council in 1947

The boundaries of Burton Constable, Ellerby, Riston, Rise, Skirlaugh, Beeford and Foston Parish Councils were adjusted in 1952

Tickton and Routh were combined as one Parish Council in 1967 but remain separate parishes

Newton-on-Derwent civil parish formed 1981

PART OF RYEDALE 4 DISTRICT

Malton ●

YORK ●

PART OF 2 SELBY DISTRICT

PART OF BOROUGH OF BOOTHFERRY 7

BOROUGH OF EAST YORKSHIRE 5

BOROUGH OF 6

BOROUGH OF BEVERLEY 1

Beverley B

PART OF SCARBOROUGH DISTRICT

J

8

C Bridlington

H

G

A KINGSTON UPON HULL

E

BOROUGH OF HOLDERNESS 3

F

D

0 km 10

0 miles 6

N

1935-1974

⋯ CIVIL PARISHES

▭ RURAL DISTRICTS
1 Beverley
2 Derwent
3 Holderness
4 Norton
5 Driffield
6 Pocklington
7 Howden
8 Bridlington

▨ URBAN AREAS
A Kingston upon Hull City and County

MUNICIPAL BOROUGHS
B Beverley
C Bridlington
D Hedon

URBAN DISTRICTS
E Haltemprice
F Withernsea
G Hornsea
H Driffield
I Norton
J Filey   Note: Hull boundary as extended 1968

1974 - 1996

▭ DISTRICT COUNCIL   ⋯⋯ Humberside/North Yorkshire County Boundary

HULL : BOUNDARY EXTENSIONS

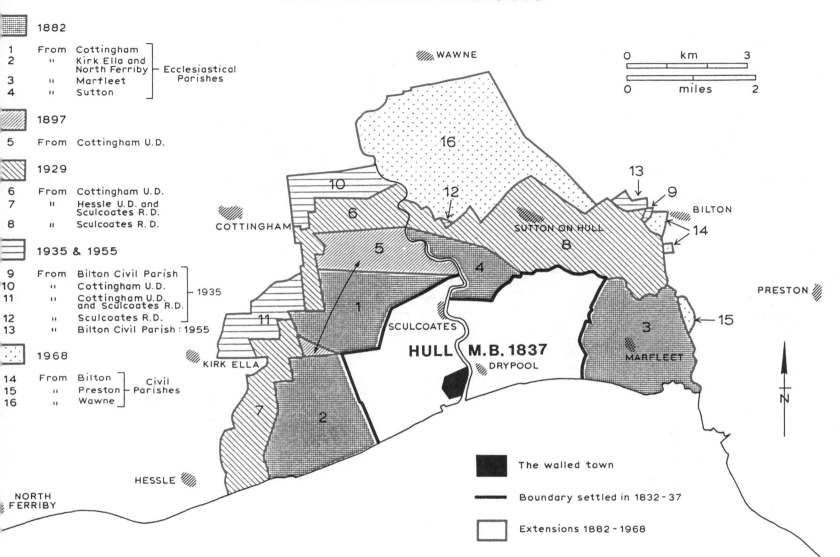

1882

1	From Cottingham	
2	" Kirk Ella and North Ferriby	Ecclesiastical Parishes
3	" Marfleet	
4	" Sutton	

1897

5 From Cottingham U.D.

1929

6 From Cottingham U.D.
7 " Hessle U.D. and Sculcoates R.D.
8 " Sculcoates R.D.

1935 & 1955

9	From Bilton Civil Parish	
10	" Cottingham U.D.	
11	" Cottingham U.D. and Sculcoates R.D.	1935
12	" Sculcoates R.D.	
13	" Bilton Civil Parish : 1955	

1968

14	From Bilton	Civil Parishes
15	" Preston	
16	" Wawne	

WAWNE

COTTINGHAM

BILTON

PRESTON

SUTTON ON HULL

KIRK ELLA

SCULCOATES

HULL M.B. 1837

DRYPOOL

MARFLEET

HESSLE

NORTH FERRIBY

0 km 3
0 miles 2

N

The walled town

Boundary settled in 1832-37

Extensions 1882-1968

137

BRIDLINGTON : BOUNDARY EXTENSIONS

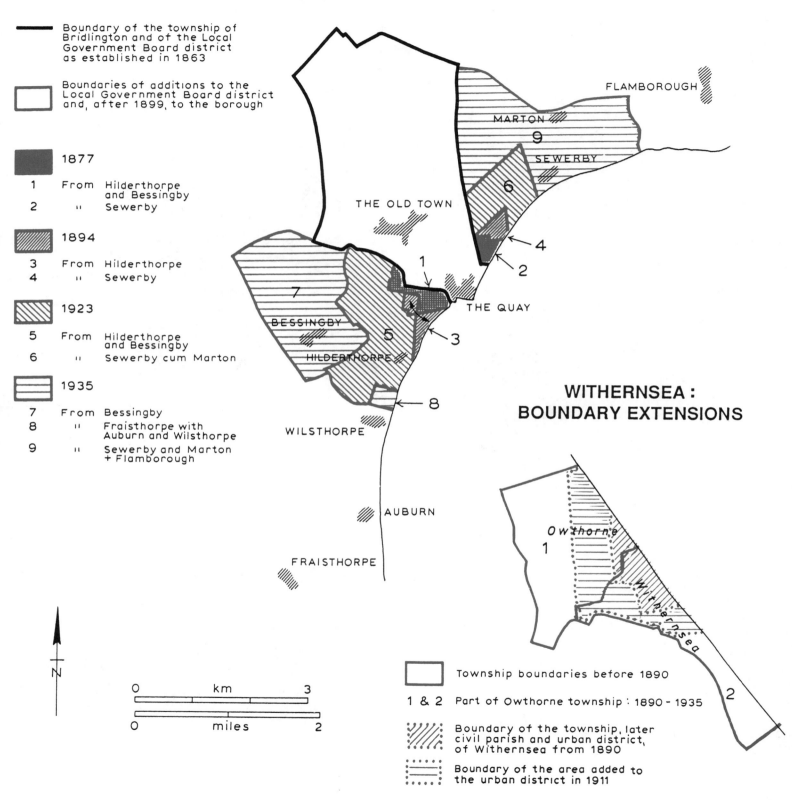

Boundary of the township of Bridlington and of the Local Government Board district as established in 1863

Boundaries of additions to the Local Government Board district and, after 1899, to the borough

1877
1   From   Hilderthorpe and Bessingby
2   "   Sewerby

1894
3   From   Hilderthorpe
4   "   Sewerby

1923
5   From   Hilderthorpe and Bessingby
6   "   Sewerby cum Marton

1935
7   From   Bessingby
8   "   Fraisthorpe with Auburn and Wilsthorpe
9   "   Sewerby and Marton + Flamborough

FLAMBOROUGH

MARTON

SEWERBY

9

6

4

2

THE OLD TOWN

1

THE QUAY

7

BESSINGBY

5

3

HILDERTHORPE

8

WILSTHORPE

AUBURN

FRAISTHORPE

N

0   km   3

0   miles   2

WITHERNSEA : BOUNDARY EXTENSIONS

Owthorne

1

Withernsea

2

Township boundaries before 1890

1 & 2   Part of Owthorne township : 1890 - 1935

Boundary of the township, later civil parish and urban district, of Withernsea from 1890

Boundary of the area added to the urban district in 1911

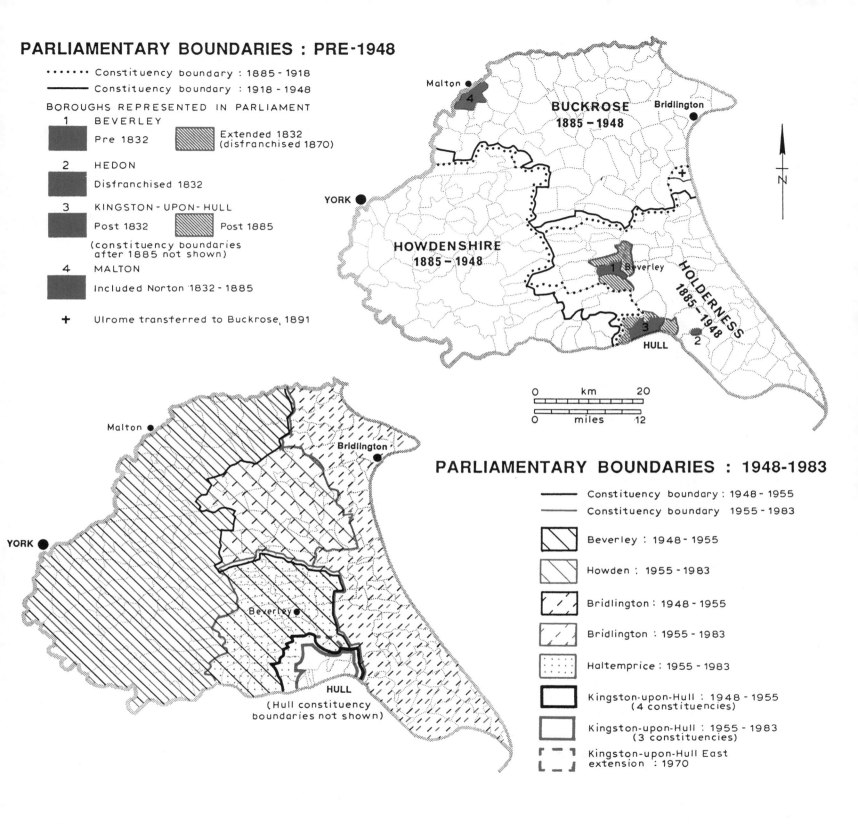

PARLIAMENTARY BOUNDARIES : PRE-1948

······ Constituency boundary : 1885 - 1918
——— Constituency boundary : 1918 - 1948

BOROUGHS REPRESENTED IN PARLIAMENT

1   BEVERLEY

Pre 1832   Extended 1832
(disfranchised 1870)

2   HEDON

Disfranchised 1832

3   KINGSTON - UPON - HULL

Post 1832   Post 1885

(constituency boundaries
after 1885 not shown)

4   MALTON

Included Norton 1832 - 1885

+   Ulrome transferred to Buckrose, 1891

BUCKROSE
1885 - 1948

HOWDENSHIRE
1885 - 1948

HOLDERNESS
1885 - 1948

Malton
Bridlington
YORK
Beverley
HULL

0   km   20
0   miles   12

PARLIAMENTARY BOUNDARIES : 1948-1983

——— Constituency boundary : 1948 - 1955
——— Constituency boundary   1955 - 1983

Beverley : 1948 - 1955

Howden : 1955 - 1983

Bridlington : 1948 - 1955

Bridlington : 1955 - 1983

Haltemprice : 1955 - 1983

Kingston-upon-Hull : 1948 - 1955
(4 constituencies)

Kingston-upon-Hull : 1955 - 1983
(3 constituencies)

Kingston-upon-Hull East
extension : 1970

Malton
Bridlington
YORK
Beverley
HULL
(Hull constituency
boundaries not shown)

NOTES AND BIBLIOGRAPHY

ENVIRONMENT

PHYSIOGRAPHY

Bibliography

G. de Boer, 'Physiographic Evolution' in D.H. Rayner and J.E. Hemingway (eds), *The Geology and Mineral Resources of Yorkshire* (Leeds, 1974), 271-92.

J.R. Flenley, 'Vegetational History' in S. Ellis and D.R. Crowther (eds), *Humber Perspectives: a region through the ages* (Hull, 1990), 43-53.

J. Lewin, *The Yorkshire Wolds: a study in geomorphology* (Hull, 1969).

J.S. Pethick, 'The Humber Estuary' in S. Ellis and D.R. Crowther (eds), *Humber Perspectives: a region through the ages* (Hull, 1990), 54-67.

J.A. Sheppard, *The Draining of the Hull Valley* (East Yorkshire Local History Society Series 8, 1958).

J.A. Sheppard, *The Draining of the Marshlands of South Holderness and the Vale of York* (East Yorkshire Local History Society Series 20, 1966).

A. Straw and K.M. Clayton, *Eastern and Central England* (London, 1979).

GEOLOGY

Bibliography

British Geological Survey, *Quaternary Map of the United Kingdom (South)*, 1:625,000 scale (Southampton, 1977).

J.A. Catt, 'Geology and Relief' in S. Ellis and D.R. Crowther (eds), *Humber Perspectives: a region through the ages* (Hull, 1990), 13-28.

N. Eyles, A.M. McCabe and D.Q. Bowen, 'The Stratigraphic and Sedimentological Significance of Late Devensian Ice Sheet Surging in Holderness, Yorkshire, U.K', *Quaternary Science Reviews* 13 (1994), 727-59.

P. Kent, *British Regional Geology: eastern England from the Tees to The Wash* (London, 1980).

J.W. Neale, 'The Geology of the Humber Area' in N. Jones (ed.), *A Dynamic Estuary: man, nature and the Humber* (Hull, 1988), 1-15.

D.H. Rayner and J.E. Hemingway (eds), *The Geology and Mineral Resources of Yorkshire* (Leeds, 1974).

COASTAL EROSION OF HOLDERNESS

Bibliography

G. de Boer and R.A. Skelton, 'The Earliest English Chart with Soundings', *Imago Mundi* 23 (1969), 9-16.

C.E. De Rance, 'The Rate of Erosion of the Sea-coasts of England and Wales, and the Influence of the Artificial Abstraction of Shingle or Other Material in that Action. Fourth Report of the Committee', *Report of the British Association for the Advancement of Science* (1895), 352-87.

R. Pickwell, 'The Encroachments of the Sea from Spurn Point to Flamborough Head, and the Works Executed to Prevent the Loss of Land', *Proceedings of the Institution of Civil Engineers* 51 (1878), 191-212.

Royal Commission on Coast Erosion, *Royal Commission on Coast Erosion (1907-11), Third and Final Report* (London, 1911).

T. Sheppard, *The Lost Towns of the Yorkshire Coast* (London, 1912).

H. Valentin, 'Der Landverlust in Holderness, Ostengland, von 1852 bis 1952', *Erde, Berlin* 6 (1954), 296-315. Translated and reprinted as:

H. Valentin, 'Land Loss at Holderness' in J.A. Steers (ed.), *Applied Coastal Geomorphology* (London, 1971), 116-37.

THE HISTORY OF SPURN POINT

Bibliography

G. de Boer, 'Spurn Head: its history and evolution', *Transactions of the Institute of British Geographers*, 34 (1964), 71-89.

G. de Boer, *A History of the Spurn Lighthouses* (East Yorkshire Local History Society Series 24, 1968).

G. de Boer, 'Spurn Point: erosion and protection after 1849' in J. Neale and J. Flenley (eds), *The Quaternary in Britain* (Oxford, 1981), 206-15.

SOILS

Bibliography

S. Ellis, 'Soils' in S. Ellis and D.R. Crowther (eds), *Humber Perspectives: a region through the ages* (Hull, 1990), 29-42.

S. Ellis and D. Newsome, 'Chalkland Soil Formation and Erosion on the Yorkshire Wolds, Northern England', *Geoderma* 48 (1991), 59-72.

R.A. Jarvis, V.C. Bendelow, R.I. Bradley, D.M. Carroll, R.R. Furness, I.N.L. Kilgour and S.J. King, *Soils and Their Use in Northern England* (Harpenden, 1984).

Soil Survey of England and Wales, *Soils of Northern England, sheet 1*, 1:250,000 scale (Southampton, 1983).

THE CHANGING DISTRIBUTION OF REPTILES SINCE THE LATE NINETEENTH CENTURY

Bibliography

B.R. Kirk, 'The Sand Lizard *Lacerta agilis* at Spurn Point: fact or fancy?', *Yorkshire Naturalists' Union Bulletin* 12 (1989), 16-18.

B.R. Kirk, 'Changes in the Distribution of Reptiles in the East Riding of Yorkshire', *The Naturalist* 119 (1994), 95-103.

WILDLIFE CONSERVATION

Bibliography

F.W. Brooks, *Domesday Book and the East Riding* (East Yorkshire Local History Society Series 21, 1966).

B. English, *The Lords of Holderness 1086 - 1260, a study in feudal society* (Oxford, 1979, Hull, 1991).

J.R. Flenley, 'Vegetational History' in S. Ellis and D.R. Crowther (eds), *Humber Perspectives: a region through the ages* (Hull, 1990), 43-53.

L.H. Matthews, *British Mammals* (London, 1968).

S. Neave, *Medieval Parks of East Yorkshire* (Cherry Burton, 1991).

ARCHAEOLOGY

Bibliography

D.J. Breeze and B. Dobson, 'Roman Military Deployment in North England', *Britannia*, 16 (1985), 1-18.

J.G.D. Clark, *Excavations at Star Carr* (Cambridge, 1954).

J.G.D. Clark, *Star Carr: a case study in bioarchaeology* (Reading Massachussets, 1972).

J.S. Dent, 'Cemeteries and Settlement Patterns of the Iron Age on the Yorkshire Wolds', *Proceedings of the Prehistoric Society*, 48 (1982), 437-57.

P. Halkon (ed.), *New Light on the Parisi: recent discoveries in Iron Age and Roman East Yorkshire* (East Riding Archaeological Society and University of Hull School of Adult and Continuing Education, 1989).

N. Loughlin and K.R. Miller, *A Survey of Archaeological Sites in Humberside* (Beverley, 1979).

T.G. Manby, 'Bronze Age Settlement in Eastern Yorkshire' in J. Barnett and R. Bradley (eds) *Settlement and Society in the Later Bronze Age* (Oxford, 1980), 307-70.

T.G. Manby, 'The Neolithic in Eastern Yorkshire' in T.G. Manby (ed.), *Archaeology in Eastern Yorkshire: essays in honour of T.C.M. Brewster* (Department of Archaeology and Prehistory, University of Sheffield, 1988), 35-88.

H. Ramm, *The Parisi* (London, 1978).

R.T. Schadla-Hall, 'The Early Post-Glacial in Eastern Yorkshire' in T.G. Manby (ed.), *Archaeology in Eastern Yorkshire: essays in honour of T.C.M. Brewster* (Department of Archaeology and Prehistory, University of Sheffield, 1988), 25-34.

I.M. Stead, *Iron Age Cemeteries in East Yorkshire*, English Heritage Archaeological Report 22 (London, 1991).

R. Van de Noort and P. Davies, *Wetland Heritage of Holderness: an archaeological assessment of the Humber wetlands* (Hull, 1993).

R. Van de Noort and S. Ellis (eds), *Wetland Heritage of Holderness: an archaeological survey* (Hull, 1995).

POPULATION AND SETTLEMENT

DOMESDAY VILLS

Notes

[1] Another common problem is that Domesday Book usually records only the basic name form, making it impossible in some cases to be certain whether all places sharing that form actually existed in 1086. In the East Riding, for instance, Domesday does not distinguish North and South Dalton, only one of which may have existed in 1086. Fortunately, this problem is not a significant one in the East Riding, so the count of 441 named places is subject only to a tiny margin of possible error.

[2] Other medieval records such as tax assessments do not, of course, tell us exactly where people lived (only archaeology can be precise about this), but most such documents are organised by townships rather than manors, which is less misleading.

[3] Domesday Book names 27 of the 28 places named by the other sources, giving a total of 441 place-names in all. Only Stamford Bridge does not appear in Domesday.

[4] Sixteen Domesday vills along the east coast have been partially or entirely lost to the sea - Aldbrough, Auburn, Cleeton, Great and Little Cowden, Dimlington, Kilnsea, Monkwith, Out Newton, Northorpe, Owthorne, Ringbrough, Waxholme, Wilsthorpe, Winkton and Withernsea. In some cases, part of the site has survived or the settlement itself has moved inland, but in a few cases (Cleeton, Northorpe, Winkton) the entire site has been lost. On the map, Cleeton and Winkton are located in the North Sea.

[5] In the Wallingfen area, e.g. Balkholme, Bellasize, Bishopsoil, Blacktoft, Broomfleet, Faxfleet, Gilberdyke, Metham, Newport, New Village and Scalby.

[6] Kexby, Full Sutton, Newton-upon-Derwent, Stamford Bridge and Wilberfoss, which, it has been argued, are concealed by the statistics for Low Catton (see *Domesday Book: Yorkshire*).

Bibliography

K.J. Allison, *The East Riding of Yorkshire Landscape* (London, 1976).

F.W. Brooks, *Domesday Book and the East Riding* (East Yorkshire Local History Society Series 21, 1966).

H.C. Darby, *Domesday England* (Cambridge, 1977).

H.C. Darby and I.S. Maxwell, *The Domesday Geography of Northern England* (Cambridge, 1977).

H.C. Darby and G.R. Versey, *Domesday Gazetteer* (Cambridge, 1975).

M.L. Faull and M. Stinson (eds), *Domesday Book: Yorkshire*, 2 vols. (Chichester, 1986).

G. Fellows-Jensen, *Scandinavian Settlement Names in Yorkshire* (Copenhagen, 1972).

A.H. Smith, *The Place-Names of the East Riding of Yorkshire and York*, English Place-Name Society 14 (Cambridge, 1937).

CASTLES AND MOATED SITES

Notes

[1] The distribution map has been compiled from information copyright of Humber Archaeology Partnership Sites and Monuments Record; National Monuments Record, R.C.H.M.E.; North Yorkshire County Council Sites and Monuments Record and from Jean Le Patourel's invaluable gazetteer (see bibliography).

[2] A moated brick lodge was mentioned in a survey of New Park, Leconfield in 1577 and described as 'made for a house of pleasure with houses of office and divers lodgings'.

[3] E.S. Eames, 'A Thirteenth Century Tile Kiln Site at North Grange, Meaux, Beverley, Yorkshire', *Medieval Archaeology* 5 (1961), 137-68.

[4] S.M. Youngs and J. Clark (eds), 'Medieval Britain in 1980', *Medieval Archaeology* 25 (1981), 216-18.

[5] Sunk Island was not embanked and reclaimed from the Humber until the seventeenth century.

Bibliography

F.A. Aberg (ed.), *Medieval Moated Sites*, Council for British Archaeology Research Report 17 (London, 1978).

R. Allen Brown, *English Castles* (3rd edition, London, 1976).

H. Clarke, *The Archaeology of Medieval England*, in particular 47-62 'Moated Sites' and 105-27 'Castles' (London, 1984).

R. Higham and P. Barker, *Timber Castles* (London, 1992).

H.E.J. Le Patourel, *The Moated Sites of Yorkshire*, Society for Medieval Archaeology Monograph 5 (London, 1973).

D. Wilson, *Moated Sites* (Princes Risborough, 1985).

MEDIEVAL HULL

Notes

[1] K.J. Allison (ed.), *The Victoria County History of Yorkshire: East Riding* vol.1 (London, 1969), 20. Contrast this low figure for Hull with that of the 1297 Lay Subsidy for Beverley, where 260 taxpayers were recorded.

[2] A. Dyer, *Decline and Growth in English Towns, 1400-1640* (London, 1991), 64.

[3] See Allison, *V.C.H. Yorkshire East Riding* vol.1, 157 and n.90.

[4] W.G. Hoskins, *Local History in England* (2nd edition, London, 1972), 238-9.

[5] For the whole period between 1370 and 1499, only 48 textile workers from Hull were admitted as freemen; in contrast, 42 weavers alone are recorded as working in Beverley during the late fifteenth century. See Allison, *V.C.H. Yorkshire East Riding* vol.1, 55-6 and Table 1 for details of the Hull freemen admissions.

[6] L.A.S. Butler, 'Medieval Urban Religious Houses' in J. Schofield, and R. Leech (eds), *Urban Archaeology in Britain*, C.B.A. Research Report 61 (London, 1987), 167-76 (and especially 169).

Bibliography

K.J. Allison (ed.), *The Victoria County History of Yorkshire: East Riding* vol.1 (London, 1969).

W.R. Childs, *The Trade and Shipping of Hull, 1300-1500* (East Yorkshire Local History Society Series 17, 1990).

See also the five volumes of 'The Hull Old Town Reports Series', in the *East Riding Archaeologist* 3-6, and 8 (1977, 1978, 1980, 1987 and 1993).

THE GEOGRAPHICAL GROWTH OF HULL

Bibliography

C.A. Forster, *Court Housing in Kingston upon Hull* (Hull, 1972).

M.T. Wild, 'The Geographical Shaping of Hull' in S. Ellis and D.R. Crowther (eds), *Humber Perspectives: a region through the ages* (Hull, 1990), 250-68.

J.E. Williams, 'Hull, 1700-1835' in K.J. Allison (ed.), *The Victoria County History of Yorkshire: East Riding* vol. 1 (London, 1969), 174-214.

MEDIEVAL BEVERLEY

Notes

[1] Charcoal recovered from a ditch at the Knights Hospitallers preceptory has been radiocarbon dated to the start of the third millennium BC; wattles from a stake and wattle fence at Annie Reed Road have been radiocarbon dated to the middle of the first millennium BC, whilst casual finds of Neolithic and Bronze Age date have been recovered from a number of locations in the town. Ditches filled with Roman pottery were found in excavations on the south side of Wylies Road in 1985 and 1990, and Roman artefacts have also been found re-deposited in medieval contexts in most excavations within the town.

[2] See P. Armstrong, D. Tomlinson and D.H. Evans, *Excavations at Lurk Lane, Beverley, 1979-1982*, Sheffield Excavation Reports 1 (Sheffield, 1991).

[3] The national rankings (excluding London) of Yorkshire towns in 1377 were:
1. York: 7,248 taxpayers
10. Beverley: 2,663
26. Hull: 1,557
30. Scarborough: 1,393
35. Pontefract: 1,085
Source: A. Dyer, *Decline and Growth in English Towns, 1400-1640* (London, 1991), 64-5.

[4] The estimates are that by the 1570s the population would have been 20% higher than in the 1560s, whilst by the 1580s it would have risen by another 12% (K.J. Allison, *The Victoria County History of Yorkshire: East Riding*, vol.6 (Oxford, 1989), 83). This is in stark contrast with the 1599 description of Beverley as 'very poore and greatly depopulated', with 400 'tenements and dwellinge-houses utterly decayed and uninhabited' (K. Miller et al., *Beverley: an archaeological and architectural study*, R.C.H.M.E. Supplementary Series 4 (London, 1982), 5).

[5] W.G. Hoskins, *Local History in England* (2nd edition, London, 1972), 238-9.

Bibliography

K.J. Allison (ed.), *The Victoria County History of Yorkshire: East Riding*, vol.6 (Oxford, 1989).

D.H. Evans, 'The Archaeology of Beverley' in S. Ellis and D.R. Crowther (eds), *Humber Perspectives: a region through the ages* (Hull, 1990), 269-82, and references therein.

K. Miller, J. Robinson, B. English and I. Hall, *Beverley: an archaeological and architectural study*, R.C.H.M.E. Supplementary Series 4 (London, 1982).

BEVERLEY IN THE EIGHTEENTH AND NINETEENTH CENTURIES

Bibliography

K.J. Allison (ed.), *The Victoria County History of Yorkshire: East Riding*, vol.6 (Oxford, 1989).

J. Crowther, *Beverley in Mid-Victorian Times* (Cherry Burton, 1990).

G. Poulson, *Beverlac* (London, 1829).

POPULATION DENSITY: 1672 AND 1743

Notes

[1] M. Drake (ed.), *Population Studies from Parish Registers* (Matlock, 1982), xxix-xxx.

[2] Public Record Office E/179/205/504, 514, 519-23; E/179/261/9-10 (microfilm in the East Riding of Yorkshire Council Archives and Records Office). For an analysis of the returns and township totals see J.D. Purdy, *Yorkshire Hearth Tax Returns* (Hull, 1991).

[3] S.L. Ollard and P.C. Walker (eds), *Archbishop Herring's Visitation Returns 1743* (Yorkshire Archaeological Society Record Series 71, 72, 75, 1928-9).

[4] Borthwick Institute of Historical Research (BIHR) Bp.V. 1764/Ret.

[5] D. Woodward (ed.), *Descriptions of East Yorkshire: Leland to Defoe* (East Yorkshire Local History Series 39, 1985), 54; BIHR Bp.V. 1764/Ret. Weaverthorpe.

[6] S. Neave, 'Rural Settlement Contraction in the East Riding of Yorkshire between the Mid-seventeenth and Mid-eighteenth Centuries', *Agricultural History Review* 41 (1993), 125-6, 135-6.

[7] E.A. Wrigley 'Urban Growth and Agricultural Change: England and the continent in the Early Modern Period' in R.I. Rotberg and T.K. Rabb (eds), *Population and History* (Cambridge, 1986), 140. The population of Hull rose from *c.*7,500 in 1700 to almost 12,000 in 1750.

[8] Neave, 'Rural Settlement Contraction' 126-8, 133-4. The fuller 1673 hearth tax returns were used for Warter and Watton.

Bibliography

D. Neave and S. Neave, 'Rural Population and Land Use in Humberside from the Sixteenth to Early Nineteenth Centuries' in S. Ellis and D.R. Crowther (eds), *Humber Perspectives: a region through the ages* (Hull, 1990), 373-87.

S. Neave 'Rural Settlement Contraction in the East Riding of Yorkshire *c.*1660-1760' (unpublished University of Hull Ph.D. thesis, 1990).

E.A. Wrigley and R.S. Schofield, *The Population History of England 1541-1871* (London, 1981).

POPULATION CHANGE: 1801-1991

Note

[1] Population counts for civil parishes are directly available in each twentieth century census. They were created simply either singly from one of the larger ecclesiastical parishes or by combining two or more of the smaller ecclesiastical parishes or 'township' divisions. After 1891, the latter ceased to be represented in published census tables.

Bibliography

K.J. Allison, *The East Riding of Yorkshire Landscape* (London, 1976).

A. Harris, *The Rural Landscape of the East Riding of Yorkshire 1700-1850* (London, 1961).

Humberside County Council, *Humberside Structure Plan: policies approved* (Beverley, 1979).

H. Mackinder *Britain and the British Seas* (Oxford, 1925).

H. Newby, *Country Life: a social history of rural England* (London, 1987).

P.J. Perry, *British Farming in the Great Depression* (Newton Abbot, 1974).

L.D. Stamp, *The Land of Britain: report of the Land Utilisation Survey of Britain, Part 48, Yorkshire (East Riding)* (London, 1942).

DESERTED SETTLEMENTS

Notes

[1] The term 'deserted' is usually applied to settlements where the number of inhabited houses has been reduced to a maximum of three.

[2] M.W. Beresford, 'The Lost Villages of Yorkshire', part 2, *Yorkshire Archaeological Journal* 38 (1955), 56-70; M. Beresford and J.G. Hurst, *Deserted Medieval Villages* (London, 1971), 207-9.

[3] Beresford, 'The Lost Villages of Yorkshire', part 2, 56.

[4] Borthwick Institute of Historical Research, CPH 5705. Documentary references for each of the individual cases of desertion mentioned in the text can be found in S. Neave 'Rural Settlement Contraction in the East Riding of Yorkshire *c.*1660-1760' (unpublished University of Hull Ph.D. thesis, 1990).

Bibliography

K.J. Allison, *Deserted Villages* (London, 1970).

M.W. Beresford, 'The Lost Villages of Yorkshire', parts 1-4, *Yorkshire Archaeological Journal* 37 (1951), 474-91; 38 (1955), 44-70, 215-40, 280-309.

M.W. Beresford, *The Lost Villages of England* (London, 1954).

M. Beresford and J.G. Hurst, *Deserted Medieval Villages* (London, 1971).

M. Beresford and J. Hurst, *Wharram Percy* (London, 1990).

B. English and K. Miller, 'The Deserted Village of Eske, East Yorkshire', *Landscape History* 13 (1991), 5-32.

S. Neave, 'Rural Settlement Contraction in the East Riding of
Yorkshire *c*.1660-1760' (unpublished University of Hull Ph.D.
thesis, 1990).

VERNACULAR BUILDING MATERIALS
Notes

[1] For a fuller discussion of East Riding building materials see N.
Pevsner and D. Neave, *Yorkshire: York and the East Riding*
(London, 1995), 23-9.

[2] H.E. Strickland, *A General View of the Agriculture of the East Riding
of Yorkshire* (York, 1812), 39.

[3] A. Lazenby, *The Cobble Stones of Holderness* (Hull, 1994). A well-
illustrated survey.

[4] J.R. Senior, 'Hildenley Limestone: a fine quality dimensional and
artifact stone from Yorkshire' in D. Parsons (ed.), *Stone
Quarrying and Building in England AD 43-1525* (Chichester,
1990), 147-68.

[5] For example 153 High Street, Hull (information from C. Ketchell).

[6] For *The Sailor* see J. Crowther (ed.), *Descriptions of East Yorkshire:
De la Pryme to Head* (East Yorkshire Local History Series 45,
1992), 49-54.

[7] S. Neave, 'Thatched Cottages of the East Riding', *Yorkshire Journal*
3 (1993), 43-9.

LANDOWNERSHIP AND LAND USE

MEDIEVAL PARKS
Notes

[1] For details of individual parks see S. Neave, *Medieval Parks of East
Yorkshire* (Cherry Burton, 1991).

[2] From *The Countrey Farm* quoted in E. Shirley, *English Deer Parks*
(London, 1867), 234.

[3] West Sussex Record Office PHA 7191.

Bibliography

L. Cantor, *The Medieval Parks of England: a gazetteer* (Department of
Education, Loughborough University, 1983).

S. Neave, *Medieval Parks of East Yorkshire* (Cherry Burton, 1991).

O. Rackham, *Trees and Woodland in the British Landscape* (1976,
reprinted London, 1983).

E. Shirley, *English Deer Parks* (London, 1867).

LANDOWNERSHIP AND PARISH TYPE, *c*.1830
Notes

[1] B.A. Holderness, '"Open" and "Close" Parishes in England in the
Eighteenth and Nineteenth Centuries', *Agricultural History
Review* 20 (1972), 127.

[2] The Land Tax was instituted in 1692, but only from *c*.1780 to 1832
were the returns deposited with the Clerk of the Peace, where they
were used to assess landowners' entitlement to the franchise. The
returns record the names of the owners and tenants of land, and the
tax paid.

[3] Before the enclosure act (1823) there had been over 20 landowners in
the village. By a process of persuasion and intimidation Hotham's
agent, John Hall, managed to buy most of the property in the
township and was able to congratulate his employer on being
'Cock of the Field'. In 1855 only one other proprietor remained.

[4] S. Bennett and N. Bennett (eds), *An Historical Atlas of Lincolnshire*
(Hull, 1993), 95.

[5] H.E. Strickland, *A General View of the Agriculture of the East Riding
of Yorkshire* (York, 1812), 31.

[6] A useful method of assessing land ownership using the returns would
take an area within ten to fifteen miles or so of a gentleman's seat
and evaluate the proportion of land tax he paid in neighbouring
townships. For example, Sir Tatton Sykes paid 60% of the tax for
East Heslerton, 21% for Eddlethorpe, 91% for Fimber, 20% for
Fridaythorpe, 25% for Helperthorpe, 55% for Kirby Grindalythe,
63% for Thixendale, 57% for Wetwang and, of course, 100% for
Sledmere.

[7] The Constables of Burton Constable, the Bethells of Rise and the
Constables of Wassand are Holderness examples.

[8] K.J. Allison, *The East Riding of Yorkshire Landscape* (London,
1976), 194.

[9] Holderness, '"Open" and "Close" Parishes', Table I, 135.

[10] J.E. Crowther, 'Enclosure, Topography and Landownership in
Eastern Yorkshire' in M.E. Turner (ed.), *Land and Property: the
English Land Tax 1692-1832* (Gloucester, 1986).

[11] Discussed in M.E. Turner, 'The Land Tax, Land and Property: old
debates and new horizons' in Turner, *Land and Property*, and
somewhat controversially in D.E. Ginter, *A Measure of Wealth:
the English Land Tax in historical analysis* (London, 1992). For a
commentary upon that study see Michael Turner's review in the
Journal of Historical Geography 19 (1993), 79-80.

SEATS OF THE GENTRY
Notes

[1] J.D. Purdy, *Yorkshire Hearth Tax Returns* (Hull, 1991), 165-73;
British Library Additional Mss 40132/109.

[2] Parliamentary Paper, *Return of Owners of Land, 1873* (England and
Wales), 1874 LXXII, pt II [C.1097-1]. The acreage and rental of
the principal East Riding landowners in 1873 is given in J.T.
Ward, *East Yorkshire Landed Estates in the Nineteenth Century*
(East Yorkshire Local History Society Series 23, 1967), 72.

[3] M.W. Barley, *Lincolnshire and the Fens* (London, 1952), 81-2.

[4] D. Neave and E. Waterson, *Lost Houses of East Yorkshire* (Hull,
1988), 8.

[5] D. Neave, *Londesborough* (Londesborough, 1977), 20-8, 32-4.

Bibliography

B. English, *The Great Landowners of East Yorkshire 1530-1910*
(Hemel Hempstead, 1990).

D. Neave and D. Turnbull, *Landscaped Parks and Gardens of East Yorkshire* (Hull, 1992).

N. Pevsner and D. Neave, *Yorkshire: York and the East Riding* (London, 1995).

THE INCIDENCE AND CHRONOLOGY OF PARLIAMENTARY ENCLOSURE

Notes

[1] The law required that owners of approximately four-fifths of the land to be enclosed had to be in agreement.

[2] See Figure 12 in A. Harris, *The Rural Landscape of the East Riding of Yorkshire, 1700-1850* (2nd edition, Wakefield, 1969).

[3] Those initiated by formal agreement followed by award and carried out by commissioners are essentially identical in their implementation and effects to those initiated by act. They are therefore also shown on the map, though not in the chronological sequence. All took place during the parliamentary enclosure period.

[4] Such a map would show that most Wolds townships had a very high proportion of their land (as much as 80% in some cases) enclosed by act, whereas in the Vale of York there were many in which the act affected only a few hundred acres, essentially a 'mopping-up' operation.

[5] Anyone seeking to discover the date of early enclosures in those townships will find a useful appendix in V. Neave, *A Handlist of East Riding Enclosure Awards* (Beverley, 1971). The Victoria County History (V.C.H.) volumes for the East Riding so far published are also an excellent source. Early enclosures are not usually well documented, references tending to occur sometimes in landowners' private papers, in parish records or in glebe terriers.

[6] The timing of parliamentary enclosure county by county is examined in Chapter 3 of Michael Turner's study, *English Parliamentary Enclosure: its historical geography and economic history* (Folkestone, 1980).

[7] Many permanent pastures were ploughed up at that time. In 1812, H.E. Strickland was highly critical of the loss of ancient sheep pastures, 'verdant sheep-walks now reduced to barren wastes', because after throwing off a few good crops they were soon exhausted, and manure could not be easily brought to such remote areas (*A General View of the Agriculture of the East Riding of Yorkshire* (York, 1812), 94-5).

Bibliography

K.J. Allison, *The East Riding of Yorkshire Landscape* (London, 1976).

J.E. Crowther, 'Parliamentary Enclosure in Eastern Yorkshire, 1730-1860' (unpublished University of Hull Ph.D. thesis, 1984).

J.E. Crowther, *Parliamentary Enclosure Commissioners and Surveyors of East Yorkshire* (East Yorkshire Local History Society Series 40, 1986).

B. English, *Yorkshire Enclosure Awards* (Hull, 1985).

A. Harris, 'The Agriculture of the East Riding of Yorkshire before the Parliamentary Enclosures', *Yorkshire Archaeological Journal* 40 (1959), 119-28.

A. Harris, *The Open Fields of East Yorkshire* (East Yorkshire Local History Society Series 9, 1959).

A. Harris, *The Rural Landscape of the East Riding of Yorkshire, 1700-1850* (2nd edition, Wakefield, 1969).

M.E. Turner, *Enclosures in Britain, 1750-1830* (London, 1984).

O. Wilkinson, *The Agricultural Revolution in the East Riding of Yorkshire* (East Yorkshire Local History Society Series 5, 1956).

AGRICULTURAL LAND USE IN 1801

Notes

[1] Maslin is a mixture of wheat and rye. The acreages of turnips and rape were counted together.

[2] The forms are kept in the Public Record Office at reference H.O. 76/26. A transcription of the English returns was made by M.E. Turner and has been printed as *Home Office Acreage Returns, List and Analysis*, being volumes 189, 190, 195 and 196 of *The List and Index Society* (1982-3). The Yorkshire returns are in 196 (1983).

[3] W.G. Hoskins, 'The Leicestershire Crop Returns of 1801', *Transactions of the Leicestershire Archaeological Society* 24 (1949), 127-53. See for Yorkshire, P.A. Churley, 'The Yorkshire Crop Returns of 1801', *Yorkshire Bulletin of Economic and Social Research* 5 (1953), 179-97, and for England, M.E. Turner, 'Arable in England and Wales: estimates from the 1801 crop returns', *Journal of Historical Geography* 7 (1981), 291-302.

[4] The coverage over England is incomplete, some counties having almost no surviving records. For Yorkshire about 77% of the parishes are covered, whilst for the East Riding 68% of the total area, or 129 of its 184 parishes (70%), are covered. Mid Holderness has the highest coverage (11 of 12 parishes) and the Low Wolds the lowest (18 of 32 parishes). Because the returns were regarded with suspicion by many farmers, some incumbents found difficulty in getting the information, and even in those parishes where returns were made there must be some doubt as to their accuracy. The unpopularity of the clergy, owing to their association with the tithes, did not help matters.

[5] For example the surveys of the East Riding commissioned by the Board of Agriculture. I. Leatham, *A General View of the Agriculture of the East Riding of Yorkshire* (London, 1794), and H.E. Strickland, *A General View of the Agriculture of the East Riding of Yorkshire* (York, 1812).

[6] The districts follow those described in A. Harris, *The Rural Landscape of the East Riding of Yorkshire, 1700-1850* (2nd edition, Wakefield, 1969), with some expansions.

[7] Wheat formed 33%, oats 26% and barley 19% in England, compared with oats 31%, wheat 27%, and barley 14% in the East Riding.

[8] Harris, *Rural Landscape*, 92.

9 Strickland, *A General View of the Agriculture of the East Riding*, 105 and 127.

10 Harris, *Rural Landscape*, 94.

11 A. Harris, 'The Rabbit Warrens of East Yorkshire in the Eighteenth and Nineteenth Centuries', *Yorkshire Archaeological Journal* 42 (1971), 429-43.

12 Turner, *Home Office Acreage Returns*, Table 1, 294; Churley, 'Yorkshire Crop Returns', 194.

13 Harris, *Rural Landscape*, 92-3.

AGRICULTURAL LAND USE IN THE MID-NINETEENTH CENTURY

Notes

1 Note from Roger Kain: Alan and I discussed what we might do for the *Atlas* in autumn 1994 and I received his suggested regional divisions just a few weeks before he died in May 1995. I offer this cameo of Alan's beloved East Riding of Yorkshire to him *In Memoriam*.

2 The tithe files are held in the Public Record Office (PRO) under pressmark IR18. Data are extant for only those districts where tithe was commuted under the Tithe Commutation Act of 1836 by voluntary agreement between local landowners and tithe owners. By 1836 almost a third of East Riding tithe districts had been exonerated from tithes under the terms of parliamentary enclosure acts; voluntary commutations were achieved in only 30 per cent of the remaining tithable districts. When reports for districts with large tracts of tithe-free land are eliminated, the number of districts with useable data falls to only 36 or just ten per cent of all East Riding districts. Thus our maps and tables should be treated with some caution and should be viewed only as indicators of the general balance of land use and of the rank order of crops. All the data from which the tables and maps have been constructed are available as a CD ROM publication: R.J.P. Kain, *A Socio-Economic Survey of Land Use and the Agricultural Economy: the 1836 national tithe files database* (Marlborough, 1995). See also R.J.P. Kain, *An Atlas and Index of the Tithe Files of Mid-Nineteenth-Century England and Wales* (Cambridge, 1986), 370-2.

3 A. Harris, *The Rural Landscape of the East Riding of Yorkshire 1700-1850* (London, 1961), 100. There is some discussion of the process of conversion of pasture to arable in the tithe file of Gransmoor: PRO IR18 11595.

4 See tithe file for Stamford Bridge West: PRO IR18 11744.

5 PRO IR18 11672.

6 Neither grassland and livestock management nor woodland and other land uses occasioned much comment in East Riding tithe files.

7 PRO IR18 11669.

8 See comments in the tithe files of Langwith and Heslington: PRO IR18 11653 and 6 11612 respectively.

9 PRO IR18 11771.

10 PRO IR18 11787.

11 PRO IR18 11751.

12 PRO IR18 11497.

Bibliography

A. Harris, *The Rural Landscape of the East Riding of Yorkshire 1700-1850* (London, 1961).

R.J.P. Kain, *An Atlas and Index of the Tithe Files of Mid-Nineteenth-Century England and Wales* (Cambridge, 1986).

R.J.P. Kain, *A Socio-Economic Survey of Land Use and the Agricultural Economy: the 1836 national tithe files database* (Marlborough, 1995) (CD ROM publication).

TRADE AND INDUSTRY

MARKETS AND TOWNS IN THE MIDDLE AGES

Notes

1 Full references cannot be given here, but the majority can be found in McCutcheon 1940 (below) and *Victoria County History: East Riding*, vols.1-6. I am grateful to Dr R.H. Britnell for the use of his unpublished list of markets.

2 C. Hart, *The Danelaw* (London, 1992), 255-9.

3 P.H. Sawyer, 'Fairs and Markets in Early Medieval England', in N. Skyum-Nielsen and N. Lund (eds), *Danish Medieval History: new currents* (Copenhagen, 1981), 159.

4 D.M. Palliser, 'An Introduction to the Yorkshire Domesday' in *The Yorkshire Domesday* (London, 1992), 21, 27. I have therefore not mapped either as a borough, and I have also excluded South Dalton, the burghal evidence for which is also doubtful. For simplicity, boroughs mapped do not have other symbols; all had also markets and fairs.

5 P.R.O. C143/4, no.21; W. Brown (ed.), *Yorkshire Inquisitions* I (Yorkshire Archaeological Society Record Series 12, 1892 for 1891), 187.

6 *Cal. Charter Rolls* V, 178.

7 H.C. Darby (ed.), *A New Historical Geography of England before 1600* (Cambridge, 1976), 184; A. Dyer, *Decline and Growth in English Towns, 1400-1640* (London, 1991), 64.

Bibliography

K.J. Allison (ed.), *The Victoria County History of Yorkshire: East Riding*, vols. 1-6 (Oxford and London, 1969-89).

K.L. McCutcheon, *Yorkshire Fairs and Markets to the End of the Eighteenth Century* (Thoresby Society 39, 1940 for 1939).

M. Noble, 'Urban Settlement' in B. Dyson (ed.), *A Guide to Local Studies in East Yorkshire* (Cherry Burton, 1985), 103 (map of markets *c*.1400).

MARKETS AND FAIRS: 1500-1928

Notes

1 Information on markets and fairs can be gained from the bibliography and the following sources: British Parliamentary Papers, c.5550 Iiii Royal Commission on Market Rights and Tolls

1888; W. Owen, *Book of Fairs* (6th edition, London, 1770); J. Adams *Index Villaris or an Alphabetical List of all Cities, Market Towns, Parishes, Villages and Private Seats in England and Wales* (London, 1680); directories.

2 Accounts of the fair are contained in the *Hull Advertiser* and in H.E. Strickland, *A General View of the Agriculture of the East Riding of Yorkshire* (York, 1812).

3 Strickland, *A General View of the Agriculture of the East Riding*, 238.

4 J. Bigland, *The Beauties of England and Wales*, vol.16 Yorkshire (London, 1812) 411; P. Barfoot and J. Wilkes, *The Universal British Directory of Trade and Commerce*, 6 vols. (London, 1791) vol.3, 485.

Bibliography

K.J. Allison, *The East Riding of Yorkshire Landscape* (London, 1976).

A.M. Everitt, 'The Marketing of Agricultural Produce' in J. Thirsk (ed.), *The Agrarian History of England and Wales*, vol.4 (London 1967), 466-592.

K.L. McCutcheon, *Yorkshire Fairs and Markets to the End of the Eighteenth Century* (Thoresby Society 39, 1940 for 1939).

Ministry of Agriculture and Fisheries, *Markets and Fairs in England and Wales: Part 3 Northern Markets* (H.M.S.O., London, 1928).

M. Noble, 'Growth and Development of Country Towns: the case of Eastern Yorkshire 1700-1800' (unpublished University of Hull Ph.D. thesis, 1983).

M. Noble, 'The Market Towns of the Humber North Bank' in S. Ellis and D.R. Crowther (eds), *Humber Perspectives: a region through the ages* (Hull, 1990), 307-20.

WINDMILLS AND WATERMILLS

Notes

1 L. White, *Medieval Technology and Social Change* (Oxford, 1962), 87. See also R. Holt, *The Mills of Medieval England* (Oxford, 1988), Appendix 1.

2 K.J. Allison, *East Riding Water-Mills* (East Yorkshire Local History Society Series 26, 1970), 18-21.

3 R. Gregory, *East Yorkshire Windmills* (Cheddar, 1985), 71-80.

4 F. Ibaarup, 'Wind Moller', *Dansk Polytechnisk Tidskrift* (1825), 13-19.

Bibliography

K.J. Allison, *East Riding Water-Mills* (East Yorkshire Local History Society Series 26, 1970).

R. Gregory, *East Yorkshire Windmills* (Cheddar, 1985).

R. Gregory 'The Work of Norman and Smithson Millwrights of Hull 1780-1831' (unpublished University of Hull M.Phil. thesis, 1991).

J. Reynolds, *Windmills and Watermills* (London, 1970).

T.S. Reynolds, *Stronger than a Hundred Men: a history of the vertical water wheel* (Baltimore and London, 1983).

R. Wailes, *The English Windmill* (London, 1954).

BREWING AND MALTING, ROPEMAKING, TEXTILES AND TANNING

Notes

1 H.E. Strickland, *A General View of the Agriculture of the East Riding of Yorkshire* (York, 1812), 282.

2 Attempts were made to find coal at Warter, Everingham and Market Weighton in the eighteenth century. D. Neave, 'The Search for Coal in the East Riding in the Eighteenth Century', *Yorkshire Archaeological Journal* 45 (1973), 194-7.

3 The firm of William Crosskill and Son at Beverley was the riding's leading agricultural machinery manufacturer in the mid-nineteenth century, when there were 800 employees.

4 E. Baines, *History, Directory and Gazetteer of the County of York* vol.II East and North Ridings (Leeds, 1823); W. White, History, *Gazetteer of the East and North Ridings of Yorkshire* (Sheffield, 1840); E.R. Kelly (ed.), *The Post Office Directory of the North and East Ridings of Yorkshire with the City of York* (London, 1872).

5 The numbers given alongside the symbols relate to the peak figure for that trade or industry in the three directories. The information is not comprehensive and a more complete picture could be provided by the use of census enumerators' returns and Ordnance Survey plans. For example, the first edition OS plan of 1853 for Bridlington shows two tanneries.

6 Another large flax factory built at Pocklington in 1852 is not marked on the map, since it closed in 1859 and does not figure in the selected directories.

Bibliography

K.J.Allison, *East Riding Water-mills* (East Yorkshire Local History Series 26, 1970).

K.J. Allison, *The East Riding of Yorkshire Landscape* (London, 1976).

H.D. Watts, 'The Industrial Geography of East Yorkshire' (unpublished University of Hull MA thesis, 1964).

BRICK AND TILE MAKING

Notes

1 F.W. Brooks, 'A Medieval Brickyard at Hull', *Journal of the British Archaeological Association* 3rd series, 4 (1939), 151-74.

2 D. Neave, 'Artisan Mannerism in North Lincolnshire and East Yorkshire: the work of William Catlyn (1628-1709) of Hull' in C. Sturman (ed.), *Lincolnshire People and Places* (Lincoln, 1996), 18-25.

3 D. Woodward (ed.), *The Farming and Memorandum Books of Henry Best of Elmswell 1642* (London, 1984), 200.

4 W. Ann Los 'Accounts from Archives: East Yorkshire' (brickmaking at Bainton 1727-46), *British Brick Society Information* 31 (1983), 20-3.

5 K.A. MacMahon, 'The Beverley House of the Hotham Family', *Transactions of the Georgian Society for East Yorkshire* 4, pt. 3 (1959), 42.

[6] D. Neave, 'Pantiles: their early use and manufacture in the Humber region' in D. Tyszka et al. (eds.), *Land, People and Landscapes* (Lincoln, 1991), 93-8.

[7] W. Ann Los 'Brickmaking - a seasonal and dual occupation', *British Brick Society Information* 40 (1986), 4-10.

Bibliography

R. Brunskill, *Brick Building in Britain* (London, 1990).

M. Hammond, *Bricks and Brickmaking* (Princes Risborough, 1981).

N. Lloyd, *A History of English Brickwork* (London 1925, reprinted 1983).

N. Pevsner and D. Neave, *Yorkshire: York and the East Riding* (London, 1995).

J. Wight, *Brick Building in England from the Middle Ages to 1550* (Chatham, 1972).

SHIPBUILDING: 1691-PRESENT

Bibliography

A.G. Credland, *Iron and Steel Shipbuilding on the Humber: Earles of Hull* (Hull, 1982).

I. Hustwick, *Moray Firth: ships and trade* (Aberdeen, 1994).

F.H. Pearson, *The Early History of Hull Steam Shipping* (Howden, 1984).

J. Skelton, *Speybuilt* (Garmouth, 1994).

HULL'S ARCTIC WHALING TRADE FROM THE SIXTEENTH TO THE NINETEENTH CENTURY

Bibliography

A.G. Credland, *The Hull Whaling Trade, an Arctic Enterprise* (Cherry Burton, 1995).

G. Jackson, *The British Whaling Trade* (London, 1978).

B. Lubbock, *The Arctic Whalers* (Glasgow, 1937).

W. Scoresby, *An Account of the Arctic Regions, Volume 2 The Whale Fishery* (Edinburgh, 1820).

HULL FISHING IN THE NINETEENTH AND TWENTIETH CENTURIES

Notes

[1] Different dates of discovery are given for the Silver Pits: 1837-8, 1843, 1844 and 1850. Fishermen were secretive and the grounds were probably rediscovered, perhaps more than once. The Little Silver Pit is about 30 miles east of Spurn Point and the Great Silver Pit is further north, nearer the Dogger.

[2] The modern freezer trawlers encouraged an increase in long distance voyages to Greenland and Newfoundland. Increasing attempts to find new fish stocks to exploit led to co-operative ventures in Australia and New Zealand, and latterly in the Falklands.

Bibliography

A.G. Credland, *The Boxing Fleet* (Hull, 1985).

A. Gill and G. Sargeant, *Village within a City* (Hull, 1986).

E.J. March, *Sailing Trawlers* (London, 1953).

R. Robinson, *Yorkshire Coast Fishing Industry, 1780-1914* (Hull, 1987).

M. Thompson, *Fish Dock* (Cherry Burton, 1989).

THE DOCK SYSTEM OF HULL: EIGHTEENTH TO TWENTIETH CENTURIES

Bibliography

J.M. Bellamy, *The Trade and Shipping of Nineteenth-Century Hull* (East Yorkshire Local History Society Series 27, 1971).

G. Jackson, *Hull in the Eighteenth Century* (London, 1972).

E.W. Paget-Tomlinson, *The Illustrated History of Canal and River Navigations* (Sheffield, 1993).

COMMUNICATIONS

TURNPIKE TRUSTS

Notes

[1] In many parishes such a rate was already common.

[2] A turnpike was a barrier consisting of bars with one sharpened end, revolving on a pivot. The name was soon applied both to the toll-gates and to the highways repaired under the system.

[3] Shown on the map. Sources used include contemporary maps and the records of turnpike trusts. Those which have survived may be found in the East Riding of Yorkshire Council Archives and Records Office.

[4] It is notable that many townships were enclosed by parliamentary act around the same time as the nearby roads were being improved under turnpike trusts. An enclosure act enabled roads to be realigned and confined by the newly planted hedges of the adjoining fields.

[5] There seems to be no evidence that the turnpike road actually went through Pocklington, although K.A. MacMahon shows it doing so in his booklet, *Roads and Turnpike Trusts in Eastern Yorkshire* (East Yorkshire Local History Society Series 18, 1964), 38-9.

[6] York Corporation was concerned that toll-bars might be placed in situations inimical to the city's interests, Macmahon, *Roads and Turnpike Trusts*, 22-3.

[7] When the act's term expired it was not extended. North of Barmston the road was dangerously close to the cliff edge and that section is now lost to the sea. There was also an alternative route to Bridlington via Driffield. These factors probably combined to ensure the end of the trust. However, many of the mileposts remain *in situ* in the southern section.

[8] At that time the Haven was a small river port, but the development of Sunk Island and drainage improvements in southern Holderness meant that it subsequently became land-locked.

[9] The trustees probably considered that any extension of their powers further north was unnecessary on the chalky well-drained soil of the Wolds.

[10] Not, as might have been expected, as far as Market Weighton, MacMahon, *Roads and Turnpike Trusts*, 32.

Bibliography

W. Albert, *The Turnpike Road System in England, 1663-1840* (Cambridge, 1972).

W.T. Jackman, *The Development of Transportation in Modern England* (London, 1916).

K.A. MacMahon, *Roads and Turnpike Trusts in Eastern Yorkshire* (East Yorkshire Local History Series 18, 1964).

E. Pawson, *Transport and Economy: the turnpike roads of eighteenth-century Britain* (London, 1977).

T. Sheppard, 'Early Means of Transport in the East Riding', *Transactions of the East Riding Antiquarian Society 26* (1929), 1-36.

NAVIGABLE WATERWAYS AND CANALS

Notes

[1] Primary source material relating to the region's navigable waterways and canals can be found in the following: Beverley Corporation Minute Books and Account Books, East Riding of Yorkshire Council Archives and Records Office; Public Record Office; Hedon Haven Commissioners records deposited with Andrew M. Jackson & Sons Solicitors, Bowlalley Lane, Hull; Market Weighton Drainage Board, Pocklington.

[2] A short private cut, known as Sir Edward Vavasour's Canal, was made from the head of the Market Weighton Canal to the Holme to Weighton road *c*.1834.

[3] W. Slater, *Yorkshire Directory* (Leeds, 1849), 315.

[4] E. Baines, *History, Directory and Gazetteer of the County of York*, 2 vols. (Leeds, 1823), vol.2, 158.

[5] Grain from Patrington's corn market was shipped to Wakefield and other West Riding towns. An account of this is given in G. Head, *A Home Tour through the Manufacturing Districts of England in the Summer of 1835* (London, 1836), 273.

Bibliography

B. Duckham, *The Inland Waterways of East Yorkshire 1700-1900* (East Yorkshire Local History Society Series 29, 1973).

C. Hadfield, *The Canals of Yorkshire and North East England*. 2 vols. (London, 1972).

K.A. MacMahon, 'Beverley and its Beck: borough finance and a town navigation, 1700-1835', *Transport History* 4 (1971), 121-42.

M. Noble, 'Inland Navigations and Country Towns: the case of East Yorkshire *c*.1750-1850' in E.M. Sigsworth (ed.), *Ports and Resorts in the Region* (Hull, 1981), 79-100.

RAILWAYS

Bibliography

K. Hoole, *A Regional History of the Railways of Great Britain, Volume 4 The North East* (Newton Abbot, 1965).

K.A. MacMahon, revised B.F. Duckham, *The Beginnings of the East Yorkshire Railways* (East Yorkshire Local History Society Series 3, 1953, revised edition 1974).

M. Nicholson and W.B. Yeadon, *An Illustrated History of Hull's Railways* (London, 1993).

RELIGION AND SOCIAL PROVISION

MEDIEVAL PARISH CHURCHES AND CHAPELS

Notes

[1] Chapels at hospitals and manor houses are not mapped, nor are chantry chapels unless they are detached from a parish church.

[2] Occasionally a medieval church was re-sited. At Paull in 1355, Skeffling in 1470 and Withernsea in 1488 churches were built on new sites away from the depredations of the Humber or North Sea.

[3] K.J. Allison, *The East Riding of Yorkshire Landscape* (London, 1976), 58. With some certainty the nunnery where St John carried out a miracle in the early eighth century can be identified with Watton, but it is only tradition that locates the churches built by Puch and Addi and consecrated by St John, at Bishop Burton and Cherry Burton respectively.

[4] J.T. Lang, *York and Eastern Yorkshire*, Corpus of Anglo-Saxon Stone Sculpture 3 (London, 1991).

[5] M.W. Beresford and J. Hurst, *Wharram Percy Deserted Medieval Village* (London, 1990), 52-65.

[6] The six volumes of *The Victoria County History of Yorkshire: East Riding* published so far provide the best printed source for information on medieval chapels.

[7] Borthwick Institute of Historical Research Prob.Reg. 5 f.79, will of J. Hill; Public Record Office E 301/117 - information from S. Neave; East Riding of Yorkshire Council Archives and Records Service DDCC 139/65.

Bibliography

G. Lawton, *Collectio Rerum Ecclesiasticarum de Dioecesi Eboracensi; or, Collections Relative to Churches and Chapels within the Diocese of York* (London, 1842).

N. Pevsner and D. Neave, *Yorkshire: York and the East Riding* (London, 1995).

MEDIEVAL RELIGIOUS HOUSES

Notes

[1] Minor variations in the foundation dates of East Riding monastic houses occur according to the sources used.

[2] The priory at North Ferriby was for brethren of the order of the Temple of St John at Jerusalem, who followed the rule of St Augustine. The priory had no connection with the Knights Templars.

[3] In its early days Swine was apparently a double house, run on similar lines to the Gilbertine priory of Watton. See D. Knowles and R.N. Hadock, *Medieval Religious Houses* (London, 1971), 276.

Bibliography

J. Burton, *The Religious Orders in the East Riding of Yorkshire in the Twelfth Century* (East Yorkshire Local History Society Series 42, 1989).

C. Cross, *The End of Medieval Monasticism in the East Riding of Yorkshire* (East Yorkshire Local History Society Series 47, 1993).

D. Knowles and R.N. Hadock, *Medieval Religious Houses* (London, 1971).

W. Page (ed.), *The Victoria County History of Yorkshire* vol.3 (London, 1913).

N. Pevsner and D. Neave, *Yorkshire: York and the East Riding* (London, 1995).

PROTESTANT NONCONFORMITY AND ROMAN CATHOLICISM IN THE SEVENTEENTH AND EIGHTEENTH CENTURIES

Bibliography

Primary sources

Borthwick Institute of Historical Research, York, Bp.V 1764/Ret (Archbishop Drummond's Visitation Returns, 1764).

Dr William's Library, London, MS 38.4 (The John Evans List of Dissenting Congregations, 1715-1729); MS 38.5 and 6 (Josiah Thompson's Lists of Dissenting Congregations in England and Wales, 1773).

G. Lyon Turner (ed.), *Original Records of Early Nonconformity under Persecution and Indulgence* vol.2 (London, 1911).

S.L. Ollard and P.C. Walker (eds), *Archbishop Herring's Visitation Returns, 1743* (Yorkshire Archaeological Society Record Series 71, 72, 75, 77, 79, 1928-31).

Secondary sources

A. Anderson, 'From Puritanism to Nonconformity, 1660-1689: a study in the development of Protestant dissent, with special reference to Yorkshire' (unpublished University of Hull Ph.D. thesis, 1980).

H. Aveling, *Post Reformation Catholicism in East Yorkshire 1558-1790* (East Yorkshire Local History Society Series 11, 1960).

A.G. Matthews, *Calamy Revised: being a revision of Edmund Calamy's Account of the ministers and others ejected and silenced, 1660-1662* (Oxford, 1934).

D. Neave, 'Post-Reformation Religion' in B. Dyson (ed.) *A Guide to Local Studies in East Yorkshire* (Cherry Burton, 1985), 75-88.

P. Thistlethwaite, *Yorkshire Quarterly Meeting (of the Society of Friends) 1665-1966* (Harrogate, 1979).

PROTESTANT NONCONFORMIST CHAPELS AND MEETING HOUSES

Note

[1] The figures for Hull chapels and meeting houses built before 1914 are as follows: Wesleyan Methodist - 40, Primitive Methodist - 24, Other Methodist - 7, Quaker - 2, Baptist - 11, Independent/Congregational - 18, Presbyterian - 7, Other Denominations - 13. Where a building has changed hands between denominations, only the first use is recorded. For further details see D. Neave, *Lost Churches and Chapels of Hull* (Hull, 1991).

Bibliography

B.W. Blanchard, 'Nonconformist churches in the Hull District' (unpublished dissertation, Hull School of Architecture, 1955). (Copy in Hull Local Studies Library.)

D. Neave and S. Neave, *East Riding Chapels and Meeting Houses* (East Yorkshire Local History Series 44, 1990).

N. Pevsner and D. Neave, *Yorkshire: York and the East Riding* (London, 1995).

C.F. Stell, *Nonconformist Chapels and Meeting-Houses in Northern England* (London, 1994).

W.P. Thistlethwaite, *The Quaker Meeting Houses of Yorkshire 1647-1980* (Harrogate, 1982, reprinted with additions 1985).

ANGLICAN CHURCH BUILDING: 1701-1900

Notes

[1] A new church was seemingly built at Warter in the late sixteenth century. In 1586 a licence was granted for the demolition of the priory church and its rebuilding on a smaller scale. P. Evans, *Church Fabric in the York Diocese 1613-1899: the records of the Archbishop's faculty jurisdiction* (York, 1995), vi.

[2] N. Pevsner and D. Neave, *Yorkshire: York and the East Riding* (London, 1995), 398, 485. This publication is the main source of information for this section.

[3] B. English, *The Great Landowners of East Yorkshire 1530-1910* (Hemel Hempstead, 1990), 226.

[4] A. Quiney, *John Loughborough Pearson* (London, 1979). Pearson began his career as a church architect in the East Riding with Ellerker church in 1843. He was responsible for a further seven new churches in the riding and restored ten others.

[5] J. Hutchinson and P. Joyce, *George Edmund Street in East Yorkshire* (Hull, 1981).

[6] J. Allibone, *The Wallpaintings at Garton-on-the-Wolds* (London, 1991).

[7] P. Thompson, *William Butterfield*, (London, 1971), 75-9.

[8] D. Neave, *Lost Churches and Chapels of Hull* (Hull, 1991).

ATTENDANCE AT RELIGIOUS WORSHIP, 1851

Note

[1] All the figures used in this map with the exception of those for registration districts which lie across the boundaries of the East Riding have been taken from the report on the 1851 Census of Religious Worship published as a Parliamentary Paper, 1852-3, LXXXIX (1690) Population of Great Britain, 1851, Religious Worship, England and Wales. There are microfilm copies of the original returns of the Census of Religious Worship for most of the East Riding in the Local History Library at Hull Central

Library and, for the whole area, at the East Riding of Yorkshire Council Archives and Records Office, Beverley. The originals are in the Public Record Office, London: HO129/ 513, 515-26. I am indebted to Mr Kevin Watson of the Department of History, University of Hull, for his assistance in preparing the pie charts used in this map.

ELEMENTARY EDUCATION: 1850-1902
Notes
[1] The term 'Church of England school' is used to cover all those schools that were either National schools (see text) or where the denomination was thus prescribed by trust deed. 'Non-church' is used for schools that were non-Anglican. Board schools were undenominational. Information on religious denomination and ownership of schools is chiefly taken from *Tenure and Trusts of Voluntary Schools* Board of Education List 32 (London, 1907), 1041-1141.

[2] T.W. Bamford, *The Evolution of Rural Education* (Hull, 1965), 7.

[3] J. Lawson, *Primary Education in East Yorkshire 1560-1902* (East Yorkshire Local History Society Series 10, 1959), 3. This booklet provides an excellent short account of the history of primary education in the East Riding. See also J. Lawson, 'The History of Education' in B. Dyson (ed.), *A Guide to Local Studies in East Yorkshire* (Cherry Burton, 1985), 166-79.

[4] The nine schools were at Bishop Wilton, Fimber, Garton-on-the-Wolds, Kirby Grindalythe, Sledmere, Thixendale, Wansford, Weaverthorpe and Wetwang.

[5] See K.J. Allison (ed.), *The Victoria County History of Yorkshire: East Riding*, vol.6 (Oxford, 1989), 250-61.

[6] See K.J. Allison (ed.), *The Victoria County History of Yorkshire: East Riding*, vol.1 (London, 1969), 348-70.

[7] For fuller details about each board see Bamford, *Evolution of Rural Education*, 88-94.

FRIENDLY SOCIETIES: 1800-1914
Notes
[1] Brief details of all known East Riding friendly societies are given in D. Neave, *East Riding Friendly Societies* (East Yorkshire Local History Series 41, 1988). For fuller information see D. Neave, 'Friendly Societies in the Rural East Riding 1830-1912' (unpublished University of Hull Ph.D. thesis, 1986).

[2] P. Davis, *The Old Friendly Societies of Hull* (Hull, 1926).

Bibliography
P.H.J.H. Gosden, *The Friendly Societies in England 1815-1875* (Manchester, 1963).

P.H.J.H. Gosden, *Self-Help: voluntary associations in nineteenth century Britain* (London, 1973).

D. Neave, *Feasts, Fellowship and Financial Aid: South Holderness friendly societies* (Beverley, 1986).

D. Neave, *Mutual Aid in the Victorian Countryside: friendly societies in the rural East Riding 1830-1914* (Hull, 1991).

T.B. Stead, *A Short History of the Chief Affiliated Friendly Societies* (Leeds, 1880).

RIOT AND REBELLION
THE PILGRIMAGE OF GRACE: 1536-37
Notes
[1] The rising was more widespread than the East Riding, involving much of the rest of Yorkshire, parts of Lancashire, Durham, Cumberland and Westmorland. This account of the rising is drawn from M.H. and R. Dodds, *The Pilgrimage of Grace, 1536-7, and the Exeter Conspiracy, 1538*, 2 vols. (Cambridge, 1915) and *Letters and Papers of Henry VIII* xi-xii (London, 1888-91). Additional material is from M. Bush, *The Pilgrimage of Grace: a study of the rebel armies of October 1536* (Manchester, 1996), which also provides a useful summary of the many interpretations of the Pilgrimage of Grace that have been presented by historians in the past 30 years.

[2] The size of the rebel force is a contemporary estimate. For discussion of the probable size of the forces raised see Bush, 418-24.

[3] There was also a muster on Kexby Moor on 15 October.

[4] A.G. Dickens, *Lollards and Protestants in the Diocese of York 1509-1558* (2nd edition, London, 1982) gives a full account of the career of Sir Francis Bigod and the second rising.

Bibliography
M. Bush, *The Pilgrimage of Grace: a study of the rebel armies of October 1536* (Manchester, 1996).

J.C. Cox, 'William Stapleton and the Pilgrimage of Grace', *Transactions of the East Riding Antiquarian Society* 10, 1903, 80-106.

A.G. Dickens, *Lollards and Protestants in the Diocese of York 1509-1558* (2nd edition, London, 1982).

M.H. and R. Dodds, *The Pilgrimage of Grace, 1536-7, and the Exeter Conspiracy, 1538*, 2 vols. (Cambridge, 1915).

R.W. Hoyle, 'Thomas Master's Narrative of the Pilgrimage of Grace', *Northern History* 21, 1985, 53-79.

Letters and Papers of Henry VIII xi-xii (London, 1888-91).

THE CIVIL WAR IN THE EAST RIDING: 1642-45
Notes
[1] B.A. English, 'Sir John Hotham and the English Civil War', *Archives* 20, no.88 (1992), 217-24.

[2] E. Hope, *A Puritan Parish Clerk* (Beverley, n.d.), 7.

[3] P.R. Newman, 'The Defeat of John Belasyse: Civil War in Yorkshire January-April 1644', *Yorkshire Archaeological Journal* 52 (1980), 123-33.

[4] Nicholas Pearson, the parish clerk of St Mary's Beverley, records the fight as being at 'Coulam on the woulds', Hope, *Puritan Parish Clerk*, 10. Sir Henry Slingsby calls the place 'Colham' a common

variant of Cowlam. D. Parsons (ed.), *The Diary of Sir Henry Slingsby of Scriven* (London, 1836), 103.

[5] D. Johnson, 'The Battle of Bridlington: Civil War in the East Riding, February 1644', *East Yorkshire Local History Society Bulletin* 50 (1994), 19-21. Pearson dates the taking of Bridlington as 'about Jan.21st', Hope, *Puritan Parish Clerk*, 10.

[6] J.T. Cliffe, *The Yorkshire Gentry from the Reformation to the Civil War* (London, 1969), 338.

Bibliography

J. Binns, 'Scarborough and the Civil Wars 1642-1651', *Northern History* 22, 1986, 95-122.

E. Broxap, 'The Sieges of Hull during the Great Civil War', *English Historical Review* 20, 1905, 457-73.

J.W. Clay, 'The Gentry of Yorkshire at the time of the Civil War', *Yorkshire Archaeological Journal* 23, 1915, 349-94.

B.N. Reckitt, *Charles the First and Hull 1639-1645* (Hull, 1952, reprint Howden, 1988).

P. Wenham, *The Great and Close Siege of York 1644* (Kineton, 1970).

ANTI-MILITIA RIOTS: 1757

Notes

[1] The anti-militia riots of 1757, although probably most extensive in the East Riding, affected other areas, particularly Lincolnshire, Nottinghamshire and Bedfordshire. Rioting had also occurred by mid-September in Cambridgeshire, Essex, Hertfordshire, Kent, Lancashire, Middlesex, Northamptonshire, and the North and West Ridings of Yorkshire, and by early October in Derbyshire, Gloucestershire, Norfolk and Surrey. D. Neave, 'Anti-Militia Riots in Lincolnshire, 1757 and 1796', *Lincolnshire History and Archaeology* 11, 1976, 21-7; J.N. Caple, 'The Militia Riots of 1757' in A. Charlesworth (ed.), *An Atlas of Rural Protest in Britain 1548-1900* (London, 1983), 124-7.

[2] British Library (BL) Egerton Mss 3436/156.

[3] J.R. Western, *The English Militia in the 18th Century* (London, 1965), 127-40.

[4] Lincolnshire Archives Office, Anderson Deposit 5/2/1.

[5] BL Additional Mss 32874/46-7, 64.

[6] On the same day North Riding rioters, reportedly numbering 2,000, gathered in York where they pulled down the inn where the deputy lieutenants were meeting, and gutted and looted a house nearby. BL Additional Mss 32874/66 and 88.

[7] BL Additional Mss 32874/68.

[8] BL Egerton Mss 3436/191. In 1758 a bill was passed 'to better explain the Militia Act'. When balloting took place for the East Yorkshire militia two years later, at a time of lower prices, there is no record of any unrest.

ADMINISTRATIVE UNITS

Notes

[1] The Ecclesiastical Boundaries text and map were compiled by David Neave. Parish and township boundaries in the mid-nineteenth century are shown on the key map at the back of this atlas.

[2] Two peculiar jurisdictions are not shown on the map - those of the Court of the Provost of the Collegiate Church of St John, Beverley, which covered 23 scattered parishes but was not exercised after 1555, and the Prebendal Court of Givendale where probate jurisdiction was normally exercised by the dean of York.

[3] The hundreds were called Acklam, Burton, Cave, Driffield, Hessle, Holderness (North, Middle and South), Howden, 'Hunthou', Pocklington, 'Scard', 'Sneculfcros', 'Toreshou', 'Turbar', Warter, Weighton and Welton.

[4] Act for the Better Regulation of Divisions, 1828 (9 Geo.IV cap.43).

[5] Hedon Corporation and Borough Improvement Act, 1860 (23 & 24 Vict. cap.31) (Local and Private).

[6] East Riding of Yorkshire Council Archives and Records Service (hereafter ERAO) East Riding County Council Accession 357. Little Kelk was an extra-parochial district until 1929 when it was united with Lowthorpe for ecclesiastical purposes. Although considered part of Dickering wapentake, Little Kelk was linked with Lissett (North Holderness division) in land tax returns.

[7] Act for the Better Relief and Employment of the Poor, 1772 (22 Geo.III cap.83).

[8] Poor Law Amendment Act, 1834 (4 & 5 Wm.IV cap.76). The extra-parochial areas of Garrison Side and Cheapsides were added to Unions by orders of the Poor Law Commissioners in 1859 (ERAO QAT 1 & QAT 2).

[9] K.J. Allison (ed.), *The Victoria County History of Yorkshire: East Riding*, vol.1 (London, 1969), 232.

[10] Joint Committees of County Councils Orders (ERAO JCO 1 & JCO 2).

[11] Local Government Act, 1929 (19 Geo.V cap.17) Section 1.

[12] Norton was briefly transferred to Malton Rural Sanitary Authority, 1889-1890 (52 & 53 Vict. cap.71).

[13] Public Health Act, 1872 (35 & 36 Vict. cap.79). The country was to be divided into Urban and Rural Sanitary Districts.

[14] Local Government Act, 1888 (51 & 52 Vict. cap.41).

[15] Local Government Act, 1894 (56 & 57 Vict. cap.73). Those Rural Sanitary Authorities which crossed the county boundary (Malton, Scarborough, Selby and York) were split by orders of Joint Committees of County Councils (ERAO JCO 1-3).

[16] By County Council Orders: ERAO CCO 69 & CCO 70.

[17] Detached parts of townships within other parishes had been rationalised by a series of orders of the Local Government Board under the Divided Parishes and Poor Law Amendment Act, 1876 (39 & 40 Vict. cap.61), and subsequent legislation. See ERAO QAT. After 1889 the process was continued by County Council

Orders (ERAO CCO), and applied to detached parts of parishes within the North and West Ridings. Within the East Riding Lockington was combined with Lockington in Kilnwick in 1894 (CCO 6) and Auburn, Fraisthorpe and Wilsthorpe were combined as one parish in 1896 (CCO 62). Shipton civil parish was renamed Shiptonthorpe in 1922 (CCO 222).

[18] Local Government Review Order, 1935, which stemmed from the Local Government Act, 1929 (19 Geo.V cap.17), Section 46.

[19] The maps showing Hull, Bridlington and Withernsea boundary changes are based on maps in K.J. Allison (ed.), *The Victoria County History of Yorkshire: East Riding* vol.1, 7, vol.2, 31 and vol.5, 158. We are grateful to Dr C.R.J. Currie, General Editor, Victoria History of the Counties of England for permission to redraw these maps.

[20] Representation of the People Act, 1832 (2 & 3 Wm.IV cap.45).

[21] Representation of the People Act, 1867 (30 & 31 Vict. cap.102).

[22] Redistribution of Seats Act, 1885 (48 & 49 Vict. cap.23).

[23] House of Commons (Redistribution of Seats) Act, 1949 (12 & 13 Geo.VI cap.66).

[24] Statutory Instruments (SI), 1955/178 & 1955/359.

[25] Kingston-upon-Hull Order, 1968.

[26] For details of the wards within the Hull constituencies 1885-1971 see F.W.S. Craig, *Boundaries of Parliamentary Constituencies* (Chichester, 1972), *passim*.

Bibliography

The Jubilee of County Councils 1889 to 1939: fifty years of local government (London, 1939).

G. Lawton, *Collectio Rerum Ecclesiasticarum de Dioecesi Eboracensi; or, Collections relative to churches and chapels within the Diocese of York* (London, 1842).

V.D. Lipman, *Local Government Areas 1834-1935* (Oxford, 1949).

F.A. Youngs, *Guide to the Local Administrative Units of England, vol.2 Northern England* (London, 1991).

PLACE-NAME INDEX

This index refers only to East Riding settlements and administrative areas referred to in the text.

EAST RIDING PARISHES AND TOWNSHIPS IN THE MID-NINETEENTH CENTURY

Ecclesiastical parish in capitals, followed by subsidiary townships. Modern civil parish (where different from the ecclesiastical parish) in brackets. Numbers/letters refer to the accompanying map.

1	ACKLAM		20A	Ellerker (*ELLERKER*)		38	ELLERTON PRIORY (*ELLERTON*)	
1A	Leavening (*LEAVENING*)		21	BRIDLINGTON		39	ELLOUGHTON-cum-Brough	
2	ALDBROUGH		21A	Buckton (*BEMPTON*)		39A	Wauldby (*WELTON*)	
2A	East Newton		21B	Grindale (*GRINDALE*)		40	ELVINGTON	
2B	West Newton (*BURTON CONSTABLE*)		21C	Easton (*BOYNTON*)		41	ESCRICK	
3	ALLERTHORPE		21D	Hilderthorpe		41A	Deighton (*DEIGHTON*)	
3A	Waplington		21E	Sewerby w. Marton		42	ETTON	
4	ARGAM (*GRINDALE*)		21F	Speeton (*REIGHTON*)		43	EVERINGHAM	
5	ATWICK		21G	Wilsthorpe (*CARNABY*)		44	FANGFOSS	
6	AUGHTON (*ELLERTON*)		22	BUBWITH		45	FILEY	
6A	East Cottingwith (*COTTINGWITH*)		22A	Breighton-cum-Gunby		46	FLAMBOROUGH	
6B	Laytham (*FOGGATHORPE*)		22B	Foggathorpe (*FOGGATHORPE*)		47	FOLKTON	
7	BAINTON		22C	Gribthorpe (*FOGGATHORPE*)		47A	Flixton	
7A	Neswick		22D	Harlthorpe (*FOGGATHORPE*)		47B	Flotmanby	
8	BARMBY MOOR		22E	Spaldington (*SPALDINGTON*)		48	FOSTON-ON-THE-WOLDS (*FOSTON*)	
9	BARMSTON		22F	Willitoft		48A	Brigham (*FOSTON*)	
10	BEEFORD		23	BUGTHORPE		48B	Gembling (*FOSTON*)	
10A	Dunnington (*BEWHOLME*)		24	BURNBY (*HAYTON*)		48C	Great Kelk (*KELK*)	
10B	Lissett (*ULROME*)		25	BURSTWICK-cum-Skeckling		49	FOXHOLES	
11	BEMPTON		25A	Ryhill & Camerton (*THORNGUMBALD*)		49A	Boythorpe	
12	BESSINGBY (*BRIDLINGTON*)		26	BURTON AGNES		49B	Butterwick	
13A	BEVERLEY ST MARTIN		26A	Gransmoor		50	FRIDAYTHORPE	
13B	BEVERLEY ST MARY		26B	Haisthorpe (*CARNABY*)		51	FULFORDS AMBO (*FULFORD*)	
13C	BEVERLEY ST NICHOLAS		26C	Thornholme		52	FULL SUTTON	
13D	Eske (*TICKTON*)		27	BURTON FLEMING		53	GANTON	
13E	Molescroft (*MOLESCROFT*)		28	BURTON PIDSEA		54	GARTON w. Grimston (*EAST GARTON*)	
13F	Storkhill-cum-Sandholme (*TICKTON*)		29	BURYTHORPE				
13G	Tickton-cum-Hull Bridge (*TICKTON*)		30	CARNABY		55	GARTON-ON-THE-WOLDS (*GARTON*)	
13H	Thearne (*WOODMANSEY*)		30A	Fraisthorpe w. Auburn (*BARMSTON*)				
13J	Weel (*TICKTON*)		31	CATWICK		56	GOODMANHAM	
13K	Woodmansey-cum-Beverley Parks (*WOODMANSEY*)		32	CHERRY BURTON		57	GOXHILL (*HATFIELD*)	
			33	COTTINGHAM		58	GREAT DRIFFIELD (*DRIFFIELD*)	
14	BIRDSALL		34	COWLAM (*COTTAM*)		58A	Elmswell (*GARTON*) w. Kellythorpe (*KIRKBURN*) & Little Driffield (*DRIFFIELD*)	
15	BISHOP BURTON		35	DUNNINGTON				
16	BISHOP WILTON w. Belthorpe		35A	Grimston				
16A	Bolton (*FANGFOSS*)		36	EASINGTON		59	GREAT GIVENDALE w. Grimthorpe (*MILLINGTON*)	
16B	Youlthorpe w. Gowthorpe		36A	Out Newton				
17	BLACKTOFT		37	EASTRINGTON		60	HALSHAM	
17A	Scalby (*GILBERDYKE*)		37A	Bellasize (*BLACKTOFT*)		61	HARPHAM	
18	BOYNTON		37B	Bishopsoil (*GILBERDYKE*)		62	HARSWELL (*EVERINGHAM*)	
19	BRANDESBURTON		37C	Gilberdyke (*GILBERDYKE*)		63	HAYTON	
19A	Moor Town		37D	Portington & Cavil		63A	Bielby (*BIELBY*)	
20	BRANTINGHAM w. Thorpe		37E	Newport-Wallingfen (*NEWPORT*)		64	HEDON	

65	HELPERTHORPE (*LUTTONS*)	84	KILNSEA (*EASINGTON*)	105	MARFLEET (*KINGSTON UPON HULL*)
66	HEMINGBROUGH	85	KILNWICK-ON-THE-WOLDS (*BESWICK*)		
66A	Barlby (*BARLBY*)			106	MARKET WEIGHTON w. Arras
66B	Brackenholme w. Woodhall	85A	Beswick (*BESWICK*)	106A	Shipton (*SHIPTONTHORPE*)
66C	Cliffe-cum-Lund (*CLIFFE*)	85B	Bracken (*WATTON*)	107	MIDDLETON-ON-THE-WOLDS
66D	Menthorpe (*NORTH DUFFIELD*) & Bowthorpe (*CLIFFE*)	86	KILNWICK PERCY (*NUNBURNHOLME*)	108	MILLINGTON w. Little Givendale
66E	Osgodby (*BARLBY*)	87A	KINGSTON-UPON-HULL DRYPOOL	109	MUSTON
66F	South Duffield (*CLIFFE*)			110	NABURN
67	HESLINGTON	87B	KINGSTON-UPON-HULL HOLY TRINITY	111	NAFFERTON
68	HESSLE			111A	Wansford (*SKERNE*)
69	HILSTON (*ROOS*)	87C	KINGSTON-UPON-HULL ST MARY	112	NEW VILLAGE (*NEWPORT*)
70	HOLLYM			113	NORTH CAVE
70A	Withernsea (*WITHERNSEA*)	87D	KINGSTON-UPON-HULL SCULCOATES	113A	Everthorpe
71	HOLME-UPON-SPALDING MOOR			113B	Drewton (*SOUTH CAVE*)
72	HOLME-ON-THE-WOLDS (*DALTON HOLME*)	88	KIRBY GRINDALYTHE	113C	South Cliffe (*SOUTH CLIFFE*)
		88A	Duggleby	114	NORTH DALTON
73	HOLMPTON	88B	Thirkleby	115	NORTH FERRIBY
74	HORNSEA	89	KIRBY UNDERDALE	115A	Swanland (*SWANLAND*)
75	HOTHAM	90	KIRKBURN	116	NORTH FRODINGHAM
76	HOWDEN	90A	Eastburn	117	NORTH GRIMSTON (*BIRDSALL*)
76A	Asselby (*ASSELBY*)	90B	Southburn	118	NORTH NEWBALD (*NEWBALD*)
76B	Balkholme (*KILPIN*)	90C	Tibthorpe (*TIBTHORPE*)	118A	South Newbald (*NEWBALD*)
76C	Barmby-on-the-Marsh (*BARMBY ON THE MARSH*)	91	KIRK ELLA	119	NORTON
		91A	Anlaby	120	NUNBURNHOLME
76D	Belby (*KILPIN*)	91B	West Ella	120A	Thorpe-le-Street (*HAYTON*)
76E	Cotness (*LAXTON*)	91C	Willerby	121	NUNKEELING w. Bewholme (*BEWHOLME*)
76F	Kilpin (*KILPIN*)	91D	Haltemprice		
76G	Knedlington (*ASSELBY*)	92	KIRKHAM (*FIRBY*)	122	OTTRINGHAM
76H	Laxton (*LAXTON*)	93	LANGTOFT	123	OWTHORNE (*WITHERNSEA*)
76J	Metham (*LAXTON*)	93A	Cottam (*COTTAM*)	123A	Rimswell (*RIMSWELL*)
76K	Saltmarshe (*LAXTON*)	94	LANGTON	123B	South Frodingham (*RIMSWELL*)
76L	Skelton (*KILPIN*)	94A	Kennythorpe (*BURYTHORPE*)	123C	Waxholme (*RIMSWELL*)
76M	Yokefleet (*BLACKTOFT*)	95	LECONFIELD w. Arram	124	PATRINGTON
77	HUGGATE	96	LEVEN	125	PAULL
78	HUMBLETON	96A	Hempholme (*BRANDESBURTON*)	125A	Thorngumbald (*THORNGUMBALD*)
78A	Danthorpe (*ELSTRONWICK*)	97	LITTLE KELK (*KELK*)	126	POCKLINGTON
78B	Elstronwick (*ELSTRONWICK*)	98	LOCKINGTON	126A	Ousethorpe (*MILLINGTON*)
78C	Fitling (*EAST GARTON*)	98A	Aike	126B	Yapham-cum-Meltonby (*YAPHAM*)
78D	Flinton	99	LONDESBOROUGH	127	PRESTON
79	HUNMANBY	100	LONG RISTON (*RISTON*)	127A	Lelley (*ELSTRONWICK*)
79A	Fordon (*WOLD NEWTON*)	101	LOW CATTON (*CATTON*)	128	REIGHTON
80	HUTTON CRANSWICK	101A	E. Stamford Bridge (*STAMFORD BRIDGE*)	129	RICCALL
80A	Rotsea			130	RILLINGTON
80B	Sunderlandwick	101B	High Catton (*CATTON*)	130A	Scampston (*SCAMPSTON*)
81	KEXBY	102	LOWTHORPE (*HARPHAM*)	131	RISE
81A	Scoreby-w.-Stamford Br. W.	103	LUND	132	ROOS
82	KEYINGHAM	104	MAPPLETON w. Rowlston	132A	Owstwick
83	KILHAM	104A	Cowdens Ambo	133	ROWLEY
83A	Swaythorpe			133A	Bentley
				133B	Hunsley

133C Little Weighton
133D Riplingham
133E Risby
134 ROUTH
135 RUDSTON
136 RUSTON PARVA (HARPHAM)
137 SANCTON
137A Houghton
137B North Cliffe (SOUTH CLIFFE)
138 SCORBOROUGH (LECONFIELD)
139 SCRAYINGHAM
139A Howsham (HOWSHAM)
139B Leppington
140 SEATON ROSS
141 SETTRINGTON
141A Scagglethorpe (SCAGGLETHORPE)
142 SHERBURN
143 SIGGLESTHORNE
143A Catfoss (SEATON)
143B Gt. Hatfield (HATFIELD)
143C L. Hatfield (HATFIELD)
143D Seaton & Wassand (SEATON)
144 SKEFFLING
145 SKERNE
146 SKIDBY
147 SKIPSEA
147A Bonwick (BEWHOLME)
147B Dringhoe, Upton & Brough
147C Ulrome (ULROME)
148 SKIPWITH
148A North Duffield (NORTH DUFFIELD)
149 SKIRPENBECK
150 SLEDMERE
151 SOUTH CAVE
151A Broomfleet (BROOMFLEET)
151B Faxfleet (BLACKTOFT)
152 SOUTH DALTON (DALTON HOLME)
153 SPROATLEY
154 STILLINGFLEET
154A Kelfield (KELFIELD)
154B Moreby
155 SUNK ISLAND
156 SUTTON-UPON-DERWENT
157 SUTTON-ON-HULL (KINGSTON UPON HULL)
158 SWINE
158A Benningholme
158B Bilton (BILTON)
158C Coniston (CONISTON)

158D Ellerby (ELLERBY)
158E Ganstead (BILTON)
158F Marton (BURTON CONSTABLE)
158G North Skirlaugh w. Rowton (SKIRLAUGH) & Arnold (RISTON)
158H South Skirlaugh (SKIRLAUGH)
158J Thirtleby (CONISTON)
158K Wyton (BILTON)
159 THORGANBY w. W. Cottingwith
160 THORNTON
160A Melbourne (MELBOURNE)
160B Storwood (COTTINGWITH)
161 THORPE BASSETT
162 THWING
162A Octon
163 TUNSTALL (ROOS)
164 WALKINGTON
165 WARTER
166 WATTON
167 WAWNE
167A Meaux
168 WEAVERTHORPE
168A Luttons Ambo (LUTTONS)
169 WELTON
169A Melton
170 WELWICK
171 WEST HESLERTON (HESLERTON)
171A East Heslerton (HESLERTON)
172 WESTOW
172A Eddlethorpe (BURYTHORPE)
172B Firby (FIRBY)
172C Menethorpe (BURYTHORPE)
173 WETWANG
173A Fimber (FIMBER)
174 WHARRAM-LE-STREET (WHARRAM)
175 WHARRAM PERCY (WHARRAM)
175A Raisthorpe w. Burdale (WHARRAM)
175B Thixendale (THIXENDALE)
175C Towthorpe (FIMBER)
176 WHELDRAKE
176A Langwith (HESLINGTON)
177 WILBERFOSS
177A Newton-upon-Derwent (NEWTON ON DERWENT)
178 WILLERBY
178A Binnington
178B Staxton
179 WINESTEAD (PATRINGTON)
180 WINTRINGHAM

180A Knapton (SCAMPSTON)
181 WITHERNWICK
182 WOLD NEWTON
183 WRESSLE
184 YEDINGHAM

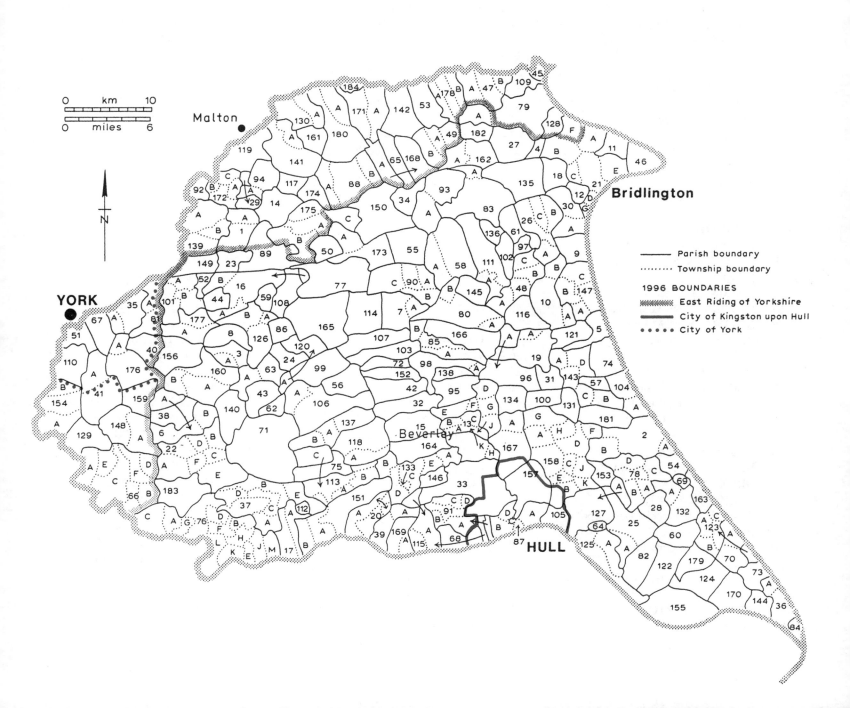

EAST RIDING OF YORKSHIRE : PARISHES AND TOWNSHIPS
IN THE MID-19th CENTURY

Malton

YORK

Beverley

Bridlington

HULL

0 km 10

0 miles 6

N

——— Parish boundary
········ Township boundary
1996 BOUNDARIES
▒▒▒▒ East Riding of Yorkshire
■■■■ City of Kingston upon Hull
●●●● City of York